Tales for an Unknown City

# Contents

Prologue   3

The Host's Tale   9

Tales of Hodja Nasrudin
*Dan Yashinsky*   12
*Celia Lottridge*   15
*Aubrey Davis*   20

A Death Is Indicated   23
*Aubrey Davis*

Four Stories of Old Men Talking   25
*Jack Nissenson*

A Lesson in Resuscitation   28
*Marvyne Jenoff*

The Tale of Uncle Dan   29
*Meryl Arbing*

Death and Baba Tsganka   32
*Ted Potochniak*

Ukrainian Fish Stories   40
*Ted Potochniak*

Nestled on the Edge   49
*Carol McGirr*

Gudrun's Dreams, from the *Laxdaela Saga*   53
*Carol McGirr*

# Contents

Martha  56
*Connie Clement*

Laura and the Lilies  68
*K. Reed Needles*

Tales of Donald Lake  71
*Pat Andrews*

The Porcupine  78
*Lenore Keeshig-Tobias*

The Gold Mine  83
*Alec Gelcer*

The New Legend of Sam Peppard  91
*Celia Lottridge*

Sugar Cane  100
*Justin Lewis*

Searching Out Moira  104
*Robert Munsch*

Andreuccio da Perugia  116
translated from Boccaccio by *Mariella Bertelli*

Tales from the Negro Leagues  123
*Lorne Brown*

The First Train and the First Bagel in Chelm  127
*Leslie Robbins*

If Not Higher  132
*Michael Wex*

Is It True?  138
An Interlude with Alice Kane

The Hare and the Lioness  141
*Alice Kane*

A Second Language  141
*Alice Kane*

The Corpse Watchers  142
*Alice Kane*

# Tales for an
# Unknown City

## Stories from One Thousand and One
## Friday Nights of Storytelling

Collected by Dan Yashinsky

McGill-Queen's University Press
Montreal & Kingston · London · Buffalo

©McGill-Queen's University Press 1990
ISBN 0-7735-0786-8

Legal deposit fourth quarter 1990
Bibliothèque nationale du Québec

Printed in Canada on acid-free paper

Funding for this book has been received from
Multiculturalism Canada

**Canadian Cataloguing in Publication Data**

Main entry under title:
Tales for an unknown city

ISBN 0-7735-0786-8
1. Tales—Ontario—Toronto.  I. Yashinsky, Dan, 1950–

GR113.5.T6T34 1990  398.2'09713'541  C90-090130-6

The typeface used in the text is Goudy Old Style
set by the Instructional Communications Centre at
McGill University.

The Dun Horse 146
*Ted Potochniak*

J. Percy Cockatoo 156
*Joan Bodger and Meg Philp*

Lord of the Deep 166
*Rita Cox*

Makonde and Moyomiti 169
*Beverley Grace*

The Singular Sister 174
*Marvyne Jenoff*

Aschenpöttel 177
adapted from Margaret Hunt's translation of Grimm by *Lynda Howes*

Schlange Hausfreund (Snake Housefriend) 184
translated from Ludwig Bechstein by *Marta Goertzen*

The Peasant's Tale 196
*Jack Nissenson*

A Duppy Tale 199
*Ray Gordezky*

The Tale of Crooker 203
adapted from Ruth Tongue by *Maggie Fehlberg*

Ownself 205
*Joan Bodger*

The Piper's Tale 212
*Jim Strickland*

Tam Lin 217
*K. Reed Needles*

The Story of Rose Latulippe 223
*Marylyn Peringer*

The Magic Cat 232
*Kate Stevens*

A Miracle on Friday 236
*Michael Wex*

# Contents

The Shivering Tree  243
*John McLeod*

Such a Land Does Not Exist  254
*Ray Gordezky*

The Sphinx and the Way to Thebes  260
translated from Wieland Schmied by *Gary Hophan*

Epilogue: The Listener's Tale  263

# Tales for an Unknown City

"But why, then, does the city exist? What line separates the inside from the outside, the rumble of wheels from the howl of wolves?"

Kublai Khan to Marco Polo in Italo Calvino's
*Invisible Cities*

# Prologue

What if Caliban was right? What if the whole place is like his island, voices everywhere, everything with a story to tell, polyphonic, "full of noises, sounds, and sweet airs"? Say this is true — what then? How do we learn to listen in such a world?

There was an Ashanti farmer once, so the story goes, and he went into his garden to dig up a yam. So far so good; many yams have been harvested in the history of the world. But this particular yam cried out indignantly: "Well, at last you're here. You never weeded me, but now you come around with your digging stick. Go away and leave me alone!"[1] The farmer, never having heard of Caliban and completely unprepared to deal with a talking vegetable, screamed and ran away. Who wouldn't do the same in that situation? We don't go around expecting to hear yams talk. We like talk to come in familiar voices. But then, says the Pit River Indian shaman, you only hear what is already familiar to you, nothing new, nothing surprising. If you want to find your power, you must be willing to hear about it from strange sources; go off alone and walk in the hills; sing some kind of a medicine song: "The dragonfly came to me / with news from my home. / I lie in the afternoon / looking toward the hills."[2] According to this way of thinking, when things begin to talk to you, don't run away screaming; stay and listen; maybe you'll hear an interesting story; maybe the story is about you.

Socrates once told a story to his companion Phaedrus, and Phaedrus scoffed: "It is easy for you, Socrates, to make up tales from

---

1  Harold Courlander, "Talk," from *The Cow-tail Switch and Other West African Stories* (New York: Holt, Rinehart, and Winston 1947).

2  Jaime de Angulo, *Indian Tales* (New York: Ballantine 1953).

Egypt or anywhere else you fancy."[3] It is neither the story's alleged provenance nor the facility of the teller that bothers him. It is the very language of Story that makes Phaedrus uneasy. He would like truth to be uttered directly. He wants a dogma to decree, a fact to report, a final "say" to be said. The problem with stories is that they tend to be the first word, not the last. They circle back to other stories. Walter Benjamin wrote that a story's counsel is not revealed as the answer to a question but rather as "a proposal concerning the continuation of a story which is just unfolding. To seek this counsel one would first have to be able to tell the story."[4] Which is to say, Phaedrus, that to hear what the story has to say you must lend it your own voice; learn it by heart; shelter it from forgetfulness; pass it along to another listener. Socrates just tells him: What does it matter if a prophecy comes from a talking oak tree in the sacred grove at Dodona – so long as the tree speaks the truth?

Then, even when you try to listen, sometimes you hear only silence. When I was growing up in a suburb of Detroit, most of my parents' friends were European Jews, survivors of the Second World War. Many of them had lost their families and were trying to build new lives for themselves. In our house they were usually cheerful, full of jokes, always ready to tease me with stories and riddles. But they never said a word about the war. I once overheard one of my adopted "uncles," the one I loved best, a man who had been in Auschwitz, describing something from the war. I heard him use the word "unspeakable." It made no sense to me. How could something be unspeakable? How could my friend have seen something that could not be spoken, even to us, even so far away from where it had happened? This was a true riddle. I wanted to ask questions, to find out more. As an adult, of course, I have learned about some of the things he must have experienced. But I could never ask him. His story remains untold, untellable.

That is one kind of silence, charged with too many stories, haunted and unutterable. There is another kind of silence that comes from a lack of stories. I once went to a funeral for an old man I hadn't really known. I listened to people talking afterwards

---

3  Plato, *Phaedrus*, translated by R. Hackforth (Cambridge and New York: Cambridge University Press 1952).

4  Walter Benjamin, "The Storyteller," from *Illuminations*, translated by H. Zohn (New York: Schocken Books 1969).

and was shocked to realize that no one had any stories to tell
about him. There were no memories, no scraps of history, no nota-
ble events to recount, even on the day he was put back into the
ground. Another riddle. How can a human being live with such
a seal on his heart, never taking or being given enough notice to
yield a single memorable story? This old man had simply passed
from one silence into another.

Then there was my mother's father. His life was, to him, pure
legend. He replayed his oral home-movies over and over again to
his most eager and devoted listener – me. My grandfather had
grown up in Romania; gone to Paris to study engineering; joined,
while there, the "Society for the Prevention of Seasickness" (and
still had a set of Indian barbells to prove it); travelled to Japan
to lay the foundations for skyscrapers (discovering there the plea-
sures of mixed-sex bathhouses); and wound up in San Francisco
designing and laying out power-lines in the High Sierras. I, a
skinny, bespectacled, middle-class kid, was enchanted by the
thought of my fiery, irascible, Romanian-Jewish grandfather riding
a mule in the mountains of California.

When he was ready to get married, he wrote to his mother back
in the old country asking her to find him a suitable wife. He had
three conditions:

1 She was to be beautiful.
2 She was to have a good singing voice.
3 She was to come from a port city.

The reason for the last was that a woman raised in a port city
could be expected to have a certain worldliness, and not be merely
a sheltered, over-refined, Eastern European bourgeoise.

The happy part of the story is that such a woman did become
his wife: beautiful, gracious, unaffected, cultured, a marvellous
singer (La Bohème was her favourite opera); and she happened to
come from the greatest port in the history of the world – Con-
stantinople (once Byzantium, now Istanbul). The sad part is that
the Romanian fascists kicked him out of the country, and he
spent the entire war separated from his wife and daughter, unable
to bring them to safety (the saddest book I own is the diary he
kept during those years). How they managed to survive on their
own in Bucharest is another story.

Perhaps not surprisingly, my grandfather had had an experience
with a ghost. Here's the story:

## The Tale of Nathan Louis Paves

He was living in San Francisco at the time, and his own grandfather had emigrated from Romania and settled in St Louis, Missouri. One night my grandfather had a dream. He dreamt that his
grandfather opened the door of his room and entered, radiant with
light. He came to the bed and spoke: "Nick, I have come to tell
you I love you very much. You are a good man. Now I must say
good-bye." So saying, he disappeared. The next morning my grandfather remembered his dream. He wanted to know how his grandfather in St Louis was doing, but he didn't have his address. He
wrote a letter back to Romania asking for news. A letter finally
arrived a few weeks later. The news was sad. His grandfather had
died. He had died on the very night of my grandfather's dream.

Why do we tell these stories? Why do we make life out to be a
kind of legend, something you can refold into a story? Why do
our otherwise catch-as-catch-can memories seize on these narratives
with such strength?

When his fellow villagers came to their local wise man, Hodja
Nasrudin, they brought a difficult and pressing question: "Which
is more important, the sun or the moon?"

To which query the wise-and-sometimes-foolish Hodja replied
without a moment's hesitation: "The moon; for the moon shines
at night when it is hard to see, and the sun shines in the daytime
when it is already light outside."

True, true, Phaedrus might have said impatiently; but look, you
noodlehead, the sun is the *source* of all the light in the first place!
Of course. And the storyteller, remembering Caliban, might say:
True, true; the sun is the source of the light, and life itself is the
source of all meaning. But to make that meaning visible, commu-
nicable, a source of good counsel, you must draw a frame of Story
around it. You must refold time and space to find out where you've
been, and when, and why. The old mother tongue, the one we
share with oak trees, dragonflies, and yams, is a language made of
stories.

The story Socrates told, the one that bothered Phaedrus so much,
went like this:

Once upon a time in Egypt, the inventor-god Theuth came to
King Thamus to show off his latest, new, improved technology; a

veritable "recipe for memory and wisdom." He called it writing. But instead of praising Theuth's creation, King Thamus was sceptical of its real worth. He warned: "If men learn this it will implant forgetfulness in their souls; they will cease to exercise memory because they rely on that which is written, calling things to remembrance no longer from within but by means of external marks. What you have discovered is a recipe not for memory, but for reminder."

What happened next?

How does it end?

The story is still unfolding. Theuth is as busy as ever, inventing ever more powerful systems of external marks. Nowadays we can not only write words on a page, we can inscribe them on electronic microcircuitry. We can record and store limitless quantities of speech. But the prophecy of King Thamus has come to pass. As we amass our vast hoard of data, we have fewer and fewer things to call to remembrance from within ourselves. We know almost nothing by heart. We forget our stories.

But not every story is lost, not every teller silenced. Even in plague times something remains. Look at Pampinea in the *Decameron*, leading her companions from the devastated, plague-struck streets of Florence out to the sanctuary of a country villa. Instead of letting them brood or mourn, she made them tell stories. Day by day, tale by tale, they managed to recollect that life was possible beyond the chaos. Even when their city had become unknowable, and history was senseless, and the future unimaginable, even in that most broken of times the storyteller's voice makes a kind of order at the centre of things. "And I hear, from your voice," says Kublai Khan to his master raconteur Marco Polo in Calvino's *Invisible Cities*, "the invisible reasons which make cities live, through which perhaps, once dead, they will come to life again."[5]

For there will always be someone who comes along and says, "Tell me a story!" Someone like Harry Bailly, for example, keeper of the Tabard Inn on the high road to Canterbury. When he spotted a likely-looking company of pilgrims one day, he challenged, provoked, and persuaded them to tell stories on their journey: "For trewely, confort ne myrthe is noon / to ride by the wey doumb as a stoon." Or the Hungarian poet George Faludy, starving

---

5 Italo Calvino, *Invisible Cities*, translated by W. Weaver (London: Picador 1979).

in a Stalinist labour camp, who gathered his fellow prisoners every
night and whispered to them stories, poems, operas, lectures on
Renaissance art. "I cannot claim," he said once, "that this saved
us from death, but it did undoubtedly save us from the despair
that inevitably resulted in death."[6] Storytellers, even when they
can only whisper, live by the belief that their stories will outlast
plagues, death camps, and the depredations of forgetfulness.

A millionaire, says the Romany proverb, is someone who has
*spent* a million dollars. So it is with stories. Countless generations
of storytellers, elders, troubadours, griots, grannies, bards, and
skalds, from earliest history until now, have felt the power of that
belief. The value of the story must survive beyond your telling of
it. Find a listener, pass it along; above all, don't hoard it! Hoarding
kills the thing. The stories themselves say it over and over again.
No fairy-tale witch or ogre is allowed to keep the secret sack of
gold forever hidden up the chimney. Everything of value must be
released, returned to life, made current again. Prince Ivan must
uncage the radiant Firebird, Princess Vasilissa must unspell the
witch-captured Prince. As for those who live only by greed, lo,
they must needs die by it as well: Ali Baba's avaricious brother
Cassim dies in the cave full of treasure because he cannot release
from his own memory the name of that most common of seeds –
sesame.

---

6 From a speech given at York University, Toronto, 1987.

# The Host's Tale

This is a book of stories told by storytellers in the city of Toronto. They were told at a gathering that meets once a week, every Friday evening. Toronto storytellers began this custom in 1978, at a café called Gaffers in Kensington Market, and have continued it in various locations ever since. These storytelling evenings came to be known as One Thousand and One Friday Nights of Storytelling.

Kensington Market was, like all markets, a good place for storytelling. You could buy on the same block Portuguese fish, Jewish cream cheese, Hungarian salami, Jamaican yams, and old clothes from places called "Exile" and "Courage My Love." You could hear on this busy city street horns blaring at a double-parked truck unloading ice-crates of fresh fish, carnival music thundering from the West Indian record store, Chinese spoken by teenagers on their way to watch *Seven Sexy Secretaries* at the Hong Kong cinema. Then there was Gaffers.

I started telling stories there in the spring of 1978. At first I was the divertissement between sets by a Dylanesque folk-singer. When more people began coming for my stories than for his songs, he was packed off and the Friday evenings belonged to me. I'd perch on a stool and tell stories from my scanty repertoire to the rather surprised diners. Artistic success was measured by the degree to which they forgot to chew their muffins and stir their espressos. I knew I was telling well when the waitress waited to ring in the bill and when Hugh, the café habitué who always read his evening paper at the table beside my stool, stopped rustling the sports section so he could hear what happened next. After some weeks of solo storytelling a friend of mine allowed as how he knew some stories and might be willing to let himself be persuaded to tell one in a week or two. So the following

Friday there were two of us. It wasn't long before the word got around that Friday evening at Gaffers Café was a storytellers' "jam" session.

The "Friday Nights" have continued to be open, informal, spontaneous. Anyone with a story is welcome to tell it. The only ritual comes at the beginning: a Host greets the crowd (I was the first Host, soon followed by others), tries to set people at their ease, and reminds them that storytelling is the order of the evening. Somehow, someone always finds the courage to tell the first story, which draws forth another, and another; and so the evening unfolds, usually unplanned, following only what Padraic Colum calls the "rhythm of reverie." Some stories have been carefully rehearsed, some spring to mind and are told impromptu. Tristan and Isolde may come after a tale about Nanabush and spark in turn a reminiscence of growing up in the Northern wilderness. An anecdote about riding on a Toronto streetcar may remind someone of a long, intricate wonder tale full of journeys and quests. A master storyteller may inspire a novice to try. The evening is like a patchwork quilt, stitched together tale by tale, its order emerging as tellers listen and respond to each other's stories.

After ten years of telling, listening, and hosting at the "Friday Nights," I wanted to make a record of this community of city-dwelling storytellers. I began to ask the storytellers to write their stories down (an odd request: our one rule, unwritten of course, has always been that every story must be told from memory, not read aloud.) I asked for stories that had stayed with me after I had heard them told; not the pleasant stories which are nice to listen to yet don't last the journey home, but the stories you wake up with the next day, still living in the landscape created by the teller's voice. These stories have a mysterious power to spark across the gap and make a place for themselves inside one's memory.

Some of the storytellers transcribed tape recordings of particular tellings; others had to recompose a written text from their memory of oral versions; still others had stories that were originally intended for the page, and afterwards were told orally at the "Friday Nights." Writing down an oral story is a little like scoring a jazz impro-visation: the tune comes across, but the timeliness is lost. I wish that you could hear for yourself the voices of these storytellers:

the clear, unaffected, youthful voice of Carol McGirr relating the fate of strong and wilful Icelanders; "Aschenpöttel" told in the prairie-raised, from-a-distance voice of Lynda Howes; the incomparably bittersweet cadence of Alice Kane's voice as she tells her tales. I can only hope that the voices of the storytellers are not lost in the translation from telling to writing.

This collection is a kind of ultimate "Friday Night," a night of nights. The stories are as various as the tellers who brought them. They come from many cultural traditions and represent many genres of oral narrative. There are Italian, German, Chinese, Trinidadian, Tanzanian, Ojibway, Quebecois, Jewish, Ukrainian, Irish, and Scottish tales. There are contemporary stories, traditional wonder tales, ghost stories, first-person reminiscences, historical chronicles, teaching tales, and an excerpt from an eight-week rendition of an Icelandic saga. Toronto is a city full of people from every part of Canada, and almost every country in the world. Storytelling is one of the ways Torontonians, both old and new, find a common ground. Stories are how we make an unknown city knowable, familiar, a proper dwelling-place.

The book begins with the wise-and-sometimes-foolish Hodja Nasrudin. (Since the Host often starts things rolling by telling his or her own story, I unapologetically place my own Hodja stories at the beginning of the book.) Following Hodja, all the stories until the interlude with Alice Kane ("Is It True?") are drawn, in one way or another, from life experience. There is no magic in them, except the magic one may find in the real circumstances and dilemmas of life itself. Then comes Alice Kane talking about the truth of fairy tales. She has been, for the storytellers in Toronto, our "master" storyteller. The ideas and values in this reflection on fairy tales have been a constant challenge and inspiration to the "Friday Night" community. It is fitting that the interlude belongs to her. After this break, you will find that the stories are all touched by the fabulous. Many of them begin in an ordinary enough fashion; then something happens: the protagonist stumbles into a world of miracles and wonders. After each story there is a storyteller's epilogue. The tellers talk about where the stories come from, how they tell them, the cultural life behind the tales, autobiographical information, and so on.

There are two very important kinds of stories I have not included in this book. Many of the best tellings at the "Friday

Nights" are of literary stories. Since these are already published, I could not have them in this collection. Let me at least name some of the authors beloved by Toronto storytellers: Alice Munro, Roch Carrier, W.O. Mitchell, Spencer Holst, Doris Lessing, e.e. cummings, Arthur Ransome, Isaac Bashevis Singer, Hans Christian Andersen, Rudyard Kipling, Diane Wolkstein, Ella Young, Padraic Colum, Italo Calvino, Joseph Jacobs. This list is long and illustrious.

I have also left out stories by the many guest tellers who have visited the "Friday Nights." In our quiet, candlelit room we have heard the finest storytellers in the world – from France, China, Scotland, the West Indies, Australia, the USA, every Canadian province, and many Native Canadian nations. There was, for example, Mr Yang Zhenyan, a professional storyteller from Shanghai, practising an art he had learned from his father. When we asked him how many stories he knew, he counted five, then noted that if he were to tell for one hour every night the story he had just done an excerpt from, it would take one year to perform (in his tradition they say it takes one month to narrate the heroine's descent down the staircase). Since this book is about a local community of storytellers, theirs are the voices you will find here.

Welcome to One Thousand and One Friday Nights of Storytelling.

❧

# Tales of Hodja Nasrudin
## Part I

### Hodja Makes It Rain

One day, the villagers of Akshahir came to Hodja. "Hodja, we're in terrible trouble! It hasn't rained for days and days, the sun is burning down like a ball of fire, we have no water left to drink! Please help us."

Hodja agreed to help. "To help you properly," he said, "I need a large basin brought into the square."

They brought a large basin into the middle of the village square. "Now," he said, "fill this basin with water."

"What do you mean, fill it with water? *What* water? Hodja, all we have left are a few drops to give to our thirsty babies!"

"Fill this basin with water," he repeated. And so they did. They each went home and searched out the vials and bottles where they had been saving a few last drops of precious water, and they brought them to the square. Then they poured this last supply of water into the basin.

"What are you going to do now, Hodja? What are you going to do with our water?" They watched in horror as Hodja Nasrudin took off his shirt, his not-very-clean shirt, and dipped it into the basin. The water turned black with the dirt of his shirt. "Hodja! You've soiled our water!" the villagers cried.

He said nothing. He washed his shirt in the basin. He squeezed out the water and shook the shirt out in the air. Then he walked with his clean shirt over to a clothesline near the village square. Very carefully, with all the villagers watching, he hung the shirt up to dry. They all waited until the shirt was almost completely dry and, just at that moment, sure enough it started to rain.


## Washing the Cat

One day Hodja took his cat down to the river and began to wash it. The villagers passing by saw this and said, "Hodja, what are you doing? You're going to kill your cat in the river!"

"I know what I'm doing," he said, and kept washing.

When people came by a little later, the cat was dead. "You see," they said, "You killed your cat!"

"Yes," said Hodja, "I killed my cat. But it wasn't when I washed it in the river. It was when I tried to wring it out."


## Sun or Moon?

They came to him one day and said, "Hodja Nasrudin, can you tell us which is more important – the sun or the moon?"

He thought about it for a while and replied, "The moon is

surely more important then the sun, for the moon shines at night when it's dark; the sun shines in the daytime when it's already light outside."

## Who Owns the Land?

One day a man who owned a field left it in the care of another man. He took good care of the land, ploughing, weeding, planting, harvesting it. When the owner came back he said to the man who had been taking care of it, "Give it back now. The land belongs to me."

"No," said the other man, "I won't. The land belongs to me. You are the owner, but I am the one who has taken care of the land all this time. The land is mine."

They went to find a judge to settle their dispute, and they came to Hodja. Each man said, "The land is mine, the land belongs to me!"

Hodja walked to the field, lay down in the dirt, and put his ear to the ground. "What are you doing, Nasrudin?" they asked.

"I'm listening."

"What are you listening to?"

"The land."

Both men laughed. "Listening to the land? So what does the land say?"

Hodja looked up and said, "The land says that both of you belong to the land."

## Hodja Keeps His Promise

Hodja lives nowadays. A rich man was dying and he wanted to take his money into the grave with him. He divided his fortune among three trustees: a lawyer, a sheik, and Hodja. He made them swear that when he died they would each bring their third and throw it in the grave. They all gave their solemn oath.

Their friend died, and the lawyer, the sheik, and Hodja met at the graveside. The lawyer said, "I've been thinking about our late friend's request. What a waste it would be to throw this money away! After all, you can't take it with you."

The sheik began to nod. "Yes," he said, "I have also decided to keep my third. It is just the amount of money I need to pay off my gambling debts."

Hodja stood there shocked. "How can you so dishonour the memory of our late friend?" he said. "Each one of us gave a solemn oath to obey his last wish, and you have both betrayed your promise! I for one have every intention of fulfilling my oath." And Hodja took out his cheque-book, wrote a cheque, and dropped it into the grave.

### Dan Yashinsky

*One of my first books came from relatives in Istanbul, where Hodja is very well known. The story of the drought came from that book.*

*The stories about the cat and the land dispute both came from Yoel Peretz, an Israeli storyteller I met in Tel Aviv. The modern story I heard from Mrs Mathilde Stephanian, an Armenian woman who owns the building where the Storytellers School of Toronto has its office.*

☙

# Tales of Hodja Nasrudin
## Part II

## Three Fridays

One of Nasrudin Hodja's duties in the village of Akshahir was to give the sermons in mosque on Fridays. Many Fridays the Hodja enjoyed preaching. He had much to say and he enjoyed looking down at the upturned faces of the congregation while he spoke words of wisdom inspired by the Koran, and by the Hodja's wide experience of village life.

There were other Fridays, however, when the Hodja had nothing to say. It was on just such a Friday that Nasrudin Hodja made his way across the village square, through the great door of the mosque, through the crowd of people who had gathered to hear him, and up into the pulpit. He looked at the beautiful mosaics on the walls, at the carpets on the floor and at the faces below him. Nothing inspired him. His mind was blank. Yet he had to speak.

The Hodja opening his mouth and said, "O people of Akshahir! Do you know and understand what I am about to say to you?"

"No," said the people. "No, we do not."

"What!" said the Hodja. "How can I speak to such ignorant people?" And he gathered his robes around him and descended from the pulpit, free − for one more week.

But this week, like all others, passed; and once again the Hodja found himself climbing into the pulpit with no idea at all of what he was going to say. He did notice that the mosque was quite crowded. There were many more faces than usual gazing up at him expectantly.

Once again the Hodja opened his mouth and spoke. "O people of Akshahir! Do you know and understand what I am about to say to you?"

"Yes, Hodja, we do," answered the people, who remembered what had happened the week before.

The Hodja beamed down at them. "Wonderful!" he said. "Then there is no need for me to speak to you today." And he gathered his robes around him and descended from the pulpit. Free − for one more week.

It was indeed rare for Nasrudin Hodja to go for three weeks without inspiration, but this time it happened. Another Friday came and the Hodja still had nothing to say. Others, however, had had much to say, and news of the Hodja's strange words had travelled far and wide. Indeed, the Hodja had some trouble pushing his way through the throng in the mosque, and looking down from the pulpit he saw many strange faces among the familiar ones from the village.

The Hodja smiled. "O people of Akshahir!" he said. "Do you know and understand what I am about to say to you?"

Now, some people in the congregation thought of the week before and they answered, "No, Hodja, we do not." But others, thinking of the week before that, said, "Yes, Hodja, we do!"

"Wonderful!" said Nasrudin Hodja. "Wonderful! Let those who know tell those who do not know."

And Nasrudin Hodja gathered his robes around him and descended from the pulpit. Free. For one more week.

## Soup of the Soup

One evening Nasrudin Hodja and his wife were just sitting down to dinner when there came a knock on the door. The Hodja opened the door to find his good friend Hassan from the next village standing on the doorstep. In Hassan's hands was a fine rabbit.

"Hodja," said Hassan, "I have brought you a gift." And he handed the rabbit to the Hodja.

This was indeed a fine gift. "Come in, come in!" said the Hodja. "We will cook the rabbit. We will make pilaf. We will have a feast."

And they did. The Hodja's wife was a very fine cook. The rabbit and all that went with it was delicious. The Hodja told stories. Hassan laughed. And when Hassan had gone home, the Hodja was pleased to be able to say to this wife, "There is plenty of rabbit and plenty of rice left. We will have rabbit pilaf tomorrow."

But the next evening, just as they were about to sit down to this fine meal, there was a knock at the door. When the Hodja opened the door, there stood a man he recognized as a neighbour of Hassan's. The Hodja observed that he carried nothing in his hands.

"Greetings, Hodja," he said. "I am a friend of Hassan from the village."

Now, the Hodja knew the customs of hospitality. "Come in," he said. "We were just about to eat our evening meal."

The meal was very good, for the Hodja's wife was indeed a good cook, but the Hodja did not tell quite so many stories. There was not as much laughter and the guest left soon after dinner.

The Hodja looked at the platters. "There are still the bones of the rabbit," he said, "and plenty of rice and vegetables to make a fine soup."

All the next day the Hodja's house smelled of the wonderful soup that was cooking, and in the evening the Hodja and his wife sat down to eat it with good appetites. But just as they picked up their spoons, there was a knock at the door.

The Hodja opened the door, and found on the doorstep a man who looked faintly familiar. "I am a friend of the friend of Hassan from the village," he said in a friendly voice.

The Hodja thought of how he had hoped to eat two bowls of that good soup which the man on the doorstep appeared to be smelling with pleasure. However, hospitality is a duty; so he said, "Come in. We were just about to eat our soup."

The guest appeared to enjoy the soup very much, but the Hodja was unusually quiet and he did not object when the man left as soon as he had eaten. He looked into the soup pot and found one large spoonful of soup. "Tomorrow," he said, "I will prepare the evening meal. I will take care of everything."

The next day there were no good smells of cooking in the Hodja's house and the Hodja and his wife did not sit down to eat at their accustomed time. But there came a knock at the door.

The Hodja flung open the door. Standing on the doorstep he saw a stranger, someone he had never seen before. But the man was smiling. "I am a friend of the friend of the friend of your friend Hassan," he said.

"Indeed," said the Hodja. "Well, you must come in and share my meal."

"I would like that very much," said the stranger. So the Hodja led him to the table. The man sniffed the air.

"Don't worry," said the Hodja. "I was just going to fetch the food." He went into the kitchen and scooped the spoonful of soup from the bottom of the pot. He carefully divided it between two bowls, filled each bowl up with hot water from the kettle, and carried the bowls to the table. He set one in front of the stranger and one in front of himself. Then he sat down and smiled happily at the man.

The man gazed into his bowl. It contained a clear liquid with two grains of rice and a shred of carrot floating in it.

The Hodja spoke: "O friend of the friend of the friend of my friend Hassan, here is the soup of the soup of the bones of the rabbit."

The next night the Hodja and his wife sat down to eat alone, in peace.

## Selling Donkeys

Every Saturday for many years Nasrudin Hodja rode a donkey to a market in a village some distance from his own village of Akshahir. There he sold the donkey for a remarkably low price, pocketed the money, and walked home with a contented look on his face.

Now it happened that there was a prosperous donkey dealer in this village, and he became annoyed because the Hodja always undersold him. One Saturday he stopped by the place in the market where the Hodja sat beside the donkey he was selling.

"I am a rich and powerful man," he said. "I am able to force the farmers to sell me fodder for my donkeys at very low prices. I also have workers who are practically slaves. I give them a miserable place to sleep and just enough food to keep them working. Yet your donkeys are always cheaper than mine. How do you do it?"

The Hodja smiled gently. "It is true," he said. "You are rich and powerful. You are able to steal food and work. I just steal donkeys."

### Celia Lottridge

*When my mother was a small girl she lived in a mission compound in the north-western part of Persia. This meant that she grew up with Mullah Nasrudin. The Turkish people in the area called him Nasrudin Hodja, but to the Persians he was Mullah and he was part of everyday life. There was a Mullah Nasrudin story for every household and village situation, and I think that the Mullah was more like a neighbour than a piece of folklore.*

*My mother, who returned to North America at the age of nine, certainly referred to him casually more than she told stories about him. "Mullah Nasrudin would call this the soup of the soup," she would say when leftovers appeared for the third time on our dinner table.*

*At some time in my childhood we found two books by Alice Kelsey:*

*Once the Hodja and Once the Mullah. Then we had whole stories
and we learned most of them by heart.*

*But I didn't realize how important Mullah Nasrudin is to me and
to the world until I visited Bukarah in Uzbekistan. From a bus window
I saw a man wearing a white robe and a white turban jogging slowly
and peacefully along on a donkey. "It's Mullah Nasrudin," I nearly
yelled. Then I realized that this name meant nothing to any of my
fellow tourists. But that afternoon our Uzbek Intourist guide told us
a Mullah Nasrudin story. I had been right. Nasrudin doesn't only
belong to my childhood or my mother's. He belongs to now. I sometimes
think it was Mullah Nasrudin who made me into a storyteller.*

༄

# Tales of Hodja Nasrudin
## Part III

## Costly

Nasrudin set up a stall and hung a sign over it which read: "Two
Questions on Any Subject Answered for $20."

A man came rushing up, slapped twenty dollars down on the
counter and said: "Twenty dollars! That's an awful lot for just
two questions, isn't it?"

"Yes," said the Mullah. "And the next question, please?"

## The Problems of Delay

The four-engined aircraft was in trouble. The pilot's voice came
over the loudspeaker:

"May I have your attention please! One of our engines is
mal-functioning. We can fly on three but we will be five minutes
late in arriving at our destination."

The passengers became worried and started to mutter among
themselves. Mullah Nasrudin was also on the plane. He called out:

"Five minutes, friends. It's only five minutes. Surely you can wait five minutes."

This calmed everyone down.

A while later, the loudspeaker clicked on and the captain spoke again:

"Attention! Another engine has ceased to function. We are now flying on two engines and will be a half-hour late in arriving."

The passengers became even more agitated than before. But once again Nasrudin spoke up:

"You know, it's only half an hour. It's much better flying in an airplane than travelling on donkey-back!"

The passengers seemed to accept this bit of philosophy and settled down once more.

Hardly half an hour passed before the pilot spoke again:

"I regret to inform you that a third engine has broken down. There will now be a one-hour delay."

"Goodness gracious!" cried the Mullah. "Let's hope the last engine does not give out, or we will be up here all day!"

## Tit for Tat

Nasrudin went into a shop to buy a pair of trousers. However, once inside he changed his mind and decided on a cloak at the same price. Picking up the cloak, the Mullah began to leave the shop.

"Stop!" cried the proprietor. "You haven't paid for that cloak!"

"No, but I left you the pants which are same value as the cloak," replied the Mullah.

"But you haven't paid for the pants either!"

"Of course not!" said Nasrudin. "Why should I pay for something I don't want to buy?"

## Never Know When It Might Come In Useful

Nasrudin used to take people for rides in his boat. One day, a very fussy schoolteacher asked to be ferried across a wide river.

As soon as they were afloat the teacher asked:

"Tell me, do you think it is going to be rough?

"Don't ask me nothing about it," said Nasrudin.

The schoolmaster was appalled. "Have you never studied gram-mar before?"

"No," said Nasrudin.

"Then half your life has been wasted," replied the scholar.

Nasrudin said nothing.

Soon a terrible storm blew up. The Mullah's crazy cockleshell was tossed all about. Waves came crashing in over the side.

Nasrudin leaned over to the teacher and yelled:

"Tell me, schoolmaster, have you ever learned to swim before?"

"No!" he cried.

"Then all your life has been wasted! We're sinking!"

## Aubrey Davis

*I was introduced to Mullah Nasrudin by a dead man. Although he'd been dead about eight hundred years, it took him only fourteen years and three thousand miles to introduce us. His name was Omar Khayyam.*

*This is how it happened. When I was seven years old, my mother took me to a movie in Midland, Ontario. It cost a quarter. It was wonderful, the best film I ever saw. That film was called Omar Khayyam.*

*Fourteen years later, while visiting a friend's stone cottage on Grand Canary Island, I was desperate for something to read. I picked up one of the three books he had on hand. Half-way through the table of contents I saw the name: Omar Khayyam. My hero! I had to investigate; I began to read.*

*This book, The Sufis by Idries Shah, was fresh, strange, and full of insight rather like Mullah (or Hodja) Nasrudin himself. It was in that book that I first met the Mullah. We hit it off right away. Perhaps it was because I felt, somewhere inside, that I had always known him. So it was that the name of a dead mathematician, astronomer, poet, and Sufi the great Omar Khayyam spanned oceans and centuries to introduce me to the Mullah Nasrudin.*

*My stories are retold, by permission of the publishers, The Octagon Press, London, from the following collections by Idries Shah: "Costly" and "The Problems of Delay" are from* The Subtleties of the Inimitable Mulla Nasrudin *(London 1983); "Tit for Tat" is from* The Pleasantries of the Incredible Mulla Nasrudin *(London 1983); "Never Know When It Might Come In Useful" is from* The Exploits of the Incomparable Mulla Nasrudin *(London 1983).*

# A Death Is Indicated

Once upon a time there was a dervish who had sixty disciples. He taught them as best he could. Then the time came for them to undergo a new phase in their study, so he called them all before him and said:

"I am about to embark upon a long journey. Something, I'm not sure what, is going to happen along the way. Those of you who have absorbed enough to enter this stage will be able to accompany me.

"But first, you must all memorize this phrase: 'I must die instead of the dervish.' Be prepared to shout this out whenever both my hands are raised in the air."

The disciples began to mutter among themselves. They were naturally very suspicious of him. "This dervish," they said, "knows we will encounter some danger along the road. He's preparing to sacrifice our lives instead of his own."

They said to the dervish: "How do we know that you're not planning some crime – perhaps even a murder! We could never follow you under terms like these!"

No less than fifty-nine of the sixty disciples deserted that dervish. So he and his sole remaining pupil went on their way.

Now shortly before they arrived in the next town, a cruel tyrant usurped the throne. In order to consolidate his rule, he decided upon a dramatic act of force. He summoned his soldiery before him and said:

"I want you to arrest some vagabond of meek appearance and bring him to the town square for judgment. I propose to sentence him as a miscreant, an evil-doer."

"We hear and obey!" said the soldiers. They went into the street and pounced upon the first wandering stranger they met. This was none other than the disciple of the dervish.

The dervish followed behind the soldiers as they dragged his young disciple away.

In the town square, the drums of death were beating. The people were already trembling with fear as the young man was hurled to the ground at the feet of the tyrant.

The King said: "I have decided to make an example of this vagabond. We will tolerate no unconformity; no attempted escape. You are to die at once!"

At that moment the dervish called out in a loud voice, "Mighty monarch, please accept my life instead of the life of this useless youth. After all, I am more blameworthy than he. It was I who induced him to embark upon his life of wandering in the first place."

And the dervish raised both of his arms into the air.

The young disciple cried out, "Munificent King, please allow me to die! I must die instead of the dervish!"

The tyrant slumped back in his throne. He called for his councillors and said to them:

"What kind of people are these, vying with one another to taste death? If this is heroism, will it not inflame the people against me? Tell me! What am I supposed to do?"

The advisers conferred for a moment and then said, "Peacock of the Age! If this is heroism, there is very little that we can do other than to increase the viciousness of our rule until the people lose heart. But we see no harm in asking this dervish why he wishes to die."

When he was asked, the dervish replied, "Your Majesty, it has been foretold that a man is to die this day on this very spot and rise again and become immortal. Naturally both I and my disciple wish to be this man."

The King thought: "Why should I make others immortal when I myself am not?"

So he gave the order for his own execution. And this was carried out. Then the worst of the King's evil advisers, wishing for their own immortality, killed themselves. Not one of them ever rose again.

Amid all the confusion that ensued, the dervish and the disciple went on their way.

*Aubrey Davis*

*I have retold this story from* Thinkers of the East *by Idries Shah (London 1982) with the permission of the publishers, The Octagon Press, London.*

# Four Stories of Old Men Talking

## A Park Bench Tale

Once upon a time there were three elderly gents sitting on a park bench. They were retired, they didn't have much to do, so they met every day and they talked about this and that. Probably just about every day they solved all of the world's problems. One day one of them said to the others, "If you had your druthers, how would you like to die?"

They thought about that for a minute until finally one of them said, "Well, you know, you see those flashy new sports cars that you see driving around. Oh, heaven knows how fast they go. I'd like to get myself the fastest of them. Nice and red, sleek and long. And I would like to take that out on the highway, get my foot pressed down to the floor, and all of a sudden all the tires would go, and I would go up in a blaze of glory. That's the way I'd like to go."

The second one said, "You're far too modest. You're not up to date at all! I would like to get myself one of those new-fangled jet planes. These jet planes go two thousand miles an hour and they fly fifty miles over the earth! When those go, it's like a comet in the sky. That's the way I would like to go."

They turned to the third one – who by the way was the oldest, probably touching ninety – and they said to him, "Well, what have you got to say for yourself?" He said, "You know, that's interesting what you say, but if I had my druthers, I would like to be shot by a jealous husband."

## Another Park Bench Tale

Now once upon a time, there were these three men, and probably not the same men, sitting on a park bench somewhere else. They were talking about various things. They were solving other problems. One day one of them said to the others, "What would you wish for, if you could have it?"

They thought about that for a few minutes and finally one of them said, "You know, I wouldn't mind having a little shop. You know, a nice little corner store and we could sell all kinds of things to the people in the village, and everyone would come and see us and we would talk. We would know everybody and we'd be able to help everybody out and we'd have a little house above the shop. We wouldn't be rich, but we'd have enough, and everybody would be our friend. That would be really nice."

Well, the second one said, "Yes, I can understand that, but personally I would prefer to be the servant of a Rabbi. Why? Well, you see a Rabbi has many books. All Rabbis have wonderful, wonderful libraries. When I worked in that house, on my off-hours I could go to that library and partake of the wisdom of the world there. That's why if I had my wish I would wish to be the servant of a Rabbi."

The third one said, "Hmm, yes, I can understand those wishes, but as for me, if I had my wish, I would like to be a great emperor of a great country. I would have a huge marble palace filled with gold and diamonds and rubies and pearls and emeralds. And I would sit on a huge golden throne. And to my right would be my six sons, each on their golden thrones, and on my left my wife and six daughters, each on their golden thrones. And we would have armies, and farms, and riches, and everything that I wanted would be at my command.

"Now one day, the king of the neighbouring country would invade my country. He would destroy my armies, level my town, burn down my fields, kill my sons and my daughters and my wife, and bring the great castle down around my ears. I would only escape with the shirt on my back."

When the others heard this they were somewhat surprised, and they said to him, "You mean you wish for all of that just so that you should escape with the shirt on your back?"

"Well," he said, "do I have a shirt?"

## The Monk's Tale

Once upon a time there were two Buddhist monks walking through the forest. And after some time they came to a stream. And at the side of the stream was a young woman, weeping bitterly. So they went up to her and said, "What's the problem?" She said that she had to get across the stream and she couldn't. So the older of the two monks, he picked her up in his arms and carried her across the stream. When they got to the other side he set her down and she thanked him very much; and off she went; and off they went.

They walked, and they walked, and they walked along their path, and finally, the younger of the two monks couldn't stand it any more. He turned on the older and he said, "How could you do it? How could you do it? You know we have sworn never to touch women, and yet you just picked her up in your arms and carried her across the stream. How could you do it?"

The older monk said, "Look, why don't you put her down? I did two hours ago."

## The Visitor's Tale

Back in the nineteenth century a very old, famous Rabbi living in Poland was visited by an American tourist. The American was surprised to find that the very famous Rabbi lived in almost a hovel. It was one room with a rickety old chair and an old bed, and piles and piles of books – books everywhere. The American was surprised, and he asked the Rabbi, "Rabbi, where is your furniture?"

And the Rabbi said to his visitor, "Well, where's yours?"

"Oh," the American said, "What would I need with furniture? I'm just a visitor here, I'm just passing through."

And the Rabbi said, "So am I."

*Jack Nissenson*

*The two "Park Bench" tales and "The Visitor's Tale" are from Jewish tradition. "The Monk's Tale" is a Zen story from Japan.*

℘

# A Lesson in Resuscitation
## (for Hedy Hill, Toronto, 1976)

I did not expect her face to be blue.

"It's nothing," she whispered from the bed. "But this morning I was dead for a moment. I had an awful pain, then nothing. Somebody shouted, 'Breathe, breathe,' and I think I heard a prayer – who am I to question? The police came, and an ambulance, too. And here I am, back again! My dear, don't be so serious. At my age you expect such things. Now, come closer and tell me how you are."

This was no time for modesty.

I whispered in her ear, "There's a man in my life."

"Ooh! Marvellous! Tell me more."

"Well, we met –"

"How exciting! How very exciting!" She sat up. "See what you are doing to me with your enthusiasm! Go on."

"Well, he said –"

"It sounds wonderful, my dear! My philosophy is, if you can talk to each other before and after, then you know it's love. But," she said, tapping off the top of a boiled egg and looking inside, "if you want my advice – I'm giving it to you anyway – I think you are spending too much time by the telephone. The best thing in your situation is to have *two* men. Don't be shocked. Find a second one now, while you are feeling so, so energetic. You know, dear, in all the excitement this morning, there was such a nice young policeman. What a pity he didn't take off his clothes! He reminded me of a delightful man I once knew in Vienna –"

"I knew a man in Winnipeg," I said,
and she said "Paris"
   and I said "Parry Sound"
and she said "The Riviera"
   and I said "Rainy River"
and she said "San Francisco"

and I said, "Are you sure it's OK for you to laugh so much?"
and she said, "Nobody forbids me to laugh."

  So I said, "Saskatoon"
and she said, "Hong Kong"
  and I said "Flin Flon."

As we sat by the window having tea
we looked out over the city lights and agreed
upon Toronto
  just in time for me to catch my train back to Mississauga.

Her hair was red again right down to the roots.
At the door she kissed both my cheeks and said,
"My dear, you look marvellous,
absolutely marvellous!
You know, the way you rushed in,
I was sure you had bad news."


                    *Marvyne Jenoff*

*This is a true story. I couldn't resist changing some of the place
names.*


                    ↻


# The Tale of Uncle Dan


I come from Prince Edward Island. It's a small place with a small
population; but there are probably more ghosts per square mile
there than any other place in Canada. My family, especially the
members of my grandmother's generation, seemed particularly close
to the spirit world, and possessed that peculiar kind of sensitivity

to events that lay on the border between the physical and the spiritual worlds. Forerunners were very common then. A forerunner is a strange happening that precedes news of a death or disaster, and only those specially blessed would be party to the other-world's warnings.

My grandmother's uncle, Dan Riley, was blessed in this way. He was a very good man, and spent his time visiting, caring for neighbours and family who were ill. Because of his goodness and generosity, he was know as "Uncle Dan" to everyone in the community.

Now, because he was so good and lived so close to God, he used to be warned whenever some tragedy was about to strike someone in the community.

Uncle Dan had a clock. I remember my grandmother telling me how he kept this clock on his mantelpiece for as long as she knew. Now, there is nothing strange about this – except that the clock did not work. Why did he keep it?

One day my grandmother, who was just in her teens at that time, was at Uncle Dan's house cleaning for him. Uncle Dan was out and, while she was in the kitchen sweeping the floor, she heard the clock strike: once … twice … three times it struck. She knew that the clock had been broken for many years. The weights that ran it were lying in the bottom of the clock, without even the cords to wind them up – but still she heard it strike.

When Uncle Dan came home she told him that she had heard his clock strike.

"How many times did it strike?" he asked.

"Three times," my grandmother answered.

"Watch," he said seriously, "within three days there will be a death."

As the forerunner had predicted, on the third day word came that a son of one of the local farmers had been killed in a farming accident. It was Uncle Dan who went to help the family because he was already prepared.

My grandmother never forgot this incident, and it confirmed in her a belief and respect for the spiritual side of existence.

But Uncle Dan was not limited to his clock. A young woman of the community had a child. She was not married, and the sensibilities of the community were offended. It was decided by others that the baby should be placed with relatives in Halifax.

Tearfully, with the babe in her arms, she was placed on the train to take her away to Nova Scotia.

It was common knowledge in the small PEI community where she had gone and why, but Uncle Dan came into his sister's house (my grandmother's mother) and said, "I've seen young Mary walking along the woods behind their land. She was singing a sad song."

My great-grandmother reminded him that she had been sent on a train that day, and no more was thought of it. Later, however, the word came that the young mother and the babe with her had stepped off the swiftly moving train and had both been killed. It was just at the same time that Uncle Dan had "seen" her.

### Meryl Arbing

*No matter how long a Maritimer has lived in Ontario, the Maritimes are always "home." We even speak of it as "Down Home," and it is a rare thing for a Maritimer not to make the yearly trip back to the red soil and the salt spray.*

*When I was a boy and spent my summers down on Prince Edward Island, there were many times when the kitchen would be full of visitors at my grandmother's home. Everyone would be telling stories and talking about the old days and the old-timers. I paid little attention to the stories that moved around me, and let them drift away on the evening breeze.*

*Now, as a storyteller and an adult (in that order) making my own pilgrimage, I am saddened to see how much of my birthright has slipped past me. It is not gone totally, however. It must be sought out more deliberately, and, when it is found, I immerse myself and try to take in as much as possible.*

෴

# Death and Baba Tsganka

I can't remember exactly when I first heard this story I am going to tell you. It was either the summer before I started high school or the summer after I finished grade nine. What I do remember for sure: it was the summer I discovered poker. Learning to play poker that summer was like being admitted through the portals of a shining, new universe. You've heard of the expression "beginner's luck." Well, I had it. And with such a cornucopia-like abundance, it verged on the miraculous. Every week on Saturday night I came rolling out of those games like a Ukrainian Croesus whose pockets were full to bulging with nickels, dimes, and quarters and even the odd dollar bill or two carefully folded away in the breast pocket of my T-shirt. Indeed, my winnings grew to be so great I took to carrying off the ill-gotten loot in a purple velvet Seagram's Crown Royal whisky bag. The mere sight of that soft, plush, gold-trimmed bag lying in wait on the table to devour even more winnings made my opponents blanch with fear.

All through that wonderful summer I kept winning and winning. It was my God-given right and my greed knew no bounds. I always tried to keep the games going on for as long as I could. The games were usually held at Bucky Burke's house two doors down from my own. The Burke family had a cottage in Port Elgin to which they would periodically disappear off the face of the earth for weeks at a time. Or so it appeared to my ethnic-coloured eyes. You see, the idea of a cottage in a port was almost incomprehensible to a West Torontonian of Ukrainian descent whose closest brush with a Canadian wilderness came in High Park. We knew from nothing about cottages in the woods.

This summer, however, was different. Bucky Burke had his first summer job and was often left in the care of his older brother Bob – a high school senior with a well-paying plant job of his own. Bob was the world's best babysitter. He required only two things of us – one, that we never touch his jazz record collection, and two, that under no circumstances were we ever to speak to him directly. It was the ideal set-up. But, too soon, all too soon, the summer was nearing its melancholy end, and, before I knew it, the second last weekend of the vacation had arrived and with it, perhaps, the last chance to add to the shoebox full of money under my bed. That Saturday night was a night I didn't want to end. My luck was phenomenal. I literally couldn't lose. I raked in pot after pot. I kept urging my friends to stay, don't go, you'll get some back, it's early. In the end, I cleaned everyone out. Every nickel that came walking into the Burke kitchen at eight o'clock that evening was sitting in my Seagram's bag. However, when I looked at the clock I realized I was in big trouble. The clock read almost four o'clock in the morning! I had to get back into my house without raising any suspicions.

Getting into our house wasn't much of a challenge. My sisters had taught me how to turn the old tumblers of our skeleton-key lock so that not even a soft clink could be heard. And from an early age I knew how to drag out the skeleton key tied to a hockey lace through the letter-box slot without so much as a whisper of a metallic rasp. Getting in was no problem. It was while I was slipping off my sneakers in the dark hallway that I saw the *real problem* I had to face – the stairs! My family lived in a very old semi-detached house that had the creakiest stairs in the whole of the west end. There were two stairs close to the bottom that screeched like cats, one in the middle that cracked like a rifle, and two near the top that groaned and moaned worse than that door on the "Inner Sanctum" radio show. I knew I couldn't get by all those traps without rousing my mother (my father worked night shifts at my uncle's bakery and my two sisters slept like logs). So I hit upon a novel strategy. I would "walk" up the stairs with my toes poking through the bars of the banister railings. It wasn't until I was half-way up that I realized this tactic had a serious flaw. The circulation in my toes was cut off and I just knew I was going to end up club-footed for the rest of my life. The pain was unbearable, but the thought of being discovered by my mother was even worse. I bore the excruciating torture and kept on climbing.

At last, I was within a leg length of the top step ... a solid quiet step. Clutching the banister post, I hauled myself up over the last two treacherous steps and stepped on to the top landing. I hadn't made a sound. Luckily, my bedroom faced the stairs. I carefully crept in, got into my pyjamas, and ever so gently lowered

myself into the bed without so much as a creak. I put my head
on the pillow and glowed with an inner pride mixed with relief.
I had made it! But, as I lay there in the dark, I became aware
of a strange shape lying next to me. It was my mother! She
rolled over on to her elbow and hissed into my ear, "And where
have we been all this time, my little cossack?" My mother's hair
was stuck up in curlers that had odd pieces of white paper sticking
out of them and her face was covered with a horrific white cream
that seemed to glow in the dark like the paint job on the Hound
of the Baskervilles. I was terrified. My heart was in my mouth.
My mother got up and standing by the bed she said to me in
a sepulchral voice, "You haven't heard the last of this." Then,
she sailed out of the room in her billowing white night dress
like a Slavic Lady Macbeth. I was doomed. I couldn't sleep a
wink. She would tell my father for sure and that would be it for
me. All through the night, for some strange reason, Edward G.
Robinson's last line in the movie *Little Caesar* – "Oh, Mother of
God and Mercy, can this be the end of little Rico!" – kept
running over and over in my mind.

In the morning, I got up and prepared for the worst. I could
hear my father downstairs eating his supper after coming off the
bakery night shift. I came down. My father greeted me warmly,
told me to hurry if I wanted to get to early Mass, and went
back to reading his beloved Racing Form. Not a word all day.
All that week, I kept waiting for the axe to fall. It never did.

Soon it was Saturday again and word was out there would be
one last game at Bucky's house. The Burke family wouldn't be
coming back until the Sunday before Labour Day. "Hurrah!" I
thought.

That evening, I buzzed around thinking of schemes, plots, ways
and means I could employ to get into the game. My mother
anticipated every move. "You are staying home tonight. I'm making
the first *studenitch* of the year and you're going to help me," she
said. I must add a word of explanation here. *Studenitch* is a very
nutritious Ukrainian delicacy made by boiling pigs' feet until a
greeny-golden broth is made. Bits of the tender, delectable pigs'
knuckle-meat are left in the broth, which smells wonderfully of
bay leaves, pepper, peppercorns, carrots, onions, and garlic. Once
the broth is bubbling to perfection the tiny metacarpal bones
that have fallen off are scooped out and dumped on newspapers

spread out on the kitchen table. Then comes my favourite part. As the bones cool, you get to suck on the last of the rich marrow juice still left in them. It is truly wonderful.

My mother and I were in the midst of this steamy work when a fierce late-summer thunderstorm broke out. You know the kind that rattles the windows near to shattering and threatens to tear the roof off the house. Then, just at the crucial moment when the heady broth was to be strained and carefully poured into the bowls that were to be put into the summer-kitchen icebox, all the lights went out. Only the blue light of the gas stove flickered in the darkness. My mother told me to get candles and by the dim yellow light we finished the making of the *studenitch*. When we were done, my mother told me to sit down, and she extinguished all the candles save one. "I'm going to tell you a little Ukrainian *byka*," she said. And it was then that I knew I was going to hear the last word on my little adventure of the week before. I sat down, began sucking the knuckle-bones that gleamed palely in the faint light of the sputtering candle, and as the storm raged I got ready to listen to my mother's Ukrainian tale.

## The Story

Once upon a time, long ago in the old and sorrowful land of the Ukraine, there stood, on a high ridge overlooking my village of Terebowlya, a cabin. The cabin was very old, but not tired, for its thatch glowed with a brilliant emerald green from the forest mosses growing on it. So beautiful was the cabin that all travellers on the high road could not help but stop and stare at it and think, "Ah *tak krasna* – Oh how lovely!" Inside the cabin lived a very old *Tsganka voroshka* – gypsy fortune-teller. Tiny as a spring peeper she was and her face was crinkled and lined like a muzhik's old boot. All the people called this ancient one "Baba Tsganka" – gypsy grandmother.

Well, as my father, your grandfather, would say, "If you fear not God and want to know what will be, go to Baba Tsganka, she knows the cards!" And oh, how they came to her, young and old alike. The path to Baba Tsganka's cabin was well worn with many footprints.

"Baba Tsganka," they asked, "will poverty camp at my door?"

"Baba Tsganka," they asked, "who will be my love?"

In answer, Baba Tsganka would shuffle her cards and shuffle her cards and once again for thrice and then gently lay them on the table – *raz, dwva, tre* – and say "Oh, ho, you are a lucky one, indeed, the coins that jingle in your pockets will always be silver," or "Ah, you will travel the roads with holes in your boots and holes in your pockets," or "Oh, ho, you will marry a young man as handsome as a Tsarevitch," or "Ah, you will marry a muzhik with bandy legs and a head shinier than the noonday sun." And whether she pleased or whether she dismayed, she was never wrong.

One winter's eve as Baba Tsganka sat by her clay stove, her little *kotyk* – cat – in her lap, she began to muse as old ones do. "I am very old. The seasons and years now pass before me like the wind and still I live. When will Death come to *my* door?" And so, because she had to know, she shuffled her cards and shuffled her cards and once again for thrice and gently she laid them on the table – *raz, dwva, tre*. She looked at the cards and then crossed herself thrice. The third card, you see, was Death's card.

"Oi," cried Baba Tsganka, "that is not what I wanted to see!" She swept the fateful card from the table. Down, down it fluttered to the floor, but, before it fell to the carpet, the little *kotyk* caught it in his paws and hid Death's card behind the clay stove. No sooner had the cat done that than there came a knocking at the cabin door.

"Who is there?" asked Baba Tsganka.

There was no reply. Baba Tsganka went to the door and opened it. There on her threshold stood Death himself, his eyes very grey, like old ice, and in his bony hands he held a scythe.

"*Dobry vatcher* – good evening – Baba Tsganka," he said in a mild voice. Death talks softly, you see, because the very sight of him speaks like thunder.

"What do you want?" asked Baba Tsganka.

"*Dobra panya* – good lady – why, I am here to offer you my hand. Take it," said Death.

"There is no warmth or comfort in a claw such as yours," said Baba Tsganka. "You keep it!"

Death smiled with his yellow teeth. "It is always the same," he thought. "They never want to go, no matter how old, and this one is surely more than old enough."

To Baba Tsganka he said, *"Dobra panya,* you have no choice. The cards have spoken."

"The cards said nothing," replied Baba Tsganka, "Go, listen to them yourself!"

Death strode into the cabin. The cards lay on the table – *raz* and *dwva,* but the third was nowhere to be seen. Death with his stiff white fingers flicked over each card in the deck and his card was not there either.

"Does your raven not fly over my table?" asked Baba Tsganka.

Death's eyes grew round and wide; he took in the whole room with one glance. But since he could not see behind the clay stove, he did not find his card. "Fear not, Baba Tsganka, my bird will find a roost in your cabin one day," replied Death. He took up his scythe and out of the cabin he swept like an ill, cold wind.

"May he roost in your black hat," muttered Baba Tsganka as she watched Death glide down the road to the village of Terebowlya.

Time passed and the wheel of the seasons turned once and all that the *Tsganka voroshka* had foretold came to pass. But, strangely, in all that year, not a single soul, either young or old, was taken by the hand of Death. The people of Terebowlya were amazed. Nothing like this had ever happened before. Old ones who should have departed still lingered. Sick ones grew thinner and more wasted, but still lingered. No one's burden was relieved, for Death always passed over Terebowlya just like the leaves and birds of autumn.

"How can this be?" asked the people of each other. They went to the priest. "Father, Death has passed us by the whole of this year. What can it mean?"

The priest could only shrug. "Life and Death are mysteries too great for the small minds of people to fathom," he said. But his eyes strayed to the high ridge where the little emerald green cabin glowed in the sun.

They did not know, you see, that Death's card lay hidden behind Baba Tsganka's clay stove. And so it might have been for all time had not Baba Tsganka said to herself one night, "I wonder, will he come again?"

And so, because she had to know, she shuffled her cards and shuffled her cards and once again for thrice and then gently she laid them on the table – *raz, dwva.* Then, just as she was about to lay the third card, her little *kotyk* leaped up on the table bearing with him the fateful calling card of Death himself.

"Oi, you wicked creature!" cried Baba Tsganka.

She snatched up the card. No sooner had she done so then there came a great and fearful knocking at her door. Quickly Baba Tsganka slipped the card under her apron. There was nothing else to do. She turned to the door.

"Who is there?" asked Baba Tsganka, knowing full well who was there.

"*Dobry vatcher, dobra panya* – Good evening, good lady," said Death, coming into the cabin. "You have called and I have heeded."

"Feh, why should I call for the likes of you!" cried Baba Tsganka. "Leave me in peace; begone. Your black bird does not perch in here!"

"Oh, Baba Tsganka," said Death, smiling his cold, yellow smile, "my pet would be very comfortable on your shoulder."

"May your bird be plucked and gutted by crows!" said Baba Tsganka. "If you've come at my calling, then show me your invitation."

Again Death strode into the cabin. He saw the cards upon the table – *raz* and *dwva*, but the third was nowhere to be seen. Death turned all the cards in the deck. He searched the cupboards. He lifted the rug. He ran his bony claw of a hand over all the shelves. He even looked behind the clay stove. He did not find his card. He did not know, you see, that the Death card was safely tucked under Baba Tsganka's apron.

"Well, where is your pet?" asked Baba Tsganka.

Death took up his scythe and, turning to look at Baba Tsganka full in the face, replied, "Next time, next time, my *dear* Baba Tsganka, my black bird will fly down your chimney." His voice chilled the marrow in Baba Tsganka's old bones. And so, for a second time Death's bony claw was empty as he left the little green cabin on the ridge.

Baba Tsganka sighed deeply. She watched Death glide down the road to Terebowlya. She waited and waited until he was well gone. She plucked the card from under her apron and looked at it. The cardboard figure grinned at her with its yellow teeth. Beside him stood a raven, its reptilian eyes glinting.

"Oh, you are a wicked pair, indeed!" moaned Baba Tsganka.

"Where you two tread bones creak, death-rattles chill, and hearts break!"

Baba Tsganka tore the card into pieces and threw the bits into the hearth-fire one by one. Then, taking the rest of the deck, she wrapped it in a red babushka, placed the bundle into a stout wooden box, locked the box and placed it high on the mantel. The *voroshka*'s days of seeing into the future were done from that day on.

All who came to her door to implore and plead were turned away.

"Go away," Baba Tsganka would say, "only the Devil dances in the future." Not another fortune would she read in the cards.

Time passed and the wheel of the seasons turned once more. One cold winter's evening Baba Tsganka sat in her chair with her little *kotyk* purring in her lap. She knitted and dozed. The hearth-fire and the warmth of the cat warmed her aching old bones. Then she awoke with a start. A strong wind came roaring down the ridge. Down, down, down it bellowed – a cold, merciless wind. Down, down, down Baba Tsganka's chimney it blew. An icy chill crept across the hearth and swirled around the cabin. The little *kotyk* leaped from Baba Tsganka's lap and hid behind the clay stove. It grew so cold Baba Tsganka felt it seep into the very marrow of her bones. She turned and there on her mantel sat a huge black raven, its reptilian eyes glinting in the firelight. The bird walked to the box. It pecked and pecked and pecked at the box of cards.

"Stop you *horoba* – you plague!" screamed Baba Tsganka.

The door to her cabin creaked and there on the threshold stood Death – dark and grim, his scythe gleaming dully.

"Oi, you might have told me you were coming," cried Baba Tsganka.

"Oh, dear lady," laughed Death, "did not my bird deliver my calling card?"

The box crashed to the floor and the raven began to croak. Baba Tsganka turned, her knees trembling. On the carpet lay all the cards of the deck. In the circle of firelight Baba Tsganka could see the faces of all the cards. And every card, every card, was a Death card.

"Come take my hand," said Death.

All light in the cabin seemed to drain away into the black

night. Baba Tsganka could only see Death's white, skeletal hand coming closer.

"Come, Baba Tsganka, I have much to do in Terebowlya this night," said Death. "Come, take my hand." Closer and closer came Death's hand towards Baba Tsganka.

At this point in the story my mother blew out the candle and in the ensuing darkness touched my tense, clutched hands with a chicken foot. After she peeled me from the ceiling, she sat me down and asked, "And now, my little cossack, do you want to go out and play cards tonight?"

You know, I never played poker again for at least six months after my mother told me her little *byka*.

### Ted Potochniak

*My version of the story-within-the-story comes from my mother's rendition, with a strong influence from Eric Kimmel's fine telling in* Mishka, Pishka, and Fishka and Other Galician Folktales *(New York: Coward, McCann and Geoghegan 1976). When I tell the tale of Death and Baba Tsganka now, I don't use my mother's ending. It's hard to touch a storytelling audience's hands collectively with a chicken foot and I don't have my mother's didactic purpose in mind when I tell it. Instead, I use Eric Kimmel's wonderful ending, which is much gentler and humorous and certainly less stressful. I acknowledge with thanks the kind permission of Eric Kimmel in letting me publish this adaptation.*

எ

# Ukrainian Fish Stories

When I was a little boy of seven or eight – I can't remember my age exactly, but I was this high and so much nicer – my father, Teofil, and my Uncle Longin would take me carp fishing on the Holland River in the spring of the year. Now, lest you think this is going to be a Slavic version of a Norman Rockwell painting come to life, I hasten to add that my presence on these fishing trips was vital for both my father and uncle; vital, because I served as their shield to deflect from them the combined wrath of my mother and my Aunt Stella, both of whom were well known for their vociferous opposition to Saturdays spent carp fishing instead of doing household chores. These expeditions always began very, very early in the morning, when my father would dress me in the dark according to an old Ukrainian formula: "Dress the child in enough clothing so that the palms of his hands cannot touch his hips no matter what he might try."

When I was sufficiently entombed within the prescribed layers of clothing, my father would pick me up and carry me downstairs to stand watch in the bay window of our living-room. I was to keep a look-out for my uncle's 1948 Dodge sedan. My father would then go into the kitchen to prepare thermoses of coffee. There was no mistaking my uncle's car, because he always came up Franklin Avenue at a slow crawl with all the headlights out, like a Chicago hit man.

I loved that car. I liked the smooth, sensuous roundness of its roof and fenders, its wide running-board, and its magnificent charging-ram hood ornament. I also liked that car because in that West Toronto neighbourhood, cars were still a rare commodity so soon after the war, and to be even tenuously connected to a car by familial bloodlines gave one a certain social cachet. At Perth Avenue Public School, for example, I was known as "the kid whose uncle owns a Dodge."

When my uncle arrived and drew abreast of our house, I would flash him the venetian-blind signal and he would make a smooth, noiseless left turn into the laneway bordering our house. His destination was an old tin-sided, tin-roofed garage that leaned tiredly against our backyard fence. It was in that garage that my father had secretly stashed all the fishing gear and fishing rods he had borrowed the night before from our neighbour, Mr Wasilyk. While my uncle was loading up, my father would carry the thermoses and me out to the street. Then, he would nip across the street to the opposite laneway, to get to Old Man Morosz's place. Old Man Morosz ran a clandestine sausage factory out of a garage in back of Mrs Bossy's house. Periodically this "factory" burnt down, but Old Man Morosz was never out of business for more than a week; and it was a good thing too, because he made the most succulent kolbassa sausage I ever tasted in my life.

Now, no sooner was my father back than the Dodge would glide quietly up to us. Quickly my father would throw in the coils of kolbassa and the thermoses of coffee; and, just as he and I were about to climb into the back seat, my mother would invariably appear on the verandah, clad in a long white dressing-gown with curling pins in her hair that had little pieces of white paper sticking out of them. She was an apparition that could have stopped anyone in their tracks. "Where are you going, you hoodlum you?" she would shout to my father.

Now you might think the jig was up and the game was over; but you would be wrong. For it was then that my father played the trump card in this ageless battle of wits: me. My father would turn to my mother and, with arms up and palms open to Heaven, he'd say, "Bernice, what can I do? Little Teddy wants to go fishing!" Then he'd knee me into the backseat and jump in after. "Liar, *bandita!*" my mother would shout. "What about the storm windows, what about …?" But we never heard the rest, because by then we would be rounding the corner of Franklin and Royce as my uncle floored the Dodge.

From there, we made a short stop at Beaver Bread – a bakery my uncle owned with many silent partners – to pick up rye bread still warm from the ovens. And we were off to the wilds of the great Canadian North – the "wilds" around Highway 9 near Bradford.

The trip to the river was very long and boring, but there were some wonderful compensations. As my uncle drove, my father sliced the rye bread, cut chunks of kolbassa, and poured steaming bitter coffee into plastic cups. It was on one of these trips that I first tasted coffee, and I loved it. We drove and we drove and, after what seemed like an eternity, we would pull over to a likely looking bank on the Holland River. My uncle and father would then race about hauling out all the fishing gear and the long, slender wooden rods that had been brought all the way from the Ukraine.

After everything was laid out in readiness, it was time for my father and uncle to engage in an old philosophical debate based on worms versus cornmeal balls. My father was a worms advocate and my uncle a zealot of the cornmeal school. Those cornmeal balls were strange. They were made from cornmeal, which my uncle called *"mama liga,"* water, and sugar. All the ingredients were boiled to make a paste, which was then formed into alley-sized balls which were chilled. These small pellets had a hard consistency which allowed them to stay on a hook for a long time. This was most important because the carp, always referred to as the "Kink of Fish" by my uncle, was a notoriously elusive and wary feeder.

Finally, the hooks were baited, the long lines cast, and the slender rods propped up on notched sticks, and my uncle and father would settle back to wait for the carp to bite. Carp fishing from that point on demanded three important qualities: patience, perseverance, and silence – three qualities entirely devoid in the make-up of a restless young child. To amuse myself, I gathered up an arsenal of rocks and sticks to throw into the river. My father would see this, of course; and, like all good Ukrainian parents, he disciplined an obstreperous, whiny child by the two cardinal principles of Slavic parental control – Fear and Terror.

"Don't throw the stones into the water," he'd say. "You will slip and tumble into the river. The water is dark and deep, and the current so strong you will be swept away before your uncle or I could save you. You will be carried to Lake Simcoe where the water is a thousand feet deep and your mother and your sisters will never see you again!"

After hearing that gruesome tale, I never came within a dozen feet of the river bank.

After what seemed like two uneventful lifetimes, one of the fishing lines would begin to bob imperceptibly. My uncle and my father would get very excited: "Ah, look, look! He's got it! He's got it!" I could see the line starting to slice through the water. Still my uncle stood, waiting for the right metaphysical moment. Then, the rod was swept up and the hook driven into the carp's mouth! What followed was a battle that could only be described as epic. The carp would shoot up the river in a powerful bull-like rush, my uncle in hot pursuit. The carp would stop, turn, and race back down the river, my uncle running alongside. Never did you actually see the fish in the initial stage of those piscatorial brawls, because the black soil of the Holland Marsh had stained the water of the river to an impenetrable darkness. But you could always sense the primordial strength of the carp as it ploughed up and down the river.

Some of the fights lasted thirty and even forty-five minutes. When the exhausted fish was finally netted, it took both my father and uncle to drag the catch up on to the steep bank. Thirty- and forty-pound carp were not uncommon.

Whenever I watched the carp gasping on shore, I always felt an ineffable sadness come over me, for the carp had such a melancholy look to their eyes. The carp were then wrestled over to the trunk of the Dodge, where a galvanized washtub was waiting, half-filled with river water. The carp were thrust into an onion or potato sack and then placed in the tub so that they could be kept alive until we got back to Toronto. Sometimes the carp were kept alive for several days longer in our family bathtub, until my mother or aunt was ready to make gefilte fish. They were tough customers, those carp; truly, a "Kink of Fish!"

Now, as I told you, my father used worms as his carp bait; and one day he caught, instead of a carp, a thrashing, violent, green monster that looked more like an alligator than a fish. I was truly frightened when my uncle pulled that denizen of the deep up on to the bank. This was no sad-eyed carp, but a malevolent looking hoodlum of a fish, with teeth a police-dog would be proud to own. It was a big pike – over three feet long! Gingerly my uncle carried the pike to the washtub. As the pike lay in the tub, it stared at me with a baleful look, and it seemed to beckon me to put my hand into the water so that it could shred the flesh from my bones. I was both horrified and fascinated by that fish.

I asked my uncle, "Voyko, did you ever have such fish in the Ukraine?" He smiled indulgently at me and said, "This fish is a Canadian pike – a Cossack of a fish true enough. But, in the Ukraine, the pike is a pike. In the Ukraine the pike were as big as logs!" And then he began to tell me how the pike was born in the Dnieper River of the Ukraine.

## The Great Pike

The night before the feast of Shvitay Ivanov a pike was born in the dark, deep waters of the Dnieper River, a pike with teeth as sharp as a Cossack's sabre. May all the saints preserve us from such as he! The night of the pike's birth was terrible indeed: the waters of the Dnieper roiled and boiled, boats were swamped, and fishermen quietly plying the river for the wary sazan scattered from the banks in fear of the heaving waves that threatened to dash them into the swirling river. All the river fish – the shad, the perch, the roach, the multitudes of minnows, and even the bugle-mouthed sazan – gathered to stare in awe at this wonder of wonders. None had seen such long teeth before, and their little hearts fluttered like birds' wings at the thought of what those teeth would do.

Now this pike grew not by the day or week or month. Oh no, he grew by the hour! Each day that passed an inch or more was added to his length. By the end of summer the pike was a monster over nine feet long. And then he began to roam.

He travelled up and down the length of the great Dnieper and none was safe from his slashing teeth. If he spied a perch from afar he had only to flick his tail once and, after a swirl of bubbles, all that could be heard was the rending of flesh and the cracking of bones. If a school of minnows was seen, the pike had only to slash once with his teeth and then engulf at his leisure the floating remnants. Such was the power of this marvel in the Dnieper!

Well, what were the little fish to do in the face of this ravenous rampager? If things went on like this, the great pike would devour them all. The whole *mir*, the whole council of the little fish would be wiped out. And so, the little fish gathered in huge schools and swam to the depths of a deep and secret pool. They all came – bream, shad, perch, roach, dace, gudgeon, and minnows in the millions. The roach tsar spoke first: "Let us destroy this mangler of our flesh. He is a brigand – the thief of our progeny!" The gudgeon with his wide, round eyes looked at the roach and gently asked, "Oh brother, you have sharp teeth yourself then?"

"Why, I have none," replied the roach; "I am a virtuous fish who leaves his neighbours in peace."

"Ah, I see," said the wise gudgeon. "Then you'd swallow him whole."

"Oh no, my mouth is too small for that," laughed the roach.

"Very well, then, do not use it to speak so stupidly!" said the gudgeon. The roach, in consternation, blushed scarlet; and, you know, that is why his fins are so red to this day.

Then the perch spoke: "I will set my spines on end across my
dorsal fin and stick them in the pike's throat. I can assure you
the monster will not like that!"

"But, dear brother," replied the gudgeon, "to accomplish this
feat you will have to swim into the monster's throat, and you'll
be gone all the same." More and more nonsense was spoken
through the night. Such is the way of the world, you see, when
frightened fools gather. Things went from bad to worse, and even
the minnows felt free enough to natter endlessly.

The wise gudgeon at last had enough. "Stop racking your feeble
wits and cudgelling your brains, which are soft enough!" he said
in a loud voice that broke all the whirling bubbles of useless
talk. All became silent. "Listen now to my words," said the
gudgeon. "Truly this ravager has sorely tried us, and truly it would
be best for him to be killed. But look about you. We are small,
and even the tsar of the minnows, the sazan who is great in size
and strength, has a mouth too small for fighting; and besides, his
teeth are in his throat. No, we cannot kill the pike, and there
is no life for us if he gobbles us up at will." "Then what are we
to do, Pan Gudgeon?" cried all the fish. The gudgeon looked at
them with his wide, round, unblinking eyes and spoke again: "Let
us leave the Dnieper! Let us swim with all of our families to the
small rivers – the Slavenka, the Konoma, the Sizma – all the
little rivers who feed the Dnieper! In the small waters we can
hide among the reeds and rushes and raise our little ones without
fear. Leave the Dnieper to the pike! When we are gone there
will be nothing for him to eat. His long, sharp teeth will grow
blunt if he has no bones to crunch. In this way we will starve
the monster!"

All the little fishes, when they heard the wisdom of the gudgeon,
leaped and danced in the deep pool. Their bubbles of joy rose
up from the depths to break on the quiet, still surface. That very
night the whole *mir* of the little fishes left the great Dnieper to
find havens in the small, shallow waters of the little rivers.

Now as for the long-toothed pike, he continued to rage up and
down the great river; but there was no tender flesh for him to
feast upon. Like a tempest he thrashed and raced about, poking
his long snout here and there, but not a fish could he find. And
soon this rascal who had caused so much trouble in the Dnieper
came to a bad end himself. With no small fish to eat he was

reduced to taking worms, and one morning he saw a long, fat worm wriggling on the bottom. The pike pounced and swallowed it in a trice. But this particular worm was attached to the end of a sharp hook, and the hook was tied to the end of a strong line, and the line was strung on a stout rod, and the rod was held in the hands of a brave fisherman. When the fisherman saw his line move, he struck the barb into the pike's jaw and the pike felt its sting. Up, up, out of the river leapt the pike, to glare with his baleful eyes at the fisherman. The fisherman did not quail or quake. Instead, harder still did he pull on his limber rod. The pike stormed up and down the river; but the line held. From dawn till dusk those two fought. Then, as the sun set, the pike meekly turned up his white belly and allowed himself to be drawn to the shore. The fisherman, with the help of his neighbours, hauled the huge fish up on to the bank. Three men carried the dead pike back to the village. The people made a great feast from the monster's flesh, and with his head and bones they made a fine fish soup that lasted three days and three nights. I know. I was there and ate the soup, but it ran down my moustache and I never got any in my mouth.

"But Uncle," I said, "you don't have a moustache."

"That's right," my uncle replied, "I shaved it off – and that is why I'll eat more of this pike your father caught than you will!" And you know, he did.

When I turned ten, years and years ago, I became an alter boy and often served at the Saturday morning masses – a duty much too important to be supplanted by frivolities such as carp fishing. With this shield gone, I think my father and uncle were always out-manoeuvred by my mother and aunt; and soon, the carp fishing expeditions were only a memory. I never fished again. I guess the associations of being bundled up, the long drives, and the boredom of waiting made it a pastime to be avoided. A few years ago, however, my wife, Patricia, and I bought a cottage on the Pine River just north of Toronto. It was a lovely parcel of land which included a one-acre pond.

The first spring we were there, we noticed fast-moving, large fish in the river. They were rainbow trout. Well, one thing led to another; and soon I was fishing in earnest. It took almost to the end of summer before I finally hooked and landed a big "bow." My father tried trout fishing once in a while, but he never really took to it. My dear uncle had died a few years before, and I think my father just wasn't in the right frame of mind. Anyway, he always said, "Call me if a *real* fish like the carp comes to this river." But I never saw any carp. Two years ago, my good father died, a week before his eighty-second birthday on St Patrick's Day; and, as I walked the banks of the Pine River that spring, I thought often of my uncle and father and their adventures on "their" river – the Holland.

In May, after high levels of spring run-offs and heavy rains, the river rose very high, and I began to see large fish flitting about in the off-coloured water. I was sure they weren't trout because there was too much bulk and breadth to them. When the river cleared somewhat I was amazed to see that these fish were spring-spawning carp! They were big – not as big as the Holland River carp but, still and all, big enough. With trembling hands I rushed back to the cottage and got my rod ready, and baited it with a long, fat dew worm, just as my father used to do. I went to the pool at the foot of our small falls, and sat down to wait, reminding myself to be silent and patient. In a short while, I saw four large carp warily nose their way into the open, and slowly swim to the recesses of the falls pool. Carefully I cast the line, and gently let the worm drift to the bottom. Then I settled back to wait, just as my father used to do. I had barely settled against a log when my line took off. I leapt to my feet and swept up the rod. The line screamed out and the rod throbbed. I had a carp!

Back and forth the carp raced in the pool. My arms ached as I fought to keep the carp from heading off downriver towards the snags and sunken logs. After half an hour, the carp began to give way, and slowly I reeled it closer to the bank. It was a large fish and I knew I couldn't net it myself, so I called my wife Pat and my son Michael. All three of us danced about trying to manoeuvre that carp into the net; but it always seemed to have just enough strength to dive deep, or take another run whenever the net was brought close to it.

Finally, the carp had had enough, and meekly went into the net. Pat and Michael scooped it up and pulled it on to the bank. In the end, it wasn't a monster of the old days; it weighed only seventeen pounds and was thirty-one inches in length. But its eyes were melancholy. My son said to me, "Let it live!" We all agreed, and the carp was released in the pond. We fed it regularly, that tsar or tsarevna in its small realm.

And whenever I caught a glimpse of the carp gliding under our dock, or in and out of our boathouse, I thought warmly of those mornings with my good father and dear uncle on the banks of the Holland River in the spring of the year.

*Ted Potochniak*

*The "frame" story is all true. My story-within-a-story is adapted from the old version in Afanas'ev, with a strong influence from Arthur Ransome's wonderful collection,* Old Peter's Russian Tales *(New York: Thomas Nelson and Sons 1944). I have given it a Ukrainian setting.*

ভ

# Nestled on the Edge

I grew up in North Bay, Ontario. One of our teachers told us that we were nestled on the edge of the pre-Cambrian Shield. Somehow that was a comforting thought.

There we were, nestled on the edge, yet the world was a mere turn of the dial away. Magic voices from the Wrigley Building in Chicago floated across our living room, not to mention southern accents from WWVA, Wheeling, West Virginia. Once, on the short wave band, we even heard from London, England.

In those days radios were not little transistors which you could tuck in your pocket, nor were they bedside clocks which blinked the time in turquoise digits. In those days a radio was A Piece of Furniture. Ours sat in the corner basking in the glow reflected from its well-polished surface. Vertical slats covered a circular patch of material in its front. "A great big radio with teeth," I thought.

I wondered how the radio knew the secret of matching the number of the dial with the right voice. Were all the voices gathered in a cacophonous cloud over our house? Were they still up there when you turned the radio off? I still don't understand radio. I just know it works.

Our radio was a many-coloured splendour. There was a little green light to tell you that the radio was on "broadcast," an amber light indicated "short wave" band. Streaks of green and amber crossed the glass window, while a bright red needle indicated the number selected.

Nestled up there on the edge of the Shield, I could imagine what it was like to live in other parts of the country. I listened to "Just Mary" stories from St John, New Brunswick. Mary Grannan promised to reply if you wrote to her. I wrote. She replied. She even sent me a booklet about her childhood in the Maritimes. I knew that she knew that I was listening.

The CBC was my window on the world. I loved the CBC with all my heart. The rich voices of John Drainie, Lorne Greene, William Needles, Jane Mallet, and many others made me want to speak well.

Sunday afternoon was the best time of all. I would gather up cushions and make a nest in front of the radio. Then I would lie in my nest and wait for the Three Great Announcements. The first sounded like this: "This is the Canadian Broadcasting Corporation." (I liked that. It had a ring of authority to it.) "We pause now for station identification." The second of the great announcements went like this: "This is CFCH, NORTH BAY, Northern Ontario's *first* radio station." I asked my father if they meant first (best) or first (the very first one there). My father told me a very interesting story.

Once there was an alderman on the North Bay City Council who went around telling everyone that some day he would be a millionaire. Everyone laughed because the man had only one suit. They joked that they would take up a collection for him. Soon everyone in town bought crystal sets and invited the neighbours in to listen to the static. Now and then a word would come in clearly. The alderman decided that he would make his fortune by starting a radio station right in North Bay. The townspeople laughed, but the alderman found an engineer who understood how to make it work. The first broadcast was from the stage of the Capitol Theatre on Main Street. The townspeople, including my parents, went to the theatre in formal dress. Everyone knew it wouldn't last. Somehow the station stayed on the air. The alderman moved to Timmins and expanded his business by purchasing the local newspaper. He made his million and many more besides. North Bay's erstwhile alderman was Roy Thomson, better known as Lord Thomson of Fleet. His newspaper empire spans the globe, but he got his start at CFCH, NORTH BAY, Northern Ontario's *first* radio station.

The last of the Three Great Announcements was simply this: "– And now from Crocus, Saskatchewan, another 'Jake and the Kid' story."

Immediately the little town of Crocus seemed to spring up around me. I knew the main street of the imaginary town as well as I knew my own home town. Jake, the hired man, and the kid would come into town and head straight for Repeat Golightly's barber shop. Repeat and Jake would argue about politics, philosophy, history, and weather. Repeat knew everything that was going on in Crocus and somehow managed to escalate it to a world-shaking scale. Repeat amused me with his sayings, which he either repeated or paraphrased. To him the British Empire was a crown and Saskatchewan was one of the jewels in the crown. When Jake asked where that left Crocus, Repeat quickly replied, "Facets, towns like Crocus, Broomhead and Brokenshell ... facets in the jewel of Saskatchewan, all part of the crown of the Empire ... part of the crown." Repeat also believed in the old saying, "As the Hist'ry's bent, so groweth the nation. Good hist'ry, good nation."

From Repeat's, it was a short journey over to McTaggart's Trading Company, owned and operated by Mayor McTaggart. Jake and the mayor would discuss the latest events in Crocus. Crocus was a small town, but a very busy one with numerous organizations. Between them, Repeat and Miss Henchbaw from Rabbit Hill School managed to run things. Jake was not too fond of Miss Henchbaw. He thought she was a stickler for the truth. When she wasn't "stickling" she was trying to run Crocus. On the other hand, Miss Henchbaw thought Jake's history was a little shaky. She did not believe that Jake made Louis Riel say "uncle" three times, once in English, once in French, and once in Cree. Jake got to the mayor first, whenever he got the chance.

Before going back to their farm just down the Government Road from Crocus, Jake would often suggest a treat at the Sanitary Café. Jake admired Old Wing, who owned the café. Old Wing fed everyone who climbed off a freight down behind Hig Wheeler's Lumber Yard. During the depression he didn't let anyone go hungry. It was Old Wing who supplied all the hockey sweaters for the teams. He sent fruit baskets to anyone who was in hospital.

W.O. Mitchell created so many characters. In some ways they were like the people I knew. In other ways they were different. Their life was different, their landscape was different, their way of speaking was different, and yet they had hopes and dreams and fears like everyone else.

In addition to "Jake and the Kid," I listened to many other Canadian plays, as well as comedies from the States. Fibber McGee would always open the closet, even though Molly warned him not to do it. The resulting clatter, predictable though it was, would always bring a chuckle. We had a closet like that too. Jack Benny, perpetually thirty-nine years old, would always threaten to play his violin. Red Skelton would make you laugh or cry. Fanny Brice was a delightful Baby Snooks.

"Lux Theatre," in which the original stars read scripts of favourite movies, came on after bedtime. In our house this was no problem. We had a hot air register between the dining room ceiling and the floor of the upper hall. The purpose of this was to carry warm air up to the chillier regions. It also carried the voices on the radio. I had perfected a quick sideways roll into my bedroom, should anyone venture upstairs. It was nice and warm lying there on the hall floor listening to the radio. I was very careful never to fall asleep, but I finally got caught. The jig was up when a shower of peanuts cascaded down through the grate and bounced off the buffet with a staccato plip ... plip ... plip ... plip. Never eat peanuts over a hot air register when listening to the radio after lights out.

The radio, the great storyteller of my childhood, taught me to conjure up my own images. It inspired me to speak well. Most important of all, it taught me that Canada was a large, diverse, and beautiful country peopled by interesting characters who seemed to possess the innate ability to laugh at themselves. The CBC in its Golden Era of the forties and fifties defined what it was to grow up Canadian. That is why when the rest of the class sang

"O Canada" at school, I sang almost under my breath. I was singing the second verse.

"O Canada, where pines and maples grow,
  Broad prairies spread and lordly rivers flow.
  How dear to us thy vast domain from east to western sea.
  Thou land of hope for all who toil, Thou true north strong
    and free."

*Carol McGirr*

*This story came about as a result of many questions I was asked about how I got interested in "Jake and the Kid" stories. One night, as I was about to tell a "Jake and the Kid" story, I recalled the way I listened to the radio as a child, and the story grew from there.*

ↄ

# Gudrun's Dreams
## From the *Laxdaela Saga*

There was a man named Osvif Helgasson. He was a great sage, and lived at Laugar in Saelingsdale. He was the son of Helgi, who was the son of Ottar, who was the son of Bjorn the Easterner, the son of Ketil Flatnose.

Osvif's wife was Thordis, the daughter of Thjodolf the Short. Osvif and Thordis had five sons called Ospak, Helgi, Vandrad, Torrad, and Thorolf. All the Osvifssons were stalwart men.

Osvif's daughter was Gudrun. She was the loveliest woman in all Iceland, and also the most intelligent. Gudrun Osvifsdaughter was a woman of such courtliness that the finery of other women seemed mere trinkets beside those things which were hers. She was shrewd, well spoken, and had a generous disposition.

A man named Gest Oddleifsson lived west, at Hagi in Bardarstrand. He was a wise chieftain, prescient in many matters. All the important people were his friends, and many there were who came to him for advice.

Each year, Gest rode to the Althing. His journey took him along the boundary of Osvif's land. In the summer of her sixteenth year, Gudrun rode out to greet her distant kinsman. They fell into a conversation, for both were fluent and intelligent talkers. Gudrun invited Gest to spend the night at Laugar. It was also her father's wish; but she had been given the privilege of bringing the invitation. Gest thanked her warmly, but said his plan was to ride to Thykkvawood, where he would spend the night at the home of his brother-in-law Armod Thorgrimsson.

Gudrun said, "I have had many dreams this winter. Four in particular have disturbed me. No one can interpret them to my satisfaction."

"Tell me your dreams," said Gest. "I will make what I can of them."

"In my first dream I was standing outside, near a stream. I was wearing a head-dress on my head, but I felt it ill became me. I was anxious to change it, but there were those who felt I should keep it. I tore the head-dress from my head and threw it into the stream. That is the end of that dream."

Gudrun continued, "In the second dream, I dreamed I was standing by a lake. A silver ring appeared on my finger and I felt it was mine. It was a wonderful treasure, and I was determined to cherish it forever. When I turned, the ring slipped off my finger and rolled into the lake. I never saw it again. I felt the loss keenly. Then I awoke."

"That was no less a dream," Gest remarked.

Gudrun went on, "In my third dream I wore a gold ring. I did not think it became me more than the first ring, though gold is more precious than silver. I stumbled and, as I tried to catch myself, the ring struck against a rock. The ring broke in two pieces and both seemed to bleed. I thought there must a flaw in the ring. When I looked at it closely, I saw that there were many flaws. I felt the ring would not have broken if I had looked after it more carefully. Then this dream came to an end."

"The dreams keep coming," said Gest.

"In the last dream, I was wearing a heavy gold helmet set with precious jewels. I had to tilt my head to keep it balanced, yet I did not want to part with it." Gudrun paused. "The helmet fell from my head and toppled into the waters of the Hvammsfjord. And now all the dreams are told."

Gest replied, "It is clear what these dreams mean, though you may find it monotonous; for I shall interpret them in the same way."

Gest explained, "You will have four husbands. The first, I suspect, will not be a love-match. The head-dress in the dream did not become you. This means you will not love him. You threw it into the water. This means you will leave him. The old saying 'thrown to the sea' means something is discarded with nothing in return."

Gest went on, "In your second dream, the silver signifies an excellent man. You will love him dearly, but for a short time. It would not surprise me if your second husband drowned, just as the ring was lost in the lake.

"In your third dream you wore a gold ring which you valued no more than the silver. Your third husband will not exceed your second. The ring is of a different metal, which I think means a change of faith. Your husband will embrace this new faith. The ring broke in two, partly because you were careless. The blood means your husband will be slain. When you look closely at the marriage, you will see that there are many flaws in it."

Gest went on, "In your fourth dream, the gold helmet was heavy to bear, but set with precious stones. Your fourth husband will be a great and wealthy chieftain. He will have the strength to dominate you completely. The marriage will last some time. Since the helmet toppled into the Hvammsfjord, I fear that this same fjord will claim your husband on the last day of his life. I shall say no more of that dream."

Gudrun's cheeks flushed red as she listened. When Gest finished she did not speak. At last she said, "You would have given me rosier prophecies if I had given you the material for them. I give you my thanks for interpreting my dreams. It is a grave thought, if all this is to come to pass."

"A grave thought indeed!" replied Gest.

### Carol McGirr

The Laxdaela Saga *is seventy-nine chapters long. It covers approximately one hundred and fifty years of events in the lives of five generations descended form Ketil Flatnose. Choosing an excerpt is difficult, since there is so much interweaving of family history. I chose this selection because it foreshadows the turbulent love triangle in which Gudrun's passion leads to a blood-feud. This feud carries on to the next generation, setting one branch of the family against the other.*

*During a visit to Iceland and the Faroe Islands I visited many places mentioned in the saga. The landscape is starkly beautiful. As in the saga, there is a spare, understated quality which is completely captivating.*

*My main source for the saga is the English translation by Magnus Magnusson and Hermann Palsson (Penguin Classics). To that I have added knowledge gained through travel, research, and comparison with other translations.*

*My first and longest telling of the saga was over eight consecutive Friday evenings. Even then I had to leave out many "side stories" about neighbours and less prominent members of the family.*

☙

# Martha

I learned this story from my grandmother. She learned it from her grandmother and she from hers. It's a story of my ancestress Martha Cory and what befell her in the winter of 1692.

At the time of the story, Martha was in her sixties. She was a stout, hard-working farm woman. Sharp-witted, she always spoke her mind. She had a habit of often being right, something for which few of her neighbours ever forgave her. Her husband, Giles, was older, in his eighties. Quick of temper, he was slow to comprehend. Unlike Martha, he couldn't use words to win fights, but he still won with his fists. They were a mixed-blessing couple, but respected. They were landowners who owned a productive farm. Martha was a covenanting elder in the church.

It was not an easy time in the small village where they lived as my story opens. Winter, as we all know, can be a hard time of year. Martha and Giles lived on the far edge of the village and feared attack by Indians in what later became known as the

French and Indian War. Their land rights were in question, for the Massachusetts Colony was then without a governor and without a charter. They didn't know how or if they'd be able to retain the farm they had eked out of the bush.

The village itself was a village fraught with dissension and argument. The new minister, who'd been there just a little over a year, was supported by no more than half of the village. This, when the minister and the church were the heart and centre of the town.

The story itself properly starts in February when Betty Ann, the nine-year-old daughter of the Reverend Samuel Parrish, started acting oddly. At first she cried to herself and whimpered. She seemed distracted and didn't always hear when people spoke to her. After a few days she began crying at night, had nightmares and woke screaming. None could comfort her or bring her back from her dreams. Then her cousin, Abigail Williams, eleven, who lived with the Parrishes, started acting the same. The household was kept awake each night by the two girls and had no peace during the day.

Soon the Reverend Samuel Parrish fetched the village doctor. Dr Griggs examined the girls, but he could find nothing physically wrong with them. Finally, Griggs said what everyone feared he might say. The doctor proclaimed that the girls were bewitched.

At a time when belief in the devil was as strong as belief in God, there was only one choice. The search for witches was on in Salem Village, Massachusetts.

No sooner had Betty Ann and Abigail been declared bewitched than the other village girls started showing the same symptoms. Before the next night had fallen, young Ann Putnam, twelve, was crying, moaning, and convulsing. By the end of the week eight or ten girls were afflicted. Throughout that first week the Minister met with the girls – singly, in pairs, and all together.

The Minister called in other ministers from neighbouring towns so they could all pray together. He hoped that their combined voices would reach God and solve the problem sooner than his lone voice might. But no matter how they alternately threatened and cajoled the girls, day in and day out, the girls did not name who it was that afflicted them. They said, "No one afflicts us. It just happens."

Finally, at the end of a long day when the girls had been questioned for ten hours without let-up, Reverend Parrish bent to pick up young Betty Ann, who was half asleep in one of the chairs. As he lifted her up to carry her to bed, she murmured, "Tituba."

The Minister caught on the word, on the name. Quickly, almost frantically, he turned to the others. "Was it Tituba? Was it Tituba?" And the girls all responded as though a spring had let loose inside them. "Tituba, Tituba, Tituba. Yes, it was Tituba. And it was Sarah Good. Sarah Good! Oh, and Sarah Osburne! It was Goody Osburne, too!" Before the evening was out they had named three women.

Sarah Good was an impoverished older woman who wandered from house to house, begging. Her own house had fallen into such a state of disrepair that she rarely stayed there. She was rude and cantankerous. Few in the village liked her. She often cursed and muttered when people wouldn't give her food or money.

Sarah Osburne had been a good, God-fearing churchwoman up until recently. But she'd lost two husbands in close succession. Now she was distraught and ill much of the time. She spent a lot of time in bed and rarely left her house. She seldom travelled the six miles to the meeting house on Sabbath any longer.

Tituba, the first to be named, was a Barbadian slave of the Reverend Samuel Parrish. Tituba, a Carib Indian, and her husband, John Indian, worked hard at the Parrish homestead. She tended the kitchen, did the hard housework, and kept the vegetable garden. The girls spent much of their time, it later turned out, in the kitchen with Tituba that winter of the fits.

It's hard to know what really happened throughout that long winter in Salem Village, but the girls did talk – later, much later – about how they had spent mornings at the Parrish house being entertained by Tituba. Tituba told stories – the kind of wonderful, imaginative stories she had grown up with on Barbados. But stories like that were not told in Puritan Massachusetts. Salem was a village where there was no dancing. There were no dolls. There was no playing. There was no theatre. There was certainly no storytelling, except readings from the Bible.

The young girls gathered, innocently enough at first, to hear Tituba's wonderful stories. Then they moved on, to reading palms perhaps. Or perhaps they learned to weave simple spells, spells to discover the name of the man they might grow to marry and what their stature in the village might be. We'll never be sure just what went on in that kitchen. Oh, today we might look at all the things they did and say it's innocent enough child's play. But in those days and those times, even the girls knew that what they did was wrong.

Most of the girls were in their teens. Although saddled with household chores, they had gained some independence. They were bored and may not have worried too much about breaking rules, might have even found some excitement in being bad. But young Betty Ann, the nine-year-old, the youngest among them, was greatly distraught. She was torn between love and fear – her strong love for Tituba and her fear of punishment, and her simultaneous love and fear of her father, God's stern representative who lived in her own home. Little Betty Ann became caught in the pull between what was right and what was wrong. It's no wonder nightmares disturbed her sleep.

Once the girls had named three women as witches, two magistrates were brought from nearby Salem Town to hear what the women had to say for themselves and to find out if they were guilty enough to be held for a later formal trial.

As you can well imagine, trying a witch is a difficult thing. The easiest witches to try are those who confess. But few witches confess willingly; instead the accused must be judged in other ways. The logic went something like this: The magistrates knew that only a witch could send out a ghost, a spirit, a spectral self. So, if anybody saw a spectral self – an image of someone wandering where that person wasn't – well, that might be evidence that the person had sent her spirit self out into the world to do mischief. Hence, the person whose spectral self had been seen must be guilty of witchcraft.

Or perhaps someone had an effigy, or a figure of a face – perhaps a dried apple doll – well, that might show they were a witch. Or a person might put a curse on someone else or swear under their breath. What if a neighbour muttered walking by you on the laneway and the next week your cow was taken ill? Now, that could be a sign of witchcraft, too. And thus it was that a memory for petty details became a virtue in Salem Village.

The three women were taken to trial. On the morning of their preliminary hearing the entire village came to watch. There were so many spectators that they couldn't fit in the inn. Everyone moved across the green to the meeting house, to hold the hearing in the house of God. Not quite everyone was present, of course. But the people who didn't go mostly kept quiet about it. One of the few outspoken in her scorn for the trial was my ancestress Martha Cory. She let on that she wasn't even sure if she believed in witches. And she was fairly sure that if she did believe in witches, they wouldn't be the likes of Sarah Osburne and Sarah Good. She was so disgusted by the goings-on that when her husband Giles wanted to go, Martha tried to talk him out of it – she was sure he'd just pick a fight with someone anyway. When he insisted on going, she hid his saddle. For all that, he just walked the eight miles into the village.

As the morning started everyone was hushed. First the magistrates turned to Goody Good. They asked if she was guilty and she pleaded her innocence. They asked how did she afflict the girls and she said she did not. But there, before everyone's eyes, the girls started writhing in pain. Surely, anyone could see that Sarah Good was afflicting them. Finally, someone had the idea of turning Sarah Good around so that she didn't face the girls. Ah, suddenly it was quiet again. The girls looked calm and out of pain. Clear proof that was that Goody Good was a witch.

Then Sarah Osburne took the stand. The magistrates were smarter now; they faced her away from the girls so she couldn't create a ruckus. The magistrates questioned and Sarah, too, declared her innocence. In her desire to answer one of the questions, she spun around to face the magistrates. And just as though the girls had been waiting, they suddenly started screaming and crying in pain, the *very* minute Goody Osburne's eyes passed over them. Sarah Osburne was turned away again. There was quiet in the room. Another witch.

Finally, on the third day of the hearing, it was Tituba's turn. Tituba, the first to be accused, gave the people of Salem Village the drama they had waited for all week. In the ten days since her accusation, Tituba had been badly beaten and whipped by her master. She had learned that the only thing she could say was the "truth" the ministers thought they wanted to hear; the truth as Tituba knew it was never spoken in the meeting house.

Instead, Tituba told of all the things that witches did. She told of meeting a tall, dark man from Boston, a leader of the witches. She told of meeting with Goody Osburne and Goody Good. She told of black hats and black rats and red cats. She told of flying from place to place on a broomstick. She described large witches' meetings.

The trials might have ended then, with just three women sent off to Boston to be held for trial and eventually hanged. But on the final day of questioning, the magistrates asked whose name was in the devil's book. Tituba couldn't read. She couldn't read in her own living self or in her spectral self, but Tituba said there were nine names in the devil's book for Salem Village. And so, the search for witches continued in Salem Village, Massachusetts.

Once again, the girls were alternately cajoled and threatened, hour after hour, to name more witches who afflicted them. Again, the girls did not name names. But finally, on March 11th after a day of fasting and prayer, young Ann Putnam named another name.

The name she named sent shivers of fear throughout the entire village. This woman was no outcast, no slave. This woman was an upstanding elder of the church, a landowner. This woman was my ancestress Martha Cory.

Martha was no ordinary witch. Two church elders rode out to her farm the very next day to have a private word with Goody Cory. Well, my ancestress had the terrible habit of putting words in people's mouths before they spoke and on that day her visitors wished she'd been quiet for just once. As they arrived, Martha opened her door and said, "I know why you've come. You've come to talk to me about being a witch." The two men looked at each other, uncomfortable now: clearly, this was a sign of clairvoyance. More likely, the rumours had travelled faster than horses.

Besides, the entire village had talked of nothing but witchcraft for weeks. By now even non-believers such as Martha were learning the ways of witches and in her next breath Martha incriminated herself beyond redemption. "Could she tell you what I'd be wearing?" Martha asked, headstrong as ever, knowing that this was something the girls had described about Sarah Osburne. Fear could be heard in Elder Cheever's voice – "Young Ann accused you of blinding her. She couldn't see what you were wearing today," he mumbled. With a snort of disgust, Martha invited her guests inside for tea.

As the elders detailed the accusations against her, Martha, God bless her soul, had the effrontery to laugh in their faces. And laugh she did. "I do not believe in witches," she said, accusing the men of gullibility; "I don't think there *are* any witches in Salem Village." Not even Sarah Osburne and Sarah Good had dared to say there were no witches working for the devil. Surely only someone who was a witch herself would dare suggest that witches did not exist at all. They wondered, too, that Martha could laugh at them. Any woman who was innocent of witchcraft, who was still pure with God, surely such a woman would cry. But everyone knew that a witch could not shed tears. Perhaps Martha did not cry because she was a witch. In any event, her stubborn righteousness was insufferable.

A warrant for Martha's arrest was issued the next Sabbath eve. Since it was the eve of the Sabbath, she could not be arrested until the Monday. So, on Sunday, Martha travelled into the village to meeting according to her usual routine. Martha saw nothing wrong with going to meeting. Being of sound and sane mind herself, Martha expected sanity to return to Salem Village.

As Martha walked into the meeting house startled whispers filled the room. The congregation could not keep their eyes off her. She created such a stir that the girls, sitting in a row of honour in the front pew, were all but ignored. But not for long. The girls' wailing was so loud and the whispering so constant that the visiting minister, come to observe the possessed for himself, could barely be heard. As he began his sermon, young Abigail Williams yelled, "Name thy text!" And the minister, surprised and daunted, did so.

"It is a long text," she sneered. And all the congregation knew it was the devil's voice speaking. Alone among the parishioners, Martha had the audacity to smile at the impertinence of the girl. During the mid-day break, a neighbour suggested that Martha go home, that she had no business sitting in God's house. Martha argued her innocence. In her faith, Martha still believed she would convince the magistrates on Monday that the afflictions were a sham. What Martha did not yet understand was that her outward profession of faith would not save her.

That very afternoon, Martha's faith and insistence were unfairly rewarded. For the first time, Martha was publicly accused. "Look," cried out Abigail Williams, "there sits Goody Cory up on the beam overhead suckling a yellow bird betwixt her fingers." Everyone strained to see. Although only the visionary young Ann

Putnam joined Abigail in claiming to see Martha – all that most people saw were cobwebs – Martha might just as well have crawled up into the rafters in her own bulky physical self, for everyone believed her spirit was roosting above them.

The next day fared no better. Martha arrived for the hearing the next morning shaken and a little afraid. The night before, for the first time, she and Giles had fought about the witch trials. But outwardly Martha appeared composed. As was her wont, she took the initiative and immediately asked the magistrates to give her leave to pray. As any minister and church-goer knows, any opinion can be aired in a prayer. But the ministers did not allow her any leeway – this was their day to try her, not hers to defend herself. Magistrate Hawthorne did not even ask her plea. The girls were already performing in the front row. He raised his voice above their moaning. "Why do you afflict these girls?"

"I do not afflict them."

"Then who doth afflict them?"

"I know not," said Martha. And throughout that long morning, question after question of the scripture was thrown at her. And Martha answered every Biblical question and reference in accurate detail. Still the magistrates continued, hammering question after question.

Finally, Martha cried out in exasperation and exhaustion, "How could I know these things? I am a gospel woman." But her tired voice was caught by the girls.

"Gospel witch ... gospel witch ... gospel witch!" they cried. And once started, the mimicry continued through the afternoon. If Martha lifted a hand, the girls lifted theirs. If Martha leaned forward, the girls leaned forward as though pulled on invisible strings. Martha could barely move but the girls echoed every movement. As Martha momentarily slumped against the railing in fatigue, one of the girls slumped forward in apparent pain. Screaming, the girl pulled off her shoe and threw it, hitting Martha in the face. Blood dribbled down her face. As Martha bit her lip in dismay, the girls all bit theirs until blood ran down the chin of every girl.

Late in the afternoon, the magistrates declared Martha guilty enough to be sent off to Boston and held. As Martha was taken from the court-house she said, "You cannot prove me guilty of witchcraft. You *cannot* prove me guilty." What Martha had not yet realized was that nobody was being asked to prove her guilty. Instead, she was being asked to do the impossible: she was being asked to prove her innocence.

After Martha was led out the door, Giles Cory, her husband, was put on the stand. Giles was well-meaning, but slow. Giles tried to answer all the questions put to him. He'd begun to doubt, after ten days of rumour, whether or not his wife was actually as innocent as he had thought. But for all the questions asked of him, Giles could come up with very little. He remembered a night when Martha had stayed up late – very late, long after he'd gone to bed. But then, he was fairly sure that all she'd done was pray at the hearth. And Giles remembered a time when they'd argued. She'd broken Puritan rule by speaking against him, had told him he was wrong. But then Giles admitted the argument had to do with his not going to meeting faithfully. So that didn't amount to much either.

The magistrates finally sent Giles on his way. But the rumours started that day. "Giles could have told more if he wanted, don't you think?"

"Nah, if he knew, he would have said."

"No, no, he must know and be hiding secrets. He's her husband. He would have had more to say if he wasn't hiding something."

"Perhaps he, too, is a wizard," someone added. And so the rumours spread.

After Martha, the next person accused of witchcraft was Dorcas Good, the five-year-old daughter of Sarah Good. Dorcas's hearing only lasted a few minutes and she, too, was sent off to Boston and held in chains to await trial.

Rebecca Nurse was next. Goody Nurse, in her seventies, was the matriarch of a large and upstanding family. When Rebecca was taken from her sick-bed, fear swept through the village. Goody Nurse was the last person living to be a witch. But then again, if Rebecca Nurse was a witch, there was no one to trust. *Anyone* could be a witch, anyone. And the fear went wider and wider.

Throughout that spring, the girls named person after person. They were unstoppable. They reached beyond the village boundaries, naming people in Topsfield and then as far away as Salem Town and even Boston. It wasn't until May that the new governor of the colony arrived. He quickly assigned judges and the trials began. The newly established court and the trials were barely distinguishable from the previous hearings. Oh, certainly they were more formal and the girls were kept quieter, but the form was much the same.

The first to stand trial was Bridget Bishop, a tavern owner from the village outskirts. On June 2nd, 1692, Bridget Bishop was found guilty of being a witch and condemned to hang, for nothing more than that she had a penchant for lace and red satin. On June 9th she was hanged.

Although one of the first to be accused, Martha was not one of the first to be tried. In the sweat of July and August, several of the women sharing Martha's prison cell were taken to trial. *All* were condemned. By the time Martha stood in the Boston courthouse, another ten had been hanged. Cotton Mather himself, New England's most famous witch-hunter, subdued the crowds the day Martha's friend Elizabeth Proctor was hanged.

On September 9th, Martha stood before the judges. The person on trial just before her had confessed and been let go. But months in jail hadn't diminished either Martha's integrity or her stubbornness. My grandmother told me that Martha was at her most eloquent that day. Martha used the pause after each question to beg the judges to question the rightness of what they were doing. She pleaded for her own innocence and also the innocence of others.

On trial the same day as Martha was Rebecca Nurse's sister Mary Esty. Instead of answering the questions put to her, Mary prayed. She prayed that the magistrates would open their eyes to God. She prayed for those still in jail to be pardoned. Even if she died, Mary reasoned, there were many others who might live. Mary's and Martha's eloquence saved neither of them: both women were condemned to die.

For Martha, the hardest blow of all in that difficult year came *after* she was already condemned. On September 14th, the Reverend Samuel Parrish and a delegation of church elders visited her in jail. Throughout her six months of imprisonment Martha's faith in God and her own church had never wavered. She had prayed and believed that whatever was happening would not continue long. But on that Wednesday, Martha was informed that she had been excommunicated. Without her God and her church, Martha had nothing left. She lived her last days without the anchor she had lived by.

On September 16th, Martha lost her husband. The rumours against Giles had grown and he, too, had been accused. Alone of all those accused, Giles Cory had proclaimed neither his innocence nor his guilt. For Giles had thought long and hard after he had testified against Martha. He had come to believe in her innocence, his own innocence, and the innocence of all others accused. He had come to realize that the courts of Massachusetts could give no justice in 1692. And so, Giles had refused to speak.

Somehow, Giles had learned that under an old British common law, his property could not be taken from him if he did not speak. Giles, who was not accused until the summer, had seen the farms, houses, and equipment stolen from those in jail by the courts of Massachusetts. His children would have nothing without the land. Thus, it came to pass that two days after Martha was excommunicated, Giles was unchained and made to lie down in the field behind the jail. There, according to old British practice, stone after stone was placed on his chest to force words of guilt or innocence from him. My grandmother told me that the only words Giles uttered all that long afternoon were an occasional "More weight. More weight," until the weight of the stones crushed him.

Six days later, Martha, along with seven other accused witches and one wizard, was taken from Boston jail. The road to Salem Village had never seemed so long. Spectators watched all along the route, for the death of a witch is an exciting thing.

As the condemned ascended Gallows Hill, the wheel of the cart they were in caught in a rut. The spectators cried out, "Ah, it is the devil's work! The devil tries to hold his own back. He cannot win! God has them now!" The cart was freed and the gallows reached.

When the noose was around Martha's neck, she began to pray. Martha prayed out loudly and without hesitation, so that all could hear her. My ancestress recited the Lord's Prayer without faltering once. For the last time, Martha Cory made her mark. Martha prayed to the instant of her death. All those listening felt fear and doubt creep into them as she died, for everyone in Salem knew that *a witch cannot pray.*

Each of my stories has an epilogue, because these real women's lives were more than the moments I choose to tell you about.

In total between two and three hundred people were accused, nearly all of them women. Nineteen were killed. The day that Martha was hanged was the last day that anyone was hanged. Public dismay had been mounting throughout the spring and summer. Increasingly, respectable and wealthy people were among those accused of witchcraft. Many of the wealthy had the resources to escape out of state (some between the accusation and the hearing; some from jail). Many relocated to New York where they convinced the government and the Dutch Reform Church to lobby the Massachusetts government. The new governor established guidelines to determine guilt or innocence.

Spectral evidence was no longer allowed as a justification for death sentence. Spectral evidence meant any action by spirits and included all the affliction of the girls. Not surprisingly, everyone brought to trial under the new guidelines was released. Towards the end of the year, everyone still in jail was pardoned.

Ann Putnam, a twelve-year-old, was the primary accuser. Her mother, Ann Putnam senior, was the only adult to join the circle of the afflicted. Between them they named approximately two-thirds of those accused. The younger Ann undertook public penance as an adult, a series of public prayers and requests for forgiveness at meeting.

But it was years before public recompense was granted by the government and church. Martha's excommunication was revoked fifteen years after her death; Giles's, twenty years. In 1711, the grandchildren of Martha and Giles were awarded twenty-one pounds in total for the loss of both grandparents. Their settlement was larger than some.

If a family member didn't seek a pardon, it wasn't granted. In some cases, the families of the accused had died off or their children had left the colony so that no one sought a pardon. Astoundingly, the government of Massachusetts granted the last pardons and changed court records to show innocence of all those condemned or accused in 1955!

### Connie Clement

*Reading a news clipping about women being burned as witches in 1985 prompted me to create a story about one of the women hanged as a witch in Salem, Massachusetts. In the course of reading half a dozen books about New England witchcraft, I chose Martha Cory from among several possible women because she was as close to cocky as a Puritan woman could be. The most useful books in my research were Marion Starkey,* The Devil in Massachusetts: A Modern Inquiry into the Salem Witchtrials *(London: Robert Hale 1949) and Paul Boyer and Stephan Nissenbaum,* Salem Possessed: The Social Origins of Witchcraft *(Cambridge, Mass.: Harvard University Press 1974).*

*As a feminist and a women's health activist, storytelling is important to me as a source of healing and as a means of creating women's culture. By using historical documents to create stories of individual women, I also find roots for myself.*

༅

# Laura and the Lilies

My mother grew lilies. Not that she was the only one in the neighbourhood who did, but hers were special; perhaps because the achievement of even four or five blooms in the midst of an extended family of teenagers, as many as fourteen at times, was remarkable. But Mother had dozens of lilies – despite the lawn fights with the hose, the midnight horse escapes, the digging dogs. The cry comes down over the years: "Not in the lilies!!" Farm life was not gentle, especially on gardens.

She grew them for herself, tending them like children, all the while professing to not much care what happened to them eventually. But, in late summer, her pride in them allowed her to pick a few blooms and display them – on the mantel in the house, on the chancel steps or the altar at church, and at the fall fair. Once, she even had some photographed and framed.

In this she was not alone, since many of her friends did the same; although not with the ferocity which seemed to accompany most of Mother's "good works." So a friendly rivalry grew in the neighbourhood, especially as the summer ended and the harvests in gardens and fields began to come in.

As teenagers, we thought of these gardens as a mild form of hysteria on Mother's part; and so we humoured her in helping to plant and weed and cut borders, and chase away the livestock.

For some reason, on the night in question Mother had gone to the city, leaving only two of us – my sister Laura and me – to look after the place. Why there were only two of us I forget. Momma simply said, "Keep the place standing," and left. Oh, she would be back late the next day, so there was nothing unnerving about her absence. So we did the chores, fed ourselves, talked and read and cleaned up, and then went to bed. Bed for Laura, as a girl, was upstairs in the house; I slept, like the rest of the boys, in a large open loft above the dairy and garage, next to the house. All the boys and visiting men slept there, in old army cots that lined the walls, with our clothes hanging over the rafters, and personal possessions in orange crates standing beside each bed. My brothers and I slept there until the first snowfall each year, when Mother finally relented and we were allowed back in the house.

I sleep well. Nothing short of the Last Judgment is likely to waken me before dawn. Laura, on the other hand, sleeps with one eye open; which is probably why this all happened.

The dogs started barking out on the porch. Not unusual, except that they kept at it with sufficient excitement to bring Laura out of bed and downstairs in her night-gown. She lit a lantern and went out on the porch. She couldn't really see anything, although the dogs by this time were hysterical. She put down the lantern, went back in the house to the gunrack, and pulled down the one weapon she knew how to use: an old Ithaca double-bore .12 gauge shotgun, with barrels as long as your arm. She broke it open, rummaged around in the drawer until she found two shells to fit it, loaded and snapped it shut, and went back out onto the porch. She called the dogs back, tucked the butt of the gun under her arm, cocked both barrels – and then couldn't remember which trigger drove which barrel. So she pulled them both.

I woke up.

By the time I got to the porch, the dogs were long gone. So, for that matter, was whatever she'd been shooting at. But Laura was still there. She was lying flat on her back with the wreckage of the screen-door under her, in the middle of the kitchen floor, holding aloft a smoking shotgun.

"Did I get it?" she asked, as I stepped through the rubble and retrieved the gun.

"Did I get it?" she asked as I helped her up off the floor and dusted her.

"Did I get it?" she demanded as she stood on the porch, rubbing her behind, while I surveyed the damage out in the yard.

Well, she hadn't exactly missed. She missed the midnight raider all right, whatever it was. Not a sign of it. But those two loads of heavy shot had sawn off the whole bed of Mother's lilies about twelve inches off the ground, just as neatly as if you'd run a mower over them.

Well, that was that, thought I. Hell to pay, death and destruction, grounded, loss of income, visions of handcuffs, prison, and dishes for months – we were not a happy pair as we went back to bed.

Next morning after chores, I set about rebuilding the screen-door, still wondering what to do about those damn flowers. I was about halfway through when a car came down the lane. Out climbed Mrs Brett, our neighbour, also our grade-school teacher. I can still recall her voice as she surveyed the carnage.

"What's happened to your door, boy, and ... gracious, child, whatever happened to your mother's lilies!!!"

We began to explain, painfully. ("Well, miz Brett, Laura was shooting at a coon, least we thought it was a coon, and she missed, well she didn't miss exactly ...") Forty years as a farm wife and teacher made Mrs. Brett a force to be reckoned with. She flapped a hand at me and I shut up. She pointed imperiously at her car. "Laura Ann, you get in that car. Boy, I want that door fixed and swinging by the time we get back!" And they drove off.

I had just finished touching up the paint when they returned. Laura got out of the car, and together she and Mrs Brett lugged a bushel-basket from the trunk and over to the flower bed.

It was full of lilies, all colours, all varieties.

"Don't just stand there, child, fetch a bucket of water. Now Laura, we'll need a shovel ..."

And in half an hour, we had removed the shattered stems and leaves of Mother's lilies and replaced them all, in neat rows, packed and watered, with the new ones.

We then stood for ten minutes, enduring Mrs Brett's wrath. Ten of the worst minutes of our lives, while she recalled with painstaking detail every misdemeanour, failing, mistake, memory loss, and boneheaded action that had ever befallen us; finishing with a despairing forecast of our future prospects. Grade-school teachers have that knack, have you ever noticed? Then she left, calling "Don't tell your mother" out the window.

The flowers, according to Laura, had been donated by the neighbours. "Donated" may be stretching it, since people seldom said no to Mrs Brett, but she got them just the same, by twos and threes, from her own and other gardens, and brought them to us. Such was the community that raised us.

Mother came in due course. She made a fuss all right, but not about the flowers. She got green paint on her hand when she opened the screen-door, and that sort of took her mind off everything else. She did thank us for weeding her flowers though.

At the fair, Momma's lilies took home first prize. Everyone congratulated her, which wasn't surprising. They were everyone's after all. But no one ever told her, then or since. To this day, I don't think Mother ever knew those weren't her lilies.

*K. Reed Needles*

*This story, for what it's worth, is true. My home life was really like that.*

જ

# Tales of Donald Lake

## Spring

Now one day, oh one day in spring I was watching the sugar snow melting on the hillside. It formed little trickles that ran down the hillside and on into the lake.

When the spring sun touched the strong winter ice it was weakened. Slowly it broke apart, the wind blowing against it, pushing the ice together in a sort of a symphony.

I went down to the lake to watch Father push his canoe out

into the bay trying to catch some fish. How long he fished I do not know for while he was out there fishing I too was fishing the bits of ice out of the bay. I would suck the water from the middle of the ice shards. Or hold the ice needles up to the sun using some for prisms and others for magnification of the far shore. It all depended on their shapes. Some didn't do anything. But always they would melt leaving me with cold hands.

After a while Father pulled his canoe ashore and said the fish weren't biting. Dinner, like breakfast, would not be served.

Well anyway my sister and I were sent to the local creek to see if we could snare some fish now that Father hadn't caught any.

We went in our rawhide moccasins for it was still too cold to go barefoot. By the time we were halfway there, my feet were wet clear through. I felt a cold numbness creeping up my legs. To relieve some of the pain I tried to think of other things.

I chose a piece of high ground under a large Spruce tree when we got to the creek. It would hide the shadows of my own darkness. I adjusted the snare on the end of the alder limb, dipping it into the water near an overhanging bank, hoping that a fish would come down the creek. I knew I would only have a second to pull the fish out.

Standing still made me more aware of the cold paining my feet. It was almost unbearable and I began to think about how in the summertime it would be so hot in this spot that I would have to move further inland. I remembered how in the summertime I would watch the painted turtle as he sunned himself on a log protruding into the water. And I would stamp my foot on the ground just to watch him jump into the water so I could catch a glimpse of his undershell colouring. I always thought of it as a gift he shared with me.

A blackbird staunchly declaring his territory brought me back to reality. The bird arrogantly flashed his red and yellow spot at me as if ordering me off his land. You know, I was pleased for his saucy company.

I glanced down at my snare silently waiting in the fast flowing water, waiting for some unsuspecting fish to come into it. And then I saw one come sliding down the creek. It wasn't a trout or a whitefish or even a pickerel. It was just an old skinny bony Jackfish, a fish that under other circumstances I would not even consider. But it was a fish and it was food. I tensed every muscle in my body. And he came within an inch of my snare. Then he stopped lazily moving his fins as if he had a lifetime to live and then he almost went into the snare but not quite.

He stopped. A pain shot up my leg and I moved it. The fish darted away leaving only the particles of dirt from the bottom of the river in the snare.

I knew I had to be even more still. I stood more quietly hoping that the next fish could not hear my pounding heart as loud as it sounded to me.

Finally another fish came sliding down the river. I saw his gill covering opening and closing, the red gills flashing brightly, and oh I could almost taste the baked fish as he came closer. Then he entered my snare and I pulled quickly, dumping him on the river bank.

Oh how glad I was! Between my sister and me we managed to get enough fish for supper and to feed the sled-dogs. We would all have full bellies when bedtime came. And my sister and I were responsible for that. Did it ever make me feel great!

## Cabbages

Now one year in the spring Mother managed to get a package of cabbage seeds. And I loved looking at the drawings on the package. In the spring we usually had just meat to eat and this year was not different. Times were lean. I would trace the lines of the cabbages on the seed packet drawings and then I would imagine how good they would taste. It had been a long hungry winter.

They were planted when the weather warmed and each day after breakfast, which consisted of oatmeal, the entire family would take a walk down to the garden to see if anything had come up overnight. It was the big event of the day. And one day ten little cabbage plants could be seen. As summer went on one little plant died. Near the end of August there were still nine cabbages the size of Macintosh apples. How I imagined the final days when we would cook them for supper along with our fish!

Now in the fall the sled-dogs were allowed to run free so they could fend for themselves. This way more fish could be dried to carry the dogs through the lean winter months. This fall was no exception. The dogs were set free. They dashed up to the house,

licking everyone, and then rushed down to the garden. There
was a growling and barking near the garden so I knew the dogs
had caught something but before I reached the garden the growling
had stopped and the dogs disappeared into the bush.

I rushed after them to see what they'd caught. I hoped it was
that pesky groundhog that had been eyeing the cabbages all summer.

Well when I got to the garden, every one of the cabbages had
been nipped off and eaten. All that was left were the frail stems
sticking up from the ground like tombstones. Oh was I mad.

Once when I was telling this story to a group of grade fours
they all cheered for the dogs 'cause every one of them hated
cabbage.

## Christmas

Usually Father would be away on his trapline for a week at a
time tending his traps. But always at Christmastime he would
come home early from looking to his traps and wait around for
the plane to come in. He didn't make any more trips until after
Christmas.

When the plane came in Father would invite the pilot up to
the cabin and show him the Northern hospitality, trying to acquire
as much news from him as he could. It had been a long time
since anyone visited Donald Lake. My family and I were interested
in news of anyone – who married within the last year, who had
a baby – and it really didn't matter if we knew the folks or not.

Father would ask after the pilot's health, and his family, then
serve him the Company Cookies and black tea. Once the pilot
finished his tea he left.

Now the excitement of Christmas was upon us, for on Christmas
Eve, my sister, brother, myself, and Father would all tramp out
into the bush looking for the perfect Christmas tree. It couldn't
be just any tree, it had to be perfect. It had to have beautifully
rounded boughs on all sides. An impossibility in the bush, where
you have one-sided trees, the top-limb-only trees, and the trees
with no limbs on at all.

But we'd find the best we could and I would run after Father,
panting hard as I dragged myself through the deep snow, the cold
of the winter catching in my throat until I coughed up a little

blood. But I would keep up and not complain for it was Christmas. And of course one did not complain at Christmastime.

Father would finally find a tree that was sort of good, and he would chop it down, cut a few extra limbs from another tree, and drag the tree home.

My sister, my brother, and I would run behind, trying to keep up. Then Father would put the tree up in the house. He'd take his brace and bit and drill holes in the tree. Then he'd add the extra limbs in to make the tree perfect.

He would start decorating from the top of the tree slowly with the glass balls, going down, down, down, until the bottom limbs were reached. Then Mary Lou, Gordie, and I were allowed to hang the plastic balls on those limbs.

Father would start hanging the icicles too, one at a time, and I would watch him transform the little green spruce into a magical tree, a beautiful tree, a work of art. But he'd never help take the ornaments down after Christmas. We children and Mother did that.

And always on Christmas Eve after we had wrapped the presents, sometimes boughten, other times home-made depending on how rich we were, Father would make doughnuts.

This was something so very special for Father believed cooking was not a man's work. It was woman's work. And even though he would come home after a long trip when he had cooked for himself, he would demand that Mother cook his supper for him.

But on Christmas Eve, oh he would cook the most beautiful doughnuts, when we had the ingredients. I really looked forward to that. I would go to bed real early with my brother and sister, and the blanket was hung up to shut out the Christmas scene. When Father cooked he would sneak me a doughnut that was all hot and sugary. I loved that. I would eat it quietly in bed, me and my sister Mary Lou. Gordie was always sound asleep by then.

Next morning we would wake up and see our presents under the tree but we had to eat breakfast before opening them. We usually had hot oatmeal, you know the rolled oats with white sugar sprinkled on top, and sometimes at Christmastime we would even have powdered milk to put on it.

After eating breakfast we would all go to the tree and slowly open our presents. This one year I got the most beautiful satin ribbon I'd ever seen. Why, it was three inches wide and it was so satiny-feeling that I ran it through my fingers, back and forth, oh it felt good. It came from the Summer-Folk. Such a lovely rose satin ribbon for my hair!

Then Mother told me to go out and play. So we all put our presents back under the tree as we were supposed to do after opening them, and we children were sent out to play. I got tired of waiting for my chance to slide on the shovel. You know the square shovels they have, well Mary Lou and I we'd sit one at a time, sitting on our rear ends on the shovel with our legs and feet wrapped around the handle, while balancing halfway so the handle of the shovel would keep up, and we could then slide down the hill. But I got so tired of waiting that I went and got a spruce bough to slide upon. My brother got a small piece of precious cardboard from Mother to slide upon.

When we came in at dinnertime there was a feast upon the table. Roast Lynx instead of the usual roast Beaver. We ate the roast lynx with stewed barley, white bread, and all the stewed applesauce we wanted, with Company Cookies as well.

After supper we children and Father would go outside in the frosty night air to watch the northern lights flicking across the sky and to point out the various groups of stars. Then we'd wind up the evening by calling to our pack of wolves and the wolves would answer us as always. Father would never ever shoot our pack of wolves even if there was a large bounty on them.

And as I howled to the wolves I remembered the time when a wolf came right to our cabin, put his nose against the window and stared into the cabin.

It was so exciting. The next day I went out and measured my foot in his footprints. How big his feet were!

I started getting so cold that I raced into the cabin to seek some warmth.

And not only that but later on at night, after supper, we would hear the Christmas Story Father had to tell.

We waited for that story all day long. Father would tell of the first Christmas he spent with Mother. Oh he hadn't had much of a life at home what with his father dying so young. His first Christmas was the most precious Christmas he'd ever spent. It happened that Mother had bought him a present. It was a garage with two cars in it, and they wound up too. Every Christmas he would get the present out and he would unwrap the yellowing tissue paper, then he would wind the cars up and let us fetch the cars when they became unwound and actually bring them back to him. Then he would wind them up again and he would tell the story about how he found the present under the Christmas tree, that first Christmas Day that he had shared with Mother.

After we would eat doughnuts sitting in the darkness by the small flickering light of the camp-stove while Father told other stories. All of Father's were true. And oh he told a lot of stories.

Christmas day had been warm and the roof had leaked a little as the snow melted on the tar-paper. The day after Christmas I woke up to find the temperature had dropped quickly. My beautiful satin ribbon was frozen to the floor. It was almost a week before another warm spell came and I managed to get my ribbon off the floor.

I guess we all love the Christmas of our childhood.

### Pat Andrews

*These stories are old photographs – verbal photographs from the past.*

*Life on Donald Lake didn't come in big adventures – the way of life came in little snippets.*

*It was waking up in the morning and going out the door for the trip to the outhouse and coming face to face with a moose and her calf on the pathway.*

*It was having a fisher run by me, almost brushing my leg as I was standing still watching a bird.*

*It was coming face to face with a black bear, so close we could touch – and turning tail and running away as fast as I could – glancing back to see the bear running away in the opposite direction. Both of us seeking our own safety.*

*It was taking the baking pans that we used to bake the fish and going down to the beach. Then taking a little sand with the short green moss – the moss that cut grease as well as any soap ... and scouring the pan.*

*Looking up while doing this and seeing a pair of otters playfully sliding down the rocks into the lake.*

*It was having the Whisky Jacks eat from my hands.*

*It was Father making the Alder Bush talk by cutting a whistle from the bush for me.*

*It was the constant hunger gnawing inside my body. Going without food for days.*

*And going out to tend my rabbit snares on such a hungry day I saw a rabbit still alive in one snare. On catching him, he bit my mitt and screamed – it was the first time I'd ever heard a rabbit make a sound and I cried for it seemed so unfair that he had to die that I would live.*

*And then the feeling that I had when I returned home bringing the rabbit which was the only food we had for three or four days. How ecstatic and proud I felt!*

∾

# The Porcupine

Dad worked in the big cities – Toronto, Niagara Falls, Buffalo, and Detroit. High steel, industrial painting, and window washing – *Indian* men have always been famous for their equilibrium in high place – something to do with the middle-ear position. Anyway, my dad was away a lot. So, Mom had to look after us kids herself and supplement Dad's earnings with her craft work.

She worked with porcupine quills and birch-bark. This she learned from Aunt Rena. Aunt Rena was a master at making quill boxes, beautiful quill boxes which she sold at the CNE (Canadian National Exhibition) each summer. Quill boxes were expensive and required an enormous amount of work. Mom made headbands, something simple, easy to make, and something tourists could pick up for a dollar or two.

Mom would sort her quills into fat ones and thin ones, and long ones and short ones. She'd dye them using crepe paper and vinegar, or a commercial product. Sometimes she would use a natural dye – berries or bark or something like that. Carefully she'd sketch designs onto strips of birch-bark, and then with an awl or darning needle she would begin to embroider, punching a hole, pushing the sharp end of a softened quill into the hole and tightening it by pulling the quill partway through with tweezers. The sharp end she'd snip off and flatten.

The embroidery done, she would then sew a strip of felt to the birch-bark, join the ends and – there was a headband. The headbands she then took to the reserve general store to buy milk and bread and other supplies.

We older kids, of course, learned quill embroidery. And soon we were making the headbands, thus giving Mom time to spend creating the pictures – blue jays, chickadees, deer, other wildlife and wildflowers. We were in awe of her artistry, and so very proud when a reporter came by to do a story about her.

She would choose her quills carefully for her pictures. The darkened end of the quills would provide the shading in her pictures. One of her finest pieces of artwork was a gift for George Armstrong, the hockey player; others were sold for fifteen or twenty dollars. The value of those pictures today runs into the thousands.

One spring Mom's supply of quills ran low and so she asked my brother Tony to go out and find a porcupine. "Down the road about a mile or so, near that big elm tree. I saw a porcupine there the other day. Must have been hit by a car. Bring it to me," she told him.

Tony went off and he walked and walked, past the elm tree and further down the road. But he didn't see any porcupine. He walked back to the elm tree a couple of times before he realized there wasn't going to be a porcupine. Someone else must have picked it up.

Tony knew how Mom needed the quills and so he decided to hunt for a porcupine. He would also prove that he too was a hunter, a good hunter. He found a good-sized rock at the side of the road and headed into the bush.

It wasn't long before he spotted a great big porcupine. Taking careful aim, he hurled the rock. It struck with a dull thud and the porcupine lay down and died. Tony pulled a length of rope form his pocket, thinking how proud Mom would be that he had fetched a porcupine for her, a big one too. But my brother's heart stopped as he reached down to tie the forepaws of the animal. There beside the dead porcupine was a little pink porcupine baby.

He wasn't sure what to do, so he tied up the dead animal as fast as he could and dragged it home. With a lump in his throat he told Mom about the porcupine kitten.

Towdy was listening. A year younger than Tony, and four years younger than me, Towdy always had a special way with animals. She could stand outside with a handful of crumbs and all kinds of birds would gather round. Some would light on her head or shoulders, others right in her hand. When she heard about the porcupine, she questioned Tony carefully, and then headed off through the bush, around the trees and over the boulders. There, curled up on the spot where its mother had died, she found the little pink baby. She scooped it up carefully, cupped it in her hands, and instinctively held it close to her heart so the baby could hear the rhythm of her heartbeat and feel the motion of her breathing. She then hurried home.

Tony was quickly sent off to the general store, with an armload of headbands. He returned with a can of baby formula and a box of pablum. That's what Towdy fed her critter. In fact, she was getting up for night-time feedings every two or three hours.

That year taught us wonderful things about porcupines. For one, porcupines purr like cats. Porki was as cuddly as a kitten and just as playful too. Towdy would hold her left hand down to Porki. Porki would crawl into the palm of her hand. Towdy would then hold him up into the air. Porki would creep along her arm, sit on her left shoulder and whisper sweet porcupine nothings into her ear. He would then nuzzle the back of her neck, perch himself on her right shoulder, and whisper more sweet nothings. Towdy would then extend her right arm, the porcupine would waddle out to her fingertips and she would lower him to the floor.

Porki played with each one of us, but slept with Towdy. He would curl up beside her pillow and sometimes on cold nights he would wiggle his way down under the blankets. And yes, sometimes Towdy did wake up to pull a quill or two from her side. This is how we learned that porcupines don't shoot quills. We all knew that, but didn't necessarily believe it.

Whenever strangers tried to pick up Porki or when people Porki didn't like tried to pick him up or whenever he was frightened by a loud or unfamiliar noise or something unfamiliar, Porki turned himself into a prickly little ball. Anyone who tried to handle this little fuzz ball ended up with a handful of prickles; everyone except Towdy, of course.

The days and weeks went by and soon Porki was going out to the garden, out to nibble yellow beans and tomatoes and lettuce. The days and weeks went by and Porki was venturing further and further into the garden. We knew it had to be. Mom said so. Porcupines needed that space, and we really couldn't expect Porki to live with us forever, although we all wished it could be.

The days and weeks went by and Porki was venturing beyond the garden, coming home late at night or the next day, and sometimes not for a couple of days.

One day Porki didn't come home. That was a sad time – for Towdy and the rest of us. Mom said Porki had heard "the call of the wild." Other times she said it was "a lady porcupine" he'd heard. And another time she told us that Porki wanted a family of his own. And we couldn't deny him that.

Months passed, and one day my brothers were heading off to the general store again. Way up in front them, they could see a small animal lumber onto the road. As they got closer they could see it was a porcupine doing its flat-footed waddle across the dirt road. "Hey, *Porki!*" they called just for fun. The porcupine stopped, turned slowly around and waddled towards them. "Hey, Porki," they shouted again and knew it *was* our pet. Porki waddled closer, grunting his porcupine greetings *kugg kugg. Kugg kugg kugg.* The boys and the porcupine talked for a while. When it was time to go, Porki turned slowly away and waddled across the road. They say he turned back for one more look before disappearing into the tall grass and the bush.

We had many pets during those years – flying squirrels, red squirrels, ducks, rabbits, raccoons, bees, and butterflies. But Porki was always the special one.

Those were good times back then when we were children. The years went by and Mom and Dad were able to build a new house, just across the yard on the other side of the white oak tree. By that time we were all on our own. But imagine nine kids and two adults and all kinds of pets in a three-bedroom house. Mom and Dad had one bedroom. *"The girls,"* all five of us, shared one with the porcupine and all of Towdy's other pets. The boys, all four of them, shared the smaller bedroom. Anyhow, Mom and Dad built a new house and the years went by.

My sisters and brothers and I went off to high school, college, and university. Tony now works for the government. I'm a storyteller and writer. Towdy is a day-care worker, has four children of her own, and still takes in and looks after injured or orphaned animals. This spring she took in *Kukky,* a baby groundhog. It was night-time feedings not only for the Kukky but her own new baby. Our youngest brother, Scoobie, found *Kukgeez* on the roadside. Its mother had been hit by a car. "Kukky" is short for "Kukgeez," which is Ojibway for groundhog.

One summer evening, not too long ago, Towdy and Mom were having a nice quiet visit, just the two of them. They were talking, listening to the crickets, talking, listening to the tree frogs. They were talking, watching the shooting stars over head and waiting for grandmother moon to rise over the limestone bluff. After a bit they became aware of a noise, a scratching noise somewhere over by the old house. They found a flashlight and quietly made their way across the lawn, past the oak tree and through the tall grass. The noise stopped briefly and then continued. Towdy and Mom crept round to the front porch of the old house. They shone the light into the corners of the porch. Nothing. They shone the light along the door frame. Nothing. Then they shone the light along the bottom of the door. And there it was – one great big *old* porcupine scratching to get in. It stiffened and blinked at the brightness of the light. "Hello, Porki," they said. And the big old porcupine relaxed, then lumbered round to look at them. There they sat for a good two hours or so, Towdy, Mom, and the porcupine. Once again Towdy and Mom listened to the sweet porcupine nothings *kugg kugg. Kugg kugg kugg.*

Porki had come back to an empty house. How many times, we wondered, how many times had he come back and scratched at the door? That old porcupine never came back again, even though Mom and Towdy waited and watched. The house is gone now, but we know that Porki had not forgotten us after all those years, and he had come back to say good-bye one last time.

### Lenore Keeshig-Tobias

*I grew up on the reserve and am the oldest of ten. Storytelling has always been an important part of our family life, not just as heritage in the traditional stories, but as a necessary function in our individual life circle and the pieces that make up that circle. Some of these stories are not flattering, but nevertheless will be told time and again – reflections of the trickster-teacher and of what not to do. Others, like the one told here, are fond remembrances of what our children now refer to as the "olden days!" Some of these stories are still growing, and will continue into the next generation.*

*At first, I was afraid to let people know this was a family story. I wasn't sure if listeners would feel comfortable with a personal story or my family history, even if the story was a good one. At the time this story began I was a gawky adolescent, thinking my life was so boring and there was nothing to write about or tell except family experiences. I see now I was in the midst of the stories growing.*

*This summer past I went home and asked permission of family members involved to continue with the story and to use their names.*

℘

# The Gold Mine

What I'm going to tell you is all true, as it was told to me by my mother and father. It takes place in South Africa, and a good title for the story would be "The Gold Mine."

My father and mother lived in Lithuania, were born there and lived there. Things had been bad in Lithuania for a long time, and not just during the First World War, but before that too. The way my mother told it, the German armies would come through, and then Russian armies would come through, and then Polish armies would come through. It ended up with everybody being able to speak half a dozen languages, but life was no fun! People wanted to get away.

Many Lithuania Jews went to America, the "Golden Land." Others said, "With so many people going there it's sure to be overcrowded," and they went to Brazil or Argentina. But others heard about South Africa. South Africa was very remote, it took months to get there by boat, and they really didn't know what they were going to find there, was it going to be jungle – lions and tigers? They knew that there was gold there, and gold was good. They knew that there were diamonds there, and diamonds were good. They knew that there were blacks there, and they weren't sure if that was good. But they were told that the blacks didn't kill Jews, that there were no pogroms in South Africa, and they knew that that was good. So, many Lithuanian Jews went there. My father went. He and my mother were in love, but there was only money for one ticket, so he went first. He arrived in Cape Town, and was immediately taken in by a "landsman." Someone who comes from your village is a landsman. And the landsman is like kin. He was taken in, and the next day he went to work. Now, he didn't speak a word of English, but that didn't matter, you didn't need to know the language to work.

He went to work, and he got his first paycheque at the end of the week – the end of the week being Saturday. For the first time in his life my father, a Jew, worked on the Sabbath, Saturday. But this was South Africa, this was his new home, and he had to fit in with its new ways. So he worked Saturday, got his paycheque, and he paid his landsman for his board and lodge, like they'd agreed. He took out a sixpence (that's like a dime), and that was his spending money for the week. And the rest he put away to save. Why? First of all, to save for a ticket for my mother, so that she could come and they could get married. And next, and even more important for him, he was saving because, he said, he wasn't going to work for other people all his life and make *them* rich. He was going to own his own business, so that he'd be working for himself and making himself rich!

Well, he did have a sixpence to spend. And that first day of rest, Sunday in this case, he went into the town to take a look around. Now, my father *looked* at things. I can remember when he was old and frail, and his life and energy were ebbing. I took him to the theatre. And he didn't want to go to the theatre but I said, "Come, you'll enjoy it."

He went and he sat there, huddled in his seat, a little old man, knowing that Death would soon touch him. As the play developed, he looked at the stage, sat upright and began to lean forward until he was focused intensely on the action that was happening on the stage; absorbed, fascinated. He looked at things. He was interested in things. So on that first Sunday he went out into the city of Cape Town, which he hadn't seen because he'd been working all week, and he looked and looked.

He saw a long line of people at a store. They were buying something, and they were eating what they were buying. They were coming out of the store with something wrapped in newspaper, which they'd open, and then dip in and eat. Well, he went and looked. And what did he see? When the people opened the newspaper there was a piece of fried fish – that he recognized, that he knew from Lithuania – and something else that he'd never seen before.

Now he knew fried fish was very good, but the people didn't eat the fried fish first, they'd eat the other things first. They'd pass the newspaper round to their friends and each person would take one of these things, gobble it up, and say "Mmm!" It was obviously something very good. So he went and looked to see how much they were spending, and it was a tickee, that's half of a sixpence (like a nickel). So he stood in line and half of his week's pocket money went to buy this packet of fish and the mystery substance.

He opened and he tasted it, and it really was delicious. Delicious! Wonderful! He ate them all up, and then he ate the fish, and that was good too. Then he hurried home to tell his landsman about this wonderful food. He (the landsman) said, "What are you talking about, it's potatoes! It's 'chips,' chips they call it! It's potatoes, that's all! What's the fuss?"

My father replied, "But it's so wonderful!"

Now he worked and worked and worked and saved. He told me that when there were holes in his shoes he didn't have them resoled. New shoes were out of the question, of course. But instead of having them resoled he put newspaper into the bottom of his shoes, because he had his budget. He had his amount that he was going to spend. And as soon as he had enough money, he bought a ticket for my mother, and she left.

When she arrived, he didn't marry her. She stayed with *her* landsman, because she came from another village, but he didn't marry her. She came expecting to be married, but it wasn't nice for a woman to say, "When are you going to marry me?" She only had a little money, just a few pounds. She tells me that she sat in the park. I know the park, I played in the park myself as a child. She sat in the park by the fountain sewing tablecloths for her trousseau. Beautifully embroidered tablecloths, which we still have.

She'd run out of money. She had one tickee left, and she spent that tickee on oranges. She said to me, "In those days you could get a lot of oranges for a tickee." And that was all she had. She ate the oranges, and then she had no more money. So she cried, and her tears wet the tablecloths she was working on. Then she went to my father and she said, "Benjamin, I have no more money."

He said, "Oh, well then, we must get married!" And they were married immediately!

Afterwards, she asked, "Why did you wait until I had no more money before you asked me to marry you?"

He said, "Well, I was living by myself and it was very cheap, and you were staying with *your* landsman and that was very cheap. I thought we could save money if we could just keep going for a month or two not together." Because he was still saving, you see.

He went on saving, and he worked. He did all kinds of things. He was a shoe salesman. Now can you imagine a shoe salesman selling shoes who can hardly speak English? Until the end of his days, my father never spoke proper English. He spoke Yiddish! But he worked hard, and when he found a better job he worked hard at that, and whenever he left a job, they always begged him to stay because he worked so hard and so well. But in the end, he had enough money to buy a business. The year was 1930. That's a year after 1929. The depression had spread everywhere, and the depression was powerful, strong, and deep in South Africa as well.

People said, "Benjamin, you must be mad to buy a business now. You've got a good job. You're going to give up a good job to buy a business now? Everybody's going bankrupt, Benjamin! Can't you see the whole world is going bankrupt?"

"No," said my father, "I will make it work." And he bought his business. The business was a fish and chip shop. Now that fish and chip shop still exists in Cape Town. It's just as old and greasy now as it was then, but the fact is that there in that little suburb of Salt River was a row of little stores. And on every single store there was a sign that said either "Bankrupt – Closed," and there was nothing left, or "Closing Sale." All except for one store, and that store was the fish and chip shop. It had a long line of people stretching out onto the pavement. At night the stores were all dark, but one store blazed with light, with a queue going out onto the sidewalk.

My mother says, "People used to be driving by in their cars, and they'd put on the brakes to find out what was going on there! What could be sold? What could they have in that store that people would be lining up for? At night! During the depression!"

They'd come and say, "What do you sell here?"

The people in the queue would answer, "Fish and chips."

And they'd say "Oh, let's get some!" And they would join the end of the line.

I heard this story when I was eight years old, and I said to my mother, "But why? Why did they all buy fish and chips, Mum?"

She said, "You see, during the depression, people went to the cinema a lot. They went to the movies. Why? Because that was the one thing that was cheap and they could enjoy. Now, during the depression they didn't have money. They couldn't go to restaurants or anything like that. They couldn't do anything. Families couldn't go on any kind of outings. But what they could do was say to the children, 'Children, tonight, we're going to go and have fish and chips!' And the children all said, 'Yay!' And then they went and got the fish and chips. It was only a tickee, but it was good food. Nutritious. And it was a fine outing that they could afford."

So my father and my mother worked in the fish shop. They woke up at five to be there by six to fry the fish and chips, because some workers would go to work early and would stop off to buy fish and chips. That would be their breakfast. So they had to be there for that. There was a slower period during the morning, but then other people would come in at lunch time. There'd be a slow period in the afternoon, and then a lot of people would come at supper time. And my parents didn't go home after supper because people went to the movies and were hungry afterwards. Perhaps after the movies a young man and a young woman who were courting would come. The young man didn't have much money, but he could say, "Do you feel like something to eat? How about fish and chips?"

The girl would say, "Oh, that would be lovely!" And they would go and they would buy fish and chips at ten-thirty at night. So my mother and my father would be frying fish and chips at ten-thirty, and they would close the store when there was no one left at eleven, and go home and sleep and wake up the next morning at five o'clock.

So it was that my father worked at the back of the store – he was the one who fried the fish and chips – and my mother, who could speak English quite well, stood at the front of the store and took the money from people and served them, wrapping up the fish and chips and so on. My father came to her one day and said, "You know, the line outside the shop is very long. It's so long that people will see that it's long and then perhaps they won't come and buy our fish and chips. And that means we'll lose business and we can't have that. You have to entertain the people, so they won't mind waiting."

My mother said, "Who, me?" My mother was about five feet one inch, just a little woman from Lithuania.

He said, "Yes, you must talk to them. You must just chat with them, that's all."

Then my mother started to do that. She would say, "Oh, hello Mrs Jones. How's your husband? I heard that he was in the hospital." And Mrs Jones, who was maybe three places back in the queue, would tell the symptoms and the treatment, and everybody in the queue would be listening and drinking in the gory details. Then she would know somebody else in the queue, and she would chat with them, perhaps about the difficulties that her son was having looking for a job, and all the people in the queue would be nodding their heads. My mother would maintain a stream of conversation with the people in the queue so that nobody would go away, because you got the news of the whole neighbourhood and all the gossip.

Then my father said, "You know, we're very busy at breakfast time, lunch time, and supper time and late at night after the movies, but in the morning and in the afternoon it's quiet. We should start selling other things. We should start selling bread, milk, and cheese. Then people will come for that, and they might buy fish and chips too." So that's what they did.

They started to sell those other things. And again, an unforgettable little anecdote was that one day somebody came into the store and said, "Can I have fourpence worth of cheese please?"

My mother took the cheese, and cut it and said, "It's fourpence ha'penny. Is that all right?"

And the person said, "Sure."

Afterwards, my father came to my mother and said, "Do you remember that person who bought the cheese? They asked for fourpence worth, and you cut off fourpence ha'penny. You can't do that. This is depression time. People don't have money. Sometimes they have only exactly enough to buy what they're asking.

If somebody comes in and asks for fourpence worth of cheese and you ask, 'Well, is fivepence all right?' they're going to be embarrassed and ashamed to say, 'No, I can't afford to pay an extra penny.' So they're going to pay that fivepence, but that might come out of their rent money! You can't do that, you've got to cut exactly fourpence. It can't be less, because then we're only selling thruppence worth of cheese, and so we're losing money. But it can't be more, because they can't afford it. You've got to cut it exactly."

My mother said, "That's impossible! You can't cut cheese exactly!"

And he said, "You have to learn." So she learned. She told me that she learned to cut the cheese exactly.

And of course I go in Toronto stores nowadays and when I say, "Give me half a pound of cheese please," they say, "Ten ounces, is that all right?"

I say, "Of course, yes, fine." But I don't want to say that. I want to say, "No! You should learn to cut it exactly!"

And so this went on until a time came when my father, who had gone to buy the fish for frying, was told by the fish wholesalers that the price of fish was going up, from fourpence a pound to fivepence. And he said, "No, I'm sorry, that's impossible. I'm not prepared to pay more."

And they said, "Mr Gelcer, you don't understand. There is no problem. We raise our price to you, and you raise your price to your customers. It doesn't cost you a thing! In fact, if you're clever, you can even make money on it, and blame it all on us!"

"No," he said. "My customers can't afford to pay more. This is depression time."

"Well, Mr Gelcer, you're a very good customer, but we can't make an exception for you."

In those days quite a lot of trek-fishing was done. In trek-fishing a rowboat with about a dozen men rows from the shore hauling a net behind it. The boat circles back to the shore with the net enclosing a circle of about three hundred yards in diameter. Then the net is laboriously pulled in to shore by hand and the fishermen, who were usually brown-skinned – mixed race – so-called coloured, would share out their catch, perhaps two hundred fish in all, and hawk them from door to door.

My father went down to the beach and watched the men

hauling in their nets. My father couldn't speak English well, but he was good at sizing up a man's character. He went up to one of the men, and said to him, "Do you know how to catch fish?"

"Yes, I know how to catch fish."

"If I buy you a boat, will you catch fish for me?"

"Yes! Yes, boss! I will do that for you!"

My father bought a boat, a little rowboat and nets, and they went out and caught fish. That man, Mr Cotton – I knew him much later when he was an old man and dying – was a coloured man, dark skin, but with bright blue eyes. He actually became the captain of my father's first trawler. Because this little fishing boat grew and grew, until eventually there was a fleet of ocean-going trawlers that were catching fish. But for that to happen the fish and chip shop had to be sold, and was. My father ended up selling the fish and chip shop and going into the fishing business with Mr Cotton and with a trawler.

I said that the title of this story is "The Gold Mine." Whenever my father would talk about this fish and chip shop, which was very dear to his heart (and very dear to mine because of the stories that came out of it), he would sometimes tell stories that I had heard before, but I certainly never tired of them. And at the end he would always say, "That fish and chip shop," shaking his head and smiling, "That fish and chip shop, it was such a gold mine!"

## Alec Gelcer

*The South African writer Pauline Smith starts one of her stories this way: "There was once an old and childless couple who were so poor that when they died they left nothing behind but this story." My parents, may they rest in peace, are both dead now, and they left behind many things, but their most precious gift to me was the story of the fish and chip shop, and all the other stories of their coming to South Africa, and of their life in a faraway land beyond the sea.*

*The night I told "The Gold Mine" I was completely unprepared. The previous teller had told a story about a couple visiting a fish and chip in rural Canada and when he had finished, the host of the evening, perhaps noting my bemused expression, asked me if I had a story. After a pause of some seconds, I said, "Yes!" and got up and told the story off the cuff. It was constructed on the spot from the*

*whole cloth of memory. I could see the audience was enjoying the
story so I began to add bits, like the embroidered tablecloths, and the
cheese cutting. It all came together well, and ended up as a homage
to my father, who, like so many other immigrants everywhere, had
the guts and the determination to carve out a niche for himself and
his family in a new world.*

ↄ

# The New Legend of Sam Peppard

There are facts in this story. Sam Peppard lived in Oskaloosa,
Kansas, from eighteen-fifty-something until he died, an old man
with a long beard and many descendants. I went to school with
some of his great-grandchildren. And what happens in the story
did happen. But why Sam did what he did do and why he never
did it again – that belongs to the legend. And the legend was
not handed down from his generation to mine. So here is a
legend for Sam Peppard.

The wind blew Sam Peppard to Oskaloosa. It was blowing strong
out of the west, and if there had been any old-timers they might
have squinted up at the dark clouds blown to rags as the wind
pushed them east and shaken their heads. But everyone in
Oskaloosa had arrived from back east not more than eighteen
months before. They were building a town in the rolling hills at
the edge of the real west and wind or no wind it was not
surprising to see a young man with a bag full of tools swing
down from one of the big wagons that hauled folks too poor to
have a wagon of their own. Sam stood in the wide, dusty street
that was destined to be the north side of the square and said,
"I just blew in from the west. Does this town need a blacksmith?"
  Oskaloosa needed wagon-wheel rims and nails and hinges. There
were always horses and mules to be shod, and besides that, like
every town it needed a blacksmith shop so that folks would have

a place to hang around. When they found out that Sam had been nearly everywhere and would tell about it, Sam's shop was always hopping.

"I like this place," said Sam. "It's right on the edge of the east and the west and the north and the south. Some day it will be dead centre of this country."

Sam lived in a room behind his shop, and every morning he would step out the front door of his shop and feel the wind. If it blew from the north, south, or west he would step right back in and start to work. But if the wind was from the east he would stand there in the middle of the street with his back to the wind and stretch his arms out until the wind whipped his shirt-tails around his ears. Folks got used to it but they teased him some: "That wind is gonna blow you straight to Denver some day." "Next time I go west that's the way I'm going," Sam would say. "No more ox-carts for me."

The country around Oskaloosa was a jumping-off place for people travelling west. Just north ran the Oregon Trail and just south ran the Santa Fe Trail. So folks had a choice of route. But, it was true, they all went by ox-cart. Prairie schooners they were called; but they lumbered over the flat prairie at a mighty slow rate.

Sam thought about all those miles of waving prairie grass. "If those were waves of water, those prairie schooners would be a pretty sight sailing before the wind," he said to his friend Joe.

One winter day, the folks who made a habit of warming themselves beside Sam's smithy fire found him building something. It looked suspiciously like a wagon box. Funny shape though. "Eight feet long, three feet wide," Sam said when they asked him, and he wouldn't explain why.

He wouldn't explain why the wheels were so high either, or why the metal rims were so thick. When they asked him why he was fiddling around with some contraption at the back off the wagon and how in tarnation he was going to hitch any horse or ox to the front, Sam just said, "This isn't a horse-cart or an ox-cart either."

One morning Joe went into Sam's shop and he found Sam fixing something that looked exactly like a mast in the front of the wagon. "What is this thing you're building?" he said. "Are you aiming to put a sail to a wagon?"

"Joe," said Sam, "I'm aiming to use the wind. There's more

wind than anything else out there on the prairie, and a lot of the time it's blowing towards the west. Why can't it take folks along with it? Some of them will want to be coming back, too. They can take the wind that blows towards the east. Think of it, Joe. Sails across the prairie."

Joe shook his head, but he caught a little of what Sam was seeing. "You gonna call it a sailing wagon?"

"A wind wagon. That's what it is. A wind wagon," said Sam Peppard.

News of what Sam was building in his shop was all over town by ten a.m. and by noon, nearly everyone who could walk had come by to look at it. Most had quite a bit to say to Sam, generally along the lines of "Sam, you're crazier than we thought you were."

Some got around to asking, "Where you planning to go in that thing?"

"Denver," said Sam. "I've heard they've made silver strikes in the mountains up behind Denver. I figured the wind wagon would be the best way to get there."

"Denver's six hundred miles!"

"There's wind all the way," said Sam.

After that, Sam got hardly a minute's peace; and, sociable as he was, he got pretty tired of admitting that he might be crazy but nevertheless, he was headed for Denver.

Some good did come of it, though. Joe decided to go with Sam. "I've taken a pretty good look at that wagon of yours," he said. "I don't see how you can manage that sail and that steering stick at the same time. I'll come along and give you a hand."

"That's a tiller," said Sam. "You're going to be glad you came."

Also, Mary Alice Bellows said she would make the sail. "Blacksmith you may be, Sam Peppard, and carpenter too; but I don't think sewing is in a man's line at all."

Sam didn't tell her about the master sail-makers he had seen back in Maine. He knew sewing wasn't his line. "I'll bring you a silver locket," He said. "I thank you kindly, Miz Bellows."

The only real aggravation Sam had was an old man who had come in from a claim to the south and west of Oskaloosa. He appeared in the door of Sam's shop one day towards closing time and leaned against the door post like a narrow gray shadow. "Thought you ought to know my shack blew away."

"Too bad," said Sam.

"Cow too."

Sam said nothing.

"Wind's mighty strong out there."

There was a long pause. "My wind wagon, she's made to go with the wind."

There was a longer pause. "There's go with," said the old man, "and then there's blown away. Can't see there's much difference."

After that he'd come and stand in the doorway every day or two and just stare at the wind wagon and shake his head.

Sam ignored him as best he could. The wind wagon was almost ready to go, and he had to work ahead to cover some of the two months he figured he'd be gone.

As he worked, he stopped now and then to add a little touch to the wind wagon. He painted her name – *Wind Wagon, Oskaloosa* – on her back panel. He polished up the brass fitting of the mast. He greased the big iron wheels until they turned sweetly, without a murmur of complaint.

One day Joe dropped by. "I've been thinking, Sam," he said. "The two of us aren't going to be enough. Think about it, Sam. Managing the sail, steering the thing, keeping a lookout for trouble, gathering buffalo chips so as we can have a fire, cooking, shooting rabbits to eat. We'll be too tired to go looking for gold and silver when we get there."

"Who did you have in mind?" said Sam.

"Well, there's the Graham boys. They don't talk much and I reckon they're a pretty good shot. One of them plays the banjo too."

Sam knew the Graham boys all right. They were the two most up and coming of a large, shiftless family that lived on the edge of town. Their names were Abraham and Isaiah, but no one ever remembered which was which; and they were both tall and lanky and silent, so they were just called the Graham boys.

"I don't guess they'd have got themselves steady jobs," said Sam. "I'll talk to them about it."

When he did, the boys looked at each other and allowed as how they weren't too busy this time of the year and they wouldn't mind setting eyes on the Rocky Mountains. But they did have one question. "How's that fool wagon of yours going to get us there?"

"She'll get us there," said Sam. "I'm just waiting for the right kind of wind."

It was a wind towards the west he needed, and all the wind that spring seemed to come from the west. Sam shook his head every morning when he came in from testing the wind. "There's one thing the wind wagon can't do, Joe," he said one day. "She can't sail into the wind. If it's coming from the northeast, now, or the southeast, we can just angle the sail a little and she'll go easy. But straight from the west, there's not much we can do."

One Saturday, when Sam went out into the street in front of the shop, the wind was from the west all right, but it was so fresh and so sweet that Sam locked up the shop and went to look for Joe and the Graham boys.

"We've got to try her out today," he told them. "I swear I can smell the snow melting in the high mountains and the flowers blooming in the foothills. One of these days the wind will be just right and we've got to be ready to go."

So they hauled the wind wagon, by hand, to a big high piece of ground just south of town. It was about as flat as any place around Oskaloosa, but it had a steep slope at the east end.

"Perfect," said Sam. "Folks think the prairie is flat as a pancake but we might have to handle a few hills."

It was a tight squeeze in the wind wagon when they were all on board, and one of the Graham boys said, "Don't know where you expect me to stick a banjo." But then Joe hoisted the sail and they were off. Sam felt the wind in his hair. There was nothing ahead of the wagon. No horse, no ox. Just the grassy field. It pulled itself under the wagon wheels smooth as silk. Well, not exactly. The wagon lurched and bumped along and the Graham boys hung on for their lives. Their faces were as white as if a raging sea awaited them if they fell overboard, instead of Old Man Hicks's pasture.

All Sam could feel was the wind pushing them. It was solid, it was strong. It could push them all the way to Denver.

Some movement against the trees caught his eye. He turned away from the onrushing pasture and saw the old man from the claim. He was watching the wind wagon with fierce eyes and Sam wondered for a second whether he wanted them to blow away or whether he hoped they wouldn't. Just then, the land sloped sharply down. The wind was under the flaring sides of the wagon body. It was ballooning the sail and lifting the wind wagon off the ground. It occurred to Sam that the wind might blow them all the way to the Missouri River. Then they were beyond the crest of the hill. The wind slackened, the wheels touched the earth again and bumped to a stop. After a minute they all got out and looked at the wind wagon. She was fine. No cracks, no bends.

"Well," said Sam, "she takes to the wind. Give her a high enough hill and she might just take off. We'll put a little ballast in front to keep her bow down. We won't take to the air again. I guarantee."

The next day Sam was painting over a few scratches on the wagon box when he looked up to see the old-timer from the claim standing in the doorway. "You'd better get that thing fixed so it stays on the ground," he said. "The wind's about to change."

Sam couldn't think of anything to say for a minute, which was unusual for him. But he collected himself. "We're ready," he said. "She'll make it to Denver. And back. I'll bring you some gold nuggets."

But the old-timer shook his head. "Just keep that wagon on the ground," he said. "The wind out there ..." He shook his head again. And then he was gone.

The wind changed the next day. It blew out of the east straight and true, as if it intended to blow that direction till Christmas. But Sam knew better. He collected Joe and the Graham boys. They packed up the sourdough and beans they had ready, found a tight corner for the banjo and a deck of cards and sent out the word that the wind wagon was ready to go.

Everyone in Oskaloosa showed up for the great send-off, except for a few sceptics who claimed they would all be home by sundown. Sam couldn't help looking for the old-timer but his lean figure and grim countenance were nowhere to be seen.

Sam stood up in the back of the wind wagon, waved his broad-brimmed hat to the crowd, and said, "Folks, if you want to beat us to Denver you should have started off three weeks ago." Then he sat down, set the hat squarely on his head to shade his eyes from the brilliant sun, and took hold of the tiller. Joe pulled the sail around till the wind caught it, several boys ran alongside to give a push, and the wind wagon, creaking a little, sailed off along the ridge road leading west out of town.

Two long days later they reached the edge of the Flint Hills where the land quits rolling and levels out into a five-hundred-mile slow upward incline to the foot on the Rocky Mountains. Before them lay the hard-packed road to Denver, rutted and worn down by the wheels of all the wagons carrying people who had headed west looking for land or gold or silver. In fact, in the distance they could see quite a swarm of prairie schooners lurching along.

"Come on, boys," said Sam Peppard, "we'll catch 'em before the sun is high!" He stretched his arms out as wide as he could and felt that strong wind from the east pulling at his shirt sleeves. This time he knew he was going with it.

For the first week or so the wind was strong and steady. The wind wagon rolled along overtaking other kinds of wagons regularly. Drivers and passengers risked falling off their seats as they stared at the oxless wind wagon careening past them.

Then there were several days of calm, and the folks in some of the slow, steady, ox-drawn wagons had the satisfaction of seeing the wind wagon drawn off the trail while its crew played cards and went rabbit hunting. They did not keep their pleasure to themselves. "Never mind," said Sam. "They'll be looking at our dust soon enough."

And Sam was right. When the wind started up again it was fresher and stronger than ever. They soon passed the main body of wagons and for days the wind wagon rolled along so fast and smooth that even the Graham boys had to admit that it looked like they would live to see the Rocky Mountains.

On one of those days Sam said, "I'd wager we're going twenty-five miles an hour." Since none of the others had any notion except that they were going mighty fast, they didn't argue with Sam; but one of the Graham boys, who happened to have the rear lookout spot, said, "Well, I sure hope those Indians can't ride twenty-five miles an hour."

They all looked where he was looking and, sure enough, there were three Indians on spotted horses riding hell for leather in their direction. Now Sam hoped he had never done anything to make any Indians sore at him, but he knew that a lot of Indians had a lot to be sore about; so he wasn't sure those Indians had friendly thoughts in their minds. And they were certainly coming on fast.

"Come on, Wind Wagon," he said, "now's the time to show

what you can do." They all hunkered down to give the sail a chance to do the most it could and Sam fiddled with the tiller. Joe lifted his head above the edge of the boards and said, "By gum, Sam, I think they're racing us."

Then they all looked at the Indians and saw that they were riding alongside the wind wagon, about a hundred yards to the south. Sam grinned. "Well, they've got themselves a race," he said.

The wind was with them that day, and after maybe ten miles of hard riding the Indians were still behind the wagon. They waved their hands over their heads in a friendly fashion and rode off to the south. That night Sam went to sleep knowing that the wind wagon could surely go with the wind.

And the wind kept getting stronger and stronger as the land rose towards the Rockies. Some days they didn't put the sail all the way up. "Either it will get blown to rags, or that wind will take us right up into the air," said Sam. And as he said it he remembered the old-timer and thought, "It's just too bad that being blown away can't get you where you're going."

After three weeks Sam said, "I reckon we're just about eighty miles from Denver." They were feeling good. The Rocky Mountains were a solid cloud on the horizon, and the Graham boys were beginning to fret about how they were ever going to climb so high. Sam was feeling a bit agitated, but he figured that it was because he hated to come to the end of the wind wagon's first voyage. He did notice that there were some dark clouds to the south-west, but there was blue sky overhead and the wind had calmed down some.

Sam was just shaking his head a little, wondering whether folks back in Oskaloosa would believe they had done it, when suddenly an immense gust of wind hit the wind wagon broadside and at the same time Joe hollered, "It's a twister!"

Sam looked. Coming out of the south-west was a thin, black finger of wind, twisting and snaking its way straight at the wind wagon, roaring like a thousand mad bulls. Sam gripped the tiller. It seemed as if he should be able to dodge something so narrow. But the next split second he knew that if that twister wanted the wind wagon, there was nothing he could do about it.

"Jump, boys!" he yelled. But there wasn't time. That twister picked up the wind wagon with Sam hanging onto the tiller and everybody else hanging onto anything they could grab. Sam felt the huge force of that wind as it lifted him and the wagon and Joe and the Graham boys and held them all twenty feet above the prairie for so long that he could have drawn a deep breath, if he had been breathing. Then it dropped them, wind wagon and all, in a heap on the ground.

Sam looked around at his crew. They were all in one piece, shaking their heads and cautiously moving their arms and legs. But the wind wagon was in a thousand pieces. Sam looked at the tangle of sail and the splintered boards and bent wheels. "Well, boys," he said, "it looks like we walk the rest of the way. But she sure gave us some ride, didn't she?"

As it turned out, one of the lumbering freight wagons came along and, with a few smirks and rude jokes, the driver offered them a ride into Denver. "Unless my team gets blowed away, of course."

Sam found the back panel with the proud words *Wind Wagon, Oskaloosa* painted on it. It was hardly scratched. Sam put it under his arm, climbed aboard the freight wagon, and rode into Denver.

That's almost the end of the story. Sam, Joe, and the Graham boys did go silver mining before they hopped another wagon back to Oskaloosa, and Sam brought home enough silver to build himself a nice little house.

"This is where I'm going to stay," he said. And he did. He married, had ten children, and lived to be known for his long white beard.

And as for the old-timer? He showed up the day Sam stoked up the fire in his shop. "You gonna build another one of them wagons?" he asked. "Or have you had enough?"

"If I build another wind wagon," said Sam, "I'd never find a wind like I found the first time. I reckon I've gotten the most out of a wind wagon that I ever could."

So Oskaloosa never did get famous for wind wagons. But it's still there, nearly dead centre of the country, just like Sam Peppard said it would be.

*Celia Lottridge*

*As I said at the beginning of the story, all of this really happened, even the twister. But it wasn't the facts that made me want to tell the story. It was the questions. What was it like to live in a new town on the edge of the west in 1860? Why would a man choose to do something as risky and uncomfortable as sail a wagon nearly six hundred miles? What would the folks in town think about it? How would it feel to sail across land? And why did someone who did something so amazing just settle down and apparently do no other memorable thing in his long life? So the story is my answer to questions.*

*Another reason the story of Sam Peppard is important to me is that it is a real prairie story. It could have happened nowhere else. When I tell the story, that great sweep of land and sky and the constant presence of the wind fill my mind.*

*I believe that many people of eccentric imagination and a willingness to try things out have lived on the prairies of the United States and Canada; but, because they are often laconic people, and because there is more space than people on the prairies, their deeds, which should have passed into legend, have been forgotten. "The New Legend of Sam Peppard" is my tribute to all those lost legends.*

*For some of the answers I had to invent characters. Sam was the only one I knew anything about. But Oskaloosa is my home town, and people seemed to enter the story naturally, as if they belonged there. I hope that all the real people who saw Sam Peppard raise a sail over a wagon would like my version of their story.*

თ

# Sugar Cane

Have you been to Kensington Market in the summer? The poet Eric Miller sees it a sprawling slaughterhouse, unidentifiable carcasses hanging in windows, dead deep-sea fish slopping about in reeking bins, pigeons in their tiny cages pecking at each other.

I prefer the way Joséphine told me about it and showed me through it the first time I was there, speaking to me calmly, *"Oui, oui, c'est comme ça,"* not to let the gypsy carnival overflow

rush to my head all at once and send me cartwheeling along the
fish-stained streets, among the gutter's mouldy oranges, bouncing
on my hands, shouting. Thousands of baskets of tomatoes, papayas,
long strange vegetables covered with brown hair, rickety stacks
of dry grey fish skins, stacks of sandals, reams of Persian rugs,
Indian spices, all growing like a jungle out onto the sidewalk on
rickety wooden stands, filling rotting boxes, creaky crates, hangers,
plastic bins. Sounds of wooden flutes. Nose-filling smells: rubber,
pepper and Spanish onions; ginger, rancid cheese, baking bread,
sweat; bananas, squid, beef patties, soap; curry, fresh paint, strawberries. Cackles and whispers and laughs and shouts from vegetable
market to seafood shop, in languages so slippery you have to look
at the people, whether they're wearing black shawls or rainbow
knitted skullcaps, what colour their eyes are, to even guess what
they're speaking. Romany? Patois? German! or Yiddish? French!
No ... Portuguese? Counter people from the meat market out in
their bright orange uniforms. Raucously whispering old men sifting
through scads of vegetables. Pale young people with painstakingly
mutilated hair. The deep brown, fat, gorgeous laughing woman
in a long blue dress with yellow and green and red polka dots
all over it. A Buddhist monk slipping through the flowing, searching crowd, quizzical, contented, barefoot in a saffron robe. Worn
fingers squeezing bulging purple eggplants. Grey eyes returning,
startled, to red mangoes.

Darken the whole scene, the light to evening and night-time,
everyone's skin and eyes to shades of brown, your mind to troubled
wonder. Take away buildings, sidewalks, streets; they're extra, the
market doesn't need them. For restaurants substitute tea stalls
selling *misty* (sweets) and *pān* (betel leaves with calcium powder).
Make the environment tropical, the odours heavier; the language
spoken varying only as village dialects will, but more foreign
to you, everyone talking: *"Keman āchen?" "Bhālo, āpni?" "Bhālo!"*
and on and on as incomprehensibly to me as those words may
be to you. You are wearing a sari, if a woman – though you'd
be the only woman there; a lungi, a wrap-around skirt, if a man.
You're sweating and smiling and eager to take in everything. You
are browsing around at the *haht*, the twice-weekly market, near
Dhandoba and Rajihar villages in District Barisāl, Bangladesh.

Wooden boats come ashore on the banks of the canal. Friends
and relatives from different villages hola each other. A raft made

of sugar canes pulls in to land. Wiry men in faded lungis strike
up the banks carrying the raft, undo the ropes, and set up the
sugar canes like a fence. Men and boys crowd around to begin
bargaining. Perpetually sneering, commanding young Narul Islam
and newly-wed, eagerly laughing Halim gesture to the sugar cane
sellers and one of them cuts off a cubit length of cane with a
sickle and hands it to Halim, who hands it to you.

"*Anek dhanyabād,*" I said, thank you very much. I held the
sugar cane and looked at it. Boys standing around watching me
tittered. "We joke, brother," Halim said. He was without any
malice, and so were they, as I was, watching them as they sold
their strange wares and held their conversations, as old men at
tea stalls began to light "hurricanes," oil lamps. The people who
were to take me to Rajihar, the next village, an old, calmly
laughing woman and a swaggering young man, had arrived.

With them in their boat, I ate sugar cane for the first time.
You bite off a chunk, chew the sweetness out, spit the fibres in
the water and take another bite. I was having the devil of a
time biting through. Later, in Rajihar, my gums bled when I ate
sugar cane and a woman explained to everyone, "Their teeth are
no good. Their countries are too cold." Here in the boat, the
old woman, squatting in the bow, looked at me wryly. The young
man was standing in the stern, turning gently, poling us along
the canal. I crouched in the middle, water slopping back and
forth under my crossed legs, the half coconut shell used to bail
floating with it. The old woman had told me her name. It was
beautiful, but I'd forgotten it. She repeated her name for me in
the course of our boat ride and was hurt, the third time, that I
couldn't remember what it was. "Bengali names are hard for me,"
I said. "Your names are hard for us – Justin." Now she took the
sugar cane and bit a mouthful easily, said something and handed it
back to me. I tried again. The demonstration hadn't made it easier.

"*A salaam moi léi koum.*" From behind us, from the market, a
long boat, four men, wiry middle-aged, paddling it, if I remember,
drew even with ours. "*Moi léi koum salaam.*" We exchanged
greetings. Then in a few strokes of the oars, if they were using
oars, their boat was alongside ours and we were gliding along the
canal together. One of the men reached over, patted my arm
lightly, and took the sugar cane from me. No words were spoken.
It seemed to be understood that we would not make the attempt

at each other's languages. From somewhere in the boat – it must have been loaded with goods from the market, you can imagine them as you like, both primitive and rare – the other men drew a sickle and a plate. A minute later the first man handed me the plate full of bite-sized pieces of sugar cane. Chewing wasn't hard. I picked up a piece and put it in my mouth. While I ate one piece of sugar cane after another – not quick eating; sucking every drop of the juice out – our boats moved along the canal side by side. It was getting darker and pleasantly cooler. When I handed back the empty plate and smiled gratefulness, the men nodded, grinned, and paddled their boat away from ours. Then we were all shouting salutations across the water and they sped off down the canal, towards their own village.

"*Bhālo?*" the old woman with the beautiful name asked me.

"*Hā bhālo,*" I said, yes, good.

The young man began to sing. "*Bhālobāsā gān?*" I asked, a love song?

"*Hā.*"

Not long after, in the darkness, we floated out onto a submerged rice-field, under an enormous sky. Over there, up there, the sunset had turned ribs of cloud dark orange, purple, and red-brown.

### Justin Lewis

*I wrote this story after spending the summer of 1983 in Bangladesh. In France the year before I met a Bangladeshi, Swapan Chowdhury, and he invited me to visit him in Bangladesh and see the work he was doing, community organizing in the villages. Through his organization, Dipshikha, I was able to spend a lot of time in the villages, and it was a new world to me. When I got back to Toronto I went through a lot of culture shock, and this story was written partly to get me through that by making a connection between Bangladesh and Toronto.*

ୠ

# Searching Out Moira

The man on the other end of the phone said that of course I probably would not like to do an author's tour of the North-West Territories. He said it as a joke before he got onto the real business of the conversation, which was going to be an offer to tour southern Alberta for Children's Book Week.

"Hold it! Hold it and stop!" says I. "I will do the North-West Territories."

Dead silence from the other end of the line. I know what he is thinking – "Shit! I had this guy figured for southern Alberta. His publisher even asked to have him sent to southern Alberta. We have even told the goddamn librarian in Lethbridge that he is probably coming."

I give my "I Have Always Wanted to Go There" speech. A quick recovery follows on the other end, and he is soon congratulating me on a great choice.

And so I end up flying into Montreal, looking at the dirty snow of the dirty city, and wondering if my clothes are warm enough. The Nordair flight to Frobisher Bay seems regular enough. Two minutes out of Montreal we run out of roads and there is only snow to look at; snow and lakes. I settle down and think what I am going to do, because they fund me as an author tour but what I do is storytelling. Lately, I have been going through a dry period and I figure that a little intercultural sort of storytelling will get my mind going again.

You see, I'm lazy. When I get a good story list I float with it. Easier to stay with what I know. Thus the North-West Territories. I figure that nothing will work up there and I will have to make up new stories. At least that is the plan.

Baffin Island comes into view. It looks like several thousand bulldozers have been working for thousands of years to make a mess. Actually, they tell me it was glaciers that did it; but the effect is the same. Off the plane, and I meet the family I'm going to stay with. (Always stay with families. That way I never get to stop storytelling. I will tell stories all day and then tell bedtime stories at night. I will get totally burned out and maybe get a new story.)

I get my first taste of the weather. I mean I just sort of walk out the door and stand there and see how cold it is – harmless sort of southern Ontario approach to the weather. I have on no gloves and no hat and no insulated pants. I just stroll out to check out the weather. It is –40 with a fifty-mile-an-hour wind, the sort of wind that blows people down the street. I stagger back inside with numb fingers and a face that feels like someone has scrubbed it with a Brillo pad; but the most amazing thing was my legs. My jeans might as well not have been there. I mean, even my legs were numb. BINGO! These kids will like stories about wind.

The next day I get my first audience. It is at the local library, and only half Inuit. I quickly find that stories about family relations (going to bed – wetting your pants – feeding your dad a playdoh cookie) run OK. Inuit families seem to run enough like southern families; or else everybody is watching "Sesame Street." On the other hand, stories with trees, subways, and two-storey houses do not go well. So far I am just fooling around with stories that I have already made up and finding elements have to change so the story will work in Baffin Island. (Did you know that if one end of Baffin Island was in Toronto the other end would be in Winnipeg?)

The next day I go to the school and there choose a girl named Allashua to make up a story about. (I was lucky to get an Inuit-sounding name. It is impolite to call an Inuit by their name so kids generally give their English name when asked.) I try out a wind story on Allashua. They love it. They should love it. Half of the Inuit kids have raw frostbite sores on their cheeks. They are highly knowledgeable about wind and cold. I later tried this story out down south. It will go in rural areas where the kids know what a real wind is. It is a dud in Toronto.

I flew out of Frobisher on a jet, landed at Hall Inlet in a blizzard. At least I would have called it a blizzard. All sorts of people from Hall Inlet were out in the dark to see the plane land. Lots of them didn't even have their hoods on. I got out and stood in the blowing snow and looked at a three-year-old girl who looked at me. When the wind blew harder I couldn't see her; neither of us said a thing. I got on a DC-3 and flew out to Spence Bay.

Spence is an almost totally Inuit community. It was dark when I got there. I stayed with Ernie and various of his relatives whose interrelations I could not figure out. I had some great lines there trying to make conversation.

"Tell me, Ernie, who founded Spence Bay?"

"You mean who started the town?" said Ernie.

"Yes."

"I did," said Ernie. Silence on my part. I mean how do you talk to the guy who founded the goddamn town?

Then there was the following: "The government built this house," said Ernie. "The windows don't open and it gets really hot no matter what I do. If you get too hot pull that towel out of the wall. I put a hole in the wall with a chain saw. Pull out the towel and the place will cool down fast."

"Right," said I. I am really good at scintillating comebacks.

Well, the next day I told stories at the local (unheated) townhall. The mayor introduced me in Inuktitut and away I go. This is clearly a different audience. Lots of the adults have the black, lined faces of Inuit who spend lots of time out on the tundra. They call it "out on the land," as in "I'm going out on the land." This audience has a really different feel to it. I fear for the success of the event, so I start with "Mud Puddle," a story that has never failed. It was a dud. When I was done a kid put up his hand and asked, "What's a mud puddle?"

One of the local teachers then spent five minutes trying to explain the idea of a mud puddle. I knew I had made it. Here was an audience that was not going to like any of my stories. I had to make up new ones. I was in an absolute panic. This was the reason for the trip. So I started telling new stories:

1 The little boy who took his father's gun and shot a caribou.

2 The two kids who climbed the radio tower and had to jump into the hoods of their mothers' parkas to get down.

3 The kid who stole the water truck and filled it with Coca-Cola.

4 Another kid who stole the water truck and ran it into a house. (It turned out that this kid really had stolen the water truck!)

5 And finally the "Mud Puddle" again, only this time it was a snowdrift that jumps on the kid.

As I told stories, the audience got up and jammed me against the wall, and we all started to list off to one side – which was OK since there was no room to fall over.

I must not forget the clapping. There wasn't any. The Inuit version of clapping is a sort of "AHHHH" sound, very light, sort of like whispering. It descends in frequency from start to finish. When one Inuit did it I could hardly hear it. With one hundred or so the effect is very pronounced. I did not know what it meant when they started doing it. For my own peace of mind I decided to assume that it meant that they liked my stories.

On to Cambridge Bay. The plane flew in heavy snow and never went very high. We just flew along and all of a sudden we landed. Cambridge Bay had mixed audiences and I told lots of stories. Only one new one grew; about Alice, who swings so high that she takes off and flies away into the sky. I still tell it sometimes. It has never gelled into a really good story but I like the idea.

Then south to Hay River. This was south to sunshine. I had been living with a week of sunsets. When I changed planes in Yellowknife, I noticed that the people getting off the plane were taking off their parkas. I walked to the door and got the sun right in my face. I took off my parka too. After all it was only –10. Much too warm to pass up a little sunshine. Actually, I got a rush; a fantastic feeling of well-being all based on *sunshine*.

I changed to the plane to Hay River and flew across the absolutely frozen Slave Lake. I dropped right into a library full of kids. I did a normal, safe storytelling and everybody liked it. I knew I was getting tired and burnt out and I was not trying very hard.

Then I went to the family I was staying with and walked into Moira's birthday party. Moira was one of the daughters of the family I was staying with. I was not happy about this. I never do birthday party storytelling. I hate birthday parties. Moira came up to me and asked very nicely if I could tell a birthday story for her party. Sometimes when a kid asks me to make up a story I get this strange feeling that something is going to happen. I got that feeling when Moira asked.

Now, this feeling is usually misleading. Often I look out at a group of kids and get this firm conviction that I *can* tell a new story about a particular kid. Usually it's not true, but I do always try a new story when I get the feeling. Usually the story is a dud.

So I started telling this story about Moira who invites grades one to six to her party and does not tell her parents. Halfway through I knew it was a winner. In fact, it was so good that it jumped up to be one of the stories I always tell; and, as sometimes happens, it turned into a book after about a hundred tellings to let it get good. (One of my favourite events is when I write a kid and say, "Remember that story I told about you? It's going to be a book. Please send me your picture if you want to be in the book." Moira sent the picture and now she is in the book.)

The effect of the constant retelling is to get the words right. For example, when I first told the birthday story, I said that Moira invited "First grade, second grade, etc." Later that switched to "Grade one, grade two, etc." The second version is much better because I can draw out the "gr" in "grade" when I tell it. That sort of revision is a result of audience reaction.

One good story is worth the whole trip. I had been waiting for a year for a really good story to zip by. It was a good day, because later I did it again. This time it was in the Dene reserve across the river (no bridge – in the winter you drive across the ice – in the summer you drive forty miles to get to the town you can see right across the river).

So there I was telling stories to about ten Dene kids. One named Tina had on brightly coloured socks. I told a story about the kid who never changes her socks. It was a very good one too. It's in a file now waiting to become a book. Tina is in a file called "Story Kids." I write her once or twice a year. She doesn't know that I write so I can find her if I need her picture for a book.

Two in one day, a record! I flew off to Yellowknife feeling very pleased. Then it happened again! This time it was at the cultural centre in Yellowknife. Two hundred kids of all ages, lots of them older than I usually tell to. Trying to keep everyone happy, I told a story about a girl named Kelly. She was about twelve, and I figured she liked to use make-up, so I told a story about make-up. I knew it was good the moment I told it. Actually, I was in shock; good stories come so rarely, and there were three in two days.

Then off to Inuvik. A very strange plane ride because we were flying up into the Arctic night. The sun was up in Yellowknife as we took off. It set behind the plane as we went north. At Norman Wells it rose again, only to set as we took off and flew north. At Inuvik it rose at 11:45.

I would like to say I made up a lot of good stories at Inuvik. I didn't. I tried but they were all bad. That happens sometimes; but it was OK. The trip was a success. I had searched out Moira. I flew out to Edmonton. Trip done, story gathered, all go home, the end.

Only it wasn't the end. I decided that this was the way to make up stories so I scheduled another North-West Territories tour. I had forgotten the major rule of my storytelling, which is: *Every time I think I have it figured out, the next story doesn't fit the plan.*

An Inuit girl named Julia Muckpah from Eskimo Point wrote me. (Eskimo Point is in Keewatin District. Keewatin is a little-visited part of the North-West Territories directly to the west of Hudson Bay. It is the coldest part of Canada, otherwise known as the Barren Lands.) I wrote back and her father sent us some Inuit hand-made jewellery. It was then that I got the idea of somehow visiting the area. I decided to take my daughter Julie, age ten. The local librarian said she could arrange a tour and have Julie go to school for a week in Rankin Inlet (population 1,126, mostly Inuit).

And that is how Julie and I came to be walking through Toronto airport on a lovely, warm, late-May morning wearing our down jackets. Winnipeg was covered with snow when we landed to change planes. The down jacket was not out of place. As we were going several hundred miles straight north, I was feeling quite smug about being so smart as to really dress for Arctic weather. I would have been less happy with myself if I had known that the Inuit would find my clothes rather the equivalent of a heavy bikini.

We changed to Calm Air (schedules may vary with weather, so somebody with a sense of humour decided to call it *Calm Air*). We got on a prop plane that had a lounge in the back. Julie loved it. She could move about and choose where to sit. We watched the flat farms turn to flat woods. First the lakes got covered with ice. Then snow cover started, and then the tree line. The flat tundra was covered with snow drifted into enormous patterns that made it look quite like clouds. In fact, it was often a matter of some dispute whether we were looking at ground or cloud cover. Next came Hudson Bay, ice covered with big cracks and pressure ridges. Finally Rankin Inlet, a small collection of buildings built on a rocky peninsula.

I have exactly two hours in Rankin before I fly out to start my tour, and I am really worried about Julie, who has never been away from Ann and me since we adopted her at age five; and here I am leaving her in the middle of nothing. We are met by Michael and Sandy Kusugak and by Lisa Oolloojuk, age ten, whom Julie will stay with. We get into the taxi, and Lisa and the driver start talking in Inuktitut. Julie looks at me and rolls her eyes. When we get to Lisa's house nobody is at home, so we walk in. Sandy Kusugak assures me that things will work out. In front of the house a mob of hungry-looking huskies is howling. (That is the last time I can remember hearing dogs howling in town. Coming across the tundra the howling is the first thing you hear but the sound gets blanked out inside town. Sort of like traffic sounds down south. ) Three-wheel all-terrain vehicles are parked beside snowmobiles and traditional Inuit sleds. Various parts of caribou bodies are scattered about, and I am starting to feel that I am dropping my daughter off the end of the earth. I am about to give her my "You Must Be Brave" speech when she comes running out of a bedroom saying that Lisa is her best friend ever and she is going to meet all Lisa's friends and goodbye. Without a kiss she is gone. I decide not to worry.

Back to the airport. The plane to Chesterfield Inlet (pop. 208) was a Twin Engine Otter (seats nineteen, all-weather versatility, quick take-off, excellent for tundra lands, no bathroom). Chesterfield is drowned in snow. It's almost up to the telephone wires. I am left off at the house of Medard Naitok (hunts all winter, odd jobs in summer) and Sue Barker ("I was a biology student. Medard came by the camp and asked if I would like to go hunting"). Medard is lying down with a hurt foot. He flipped his snowmobile three times chasing a wolf. He got the wolf (wolf equals $350.00). He has the almost-black, lined face of the Inuit who spend a lot of time on the tundra. He has sculpted the snowdrift in front of his house so that I climb up steps in the snow and then climb down steps in the snow to get to the door. The snow is windblown stuff about as hard as your average basketball court.

Here in Chesterfield Inlet, at the house of a wolf hunter married to a biologist, I begin to get the feel that all the Inuit up here are hanging between two worlds. I didn't know it, but that was the beginning of a book.

Back to Rankin Inlet, and a ride into town with me and my

sound system and my suitcase all somehow strapped to various parts of Mike Kusugak's Honda (up here Honda equals three-wheel all-terrain vehicle). I froze. On Saturday morning I took a walk out onto the sea ice, an absolute wonderland of bright blue pressure ridges and flat windswept snow. I liked it so much I went back and borrowed a Honda. I went way out to an island. In its middle was a small lake, completely frozen and absolutely clear. I think it was frozen right to the bottom, because the middle bulged up and some blocks of ice had heaved up to become sculpted by the wind. The ice gave me the feeling of walking on top of infinity. I lay down and looked into the clear, bubbly depths. I felt like I was flying. The whole island was ice-scraped. The rock looked like molasses that had suddenly gone frozen. It was the prettiest thing I have ever seen in Canada.

When I got back, Michael Kusugak told me that pressure ridges and cracks in the ice were very dangerous. The Inuit even had a monster called a Qallupilluit that grabs kids who go near cracks in the ice.

On Sunday Julie and I went ice fishing with the Kusugaks: Mike and Sandy; Bumbut, Jeffrey, and Benjy. The method of doing this is to put lots of stuff into a high-sided sled pulled by a snowmobile. Packed was food, ice drill, camera case, tool chest, three rifles, two heavy blankets, one sleeping bag, gas, various loose tools, a Coleman stove, lots and lots of extra clothes (and other stuff as I never did manage to dig down to the bottom of the sled). On top of the soft things go the adults and on top of the adults go the kids. Two or three caribou hides hold things together.

When people get done laughing at my idea of spring clothes, Sandy dug around and dressed Julie and me. We ended up in a sort of wool sock that came to mid-thigh and then tied. It was so thick and stiff that it was more like a boot than a sock. On top of that went caribou-skin things that tied about the knees. There were lots of extra and the directions were to put on more layers if we got cold. On top of these went inch-thick wool wind pants. For the torso was a pullover shirt with a parka attached. It weighed about ten pounds and was so thick it could stand up by itself. I decided to wear my own extra-warm mitts. Sandy packed some caribou-skin mitts that did not look nearly as thick as mine. She said they would work if mine didn't, which turned out to be quite true.

So off we went, the sled slamming off ice pressure ridges and rocks. It was too bumpy to do anything. All the Inuit kids went to sleep. I tried this and found that two caribou skins on a bumpy sled actually make a nice bed. We went out across the sea ice and on to the tundra. It was ice-scraped, rolling land with no sharp hills. A sort of Kansas effect with snow. I could see for miles and distances were misleading.

First crisis: Julie has to pee. She gets off the sled and looks at one hundred miles of tundra and wants to know where to go so nobody will see her. The answer is four or five miles, and she does not like that. I have this big argument with her and in the end she refuses to go. Happily, in about half an hour we come to a fishing site. A hill is nearby, and Julie and I climb over the crest. I undress her in a hurry, and she pees in a hurry, and she is still shivering by the time I get her parka back on.

Michael has only the most general sort of idea where his family is, but he will recognize the tracks of his mother's sled if he sees them. We go till we are down to half a tank of gas – much consultation – Mike decides to go over one more lake. Up the low hill on the other side there are Mike's mother and brothers happily ice fishing. Grandmother, sons, grandchildren, and in-laws; the group is about twenty people and four sleds.

I end up at an ice hole, catching nothing, while the grandmother pulls them in. She has trouble walking and would probably be in a nursing home down south. Here she is out ice fishing and bossing everybody around.

There is a tent that is warm in the sunlight and has a Coleman stove inside it. The stove is cooking a mixture of Liptons Cup-a-Soup mixed with caribou meat. It is terrible. The raw, frozen caribou that people are carving off a caribou leg turns out to taste much better than the soup. The same group is also eating caribou stomach fat. I do not have any of that.

It turns out that if you pull upon the stomach fat it separates and looks like a spider's web. One of Michael's brothers made fat webs to go along with this story:

"A spider made a web. It caught lots of flies and got bigger and bigger. It made a really large web and caught even more flies. It got so big it made a web and caught caribou. Then an Inuit came along, and the Inuit ate the spider and the web and the caribou."

I think the story has a good bit of cultural insight in it. The Inuit have a very self-conscious idea of being the boss predator. They are the ones who eat everything else. New teachers who show romantic Greenpeace films about animals are always upset that the kids see the film as a sort of food advertisement.

The group carving up the raw caribou included the assistant administrator of Keewatin District, NWT (Monday to Friday he wears a suit and has a big office in the government building), the head of Inuit Broadcasting in Rankin Inlet, and several other professional types. Sitting on the floor of the tent and eating raw meat they all looked like a group of extras from a movie about medieval Mongolia. In two weeks they will be commuting from work to the sea ice, where their families will be living in tents until the ice gets too soft.

I go back to fishing with a caribou skin to keep the wind off me. I sit and jig for the damn fish until the snow starts to drift around me. Finally it is about nine at night and we have to go. I never did catch any fish; which is terrible, because Michael Kusugak had said I could keep the carved walrus tusk lure if I caught a fish with it. It was beautiful, but I could not convince the fish that it was beautiful enough to eat.

I sit in the back of the sled and watch the snow blow along behind us. The sun starts to set and everything takes on a rose tint. The grandmother's sled is being pulled by a snowmobile driven by her five-year-old grandson. As we are going across an enormous flat ice lake that has blown clear of snow, a cross wind starts to turn the sleds sideways behind the skidoos, and several of them almost fall over. We stop, and the grandmother's sled, which is top-heavy, is pushed to the edge of the lake by hand.

While this is happening, the kids start to slide on the ice. It is perfectly smooth, absolutely clear Arctic ice that is so slippery it is almost impossible to stand. In a minute, everybody is out sliding on the ice. Then pots and pans and shovels were brought out and used as sleds. The running, yelling figures of kids and adults are set against the sun, which is setting directly over the lake, turning the ice light rose. The sliding makes everyone hungry, and people start to carve pieces of frozen flesh off a caribou. This gets a bit inefficient, and one of the men gets an axe and starts to chop at it. Bits of flesh and fat scatter out over the lake and snow. Everybody stands around till he is done, then all get down on hands and knees and fish the caribou scraps out of the snow. I note that Julie is in there with everyone else.

Before we go, each sled chops a huge block of ice out of the lake. It is for drinking water. The Inuit do not like the chlorine taste of the town water. It had seemed OK to me. We go on. Around 11:30 it starts to get dark enough for lights, and the caravan of skidoos makes a line of blinking lights strung out over several miles. The northern lights come out on schedule. Bumbut, the littlest kid in our sled, goes to sleep and wakes up screaming with pain because his hands and feet have gotten cold. We stop, and his father and mother warm him up with their own hands. Finally, very late, we get back.

On Monday Julie goes to school and I fly to Baker Lake. That night I told stories with a group of Inuit storytellers. They told in Inuktitut and I in English. Happily, there was a translator who knew both languages. They could not figure out my stories and I could not figure out theirs. Our concepts of plot were fundamentally different.

I was more than half done with the tour and I was not making up any good stories. I was trying, but nothing turned out. The next day I went to Eskimo Point. I was met by twenty kids at the airport. They took me all over town on a very disorganized tour that managed to include some of the kids' houses. Then I went to the school for a lunch of bannock and caribou stew. The classroom looked like any Toronto classroom, no Inuit content at all on the walls. Inuktitut is the main language in town, and the kids only start English in grade three.

That night I stayed with the Muckpah family. Julia, a twelve-year-old daughter, was the kid who sparked the tour by writing me. Julia turned out to be painfully shy. Her parents spoke no English. There were fourteen kids in the family. Happily, one of the older kids was a teacher. She came home that night to translate. The family listened to Inuit radio while they watched satellite TV *with the sound off.* I tried to find out how to say hello in Inuktitut, but found out the word varies with the degree of absence. Inuit words build up with infixes, and get longer and longer to express more and more in a single word. Thus, something like "I thought perhaps that I might have come and really wanted to but I could not" will be the verb "come" and a bunch of infixes all put into a single word. I did not learn any Inuktitut.

I got my own room to sleep in that night. When I woke up in the morning I found two people sleeping on the living room floor with no covers. It seems that I had kicked them out of bed. The family was so very nice to me. I felt like I was not giving them much back in return.

I left Eskimo Point and went back to Rankin Inlet. When we left for Winnipeg I was bitterly disappointed that I had no good new story. The trip was a failure.

Six months after I got back, Michael Kusugak sent me a story about his own meeting with Qallupilluit (the ice monster). I read it and something clangs in my head. I sit down at the computer and pound out the story of Allashua, who doesn't believe in Qallupilluit. I send it off to Michael, and, after editing for local content on his part, we have a book. For me, it is the perfect book because Allashua hangs between two worlds. Just the feeling I had about the Inuit. Michael and I agree to split royalties and I send it off to the publisher; they like it, and it gets published in English and Inuktitut. It's the first full-colour children's book ever done in Inuktitut.

The artist used slides from me and Michael Kusugak's brother-in-law. The book is a collage. The father had the face of Medard, the wolf hunter from Chesterfield Inlet. Allashua has the face of Julia from Eskimo Point. Everybody in the book is somebody I met on the trip; the trip where I didn't make up a story.

The book is called *A Promise Is A Promise*. It starts off like this:

On the very first nice day of spring Allashua said, "I'm going to go fishing. I'm going to go fishing in the ocean. I'm going to go fishing in the cracks in the ice."

"Ah, ah," said her mother, "Don't go fishing on the sea ice. Under the sea ice live Qallupilluit. They grab children who aren't with their parents. Go fish in a lake." "Right," said Allashua, "I promise to go fishing in the lake and not in the ocean and a promise is a promise."

Allashua pretended that she was going to go to the lake near her house, but when she got to the end of the street she didn't go to the lake. Instead she walked down the long snowy path that led to the ocean.

At the edge of the ocean were large cracks in the ice. Allashua looked very carefully and did not see any Qallupilluit. She said, "On TV I have seen Santa Claus, Fairy Godmothers, and the Tooth Fairy but never any Qallupilluit. I think my mother is wrong."

So there is Allashua, hanging between two worlds. Like me, the storyteller, hanging between story and audience, trying to build a bridge.


*Robert Munsch*

*I told this at the "Friday Nights" on September 4, 1987.*


ⁿ

# Andreuccio da Perugia


There lived in Perugia a young man by the name of Andreuccio di Pietro, a horse dealer. Having learned that in Naples there was a market that sold horses at a good price, he put *cinque-cento fiorini d'oro* – five hundred golden coins – in his purse and, leaving home for the first time in his life, he went to Naples with other merchants.

There, he soon was at the market, looking at many horses, and to show that he meant business, he pulled out his purse several times, but he failed to make a deal. One of these times, when he thoughtlessly pulled out his *fiorini d'oro*, there passed by a Sicilian girl – *bellissima* – and ready to pleasure any man for little price. She saw the purse with all the money and thought, *"Chi starebbe meglio di me se quelli fiorini fosser miei? ... yes mine."* And she walked on.

It so happened that this young woman was in the company of an older woman, who, on seeing Andreuccio, ran to embrace him tenderly. Andreuccio recognized her too and was delighted, but *il mercato* was not the best place for chatting. Couldn't she go visit Andreuccio at his inn? As soon as this was arranged the old woman rejoined the younger woman who all the while had waited a little ways off.

*La giovane* – having seen first Andreuccio's money, then his friendship with her old servant – quickly schemed that she could easily make that money her own. With this in mind she started to question the older woman about Andreuccio, and learned many things about him, *chi era* and why he was here, and discovered many details about his life and his relatives.

Back home the young woman put the old woman to work for the whole day so that she could not find time to visit Andreuccio. *La bella* then called a little servant girl whom she had trained especially for these sorts of affairs, and around vespers sent her to Andreuccio's inn. No sooner was she there than *la fanticella* asked for Andreuccio, to Andreuccio himself, who by chance was standing at the gate. "*Io son Andreuccio*" – "Ah, Messere, a Lady of this country would gladly speak to you." At these words Andreuccio became very interested, for he thought himself quite a handsome fellow and was certain that the lady was seeking him because she was in love with him. He readily accepted: "*Per certo che le parlerò*, but when and where?" "*Messere, quando di venir vi piaccia* she is already waiting for you, at her place" – "*Or via mettiti avanti*, I'll follow you." And without uttering a single word to anyone Andreuccio left the inn.

*La fanticella* led him to her mistress's house in an area of town called *Malpertugio* – Evil Hole – the name indicative of its character.

Andreuccio, not suspecting anything, and believing that he was going to see a sweet lady, followed the girl right inside the house.

"*Ecco Andreuccio!*" – The lady was waiting for him, at the top of the stairs. She was very beautiful, rosy and fresh, standing tall and very richly dressed. As Andreuccio approached she met him with open arms and embraced him tightly but was silent, as if overtaken by emotion; then bursting into a flood of tears she kissed him tenderly on the forehead – "*O Andreuccio mio tu sii il benvenuto*, welcome, welcome my Andreuccio."

Andreuccio was dumbfounded by such display of emotion. "*Madonna, voi siate la bentrovata*," he could only answer, "Madam, well met, madam."

She then took him by the hand and led him into her chamber which was scented with roses and orange blossoms and looked like the room of a great lady.

"You are in truth surprised by our meeting and by my welcoming you, but now that I shall tell you the reason, you will be even more astonished – *E perciò sappia ch'io sono tua sorella* – I am your sister!" and giving all sorts of detail, she described how his father had also fathered her, when he had lived in Palermo during the years of his youth, and how, when back in Perugia, he had forgotten all about her and her mother, but no matter – now that God had granted her the great wish to see and meet one of her brothers, all was forgiven. As she talked she offered him sweets and wine and kissed him and embraced him tenderly.

On seeing her sweet tears and delighting in such loving expressions, Andreuccio believed her completely: "*Madonna*, I am indeed astonished for I had no knowledge of your existence ... *Ed emmi tanto più caro l'avervi qui mia sorella trovata* ... to have found you here! But pray, do tell me, how did you find out I was here?"

"*Mel fe sapere una povera femena*, an old woman who works for me, she met you at the market."

She then cleverly turned the conversation and asked after many of his relations, naming them one by one, dispelling any doubt that Andreuccio might have had, although he already believed her unquestioningly.

She continued to converse with him, entertaining him for a long time, enticing him first to stay to supper then to sleep the night, pretending to send word at the inn not to wait for him, for surely he would not dare to stay at an inn in a city in which he had a sister ... *una sorella* ... who could rightly honour him.

They talked well into the night before *la Siciliana* bid him good night. She left him in her chamber with a little boy to assist him and retired into another chamber with her women. It was very hot, and so Andreuccio took off his clothes, and, in his undergarments, having to relieve himself after many hours of eating and drinking, asked the boy where he might do so. He was shown a door in a corner of the room "*Andate là entro.*"

On opening the door Andreuccio found himself in a toilet room which was but an arrangement of planks across a narrow alley. The unfortunate Andreuccio set his foot on a defective plank and fell with it to the ground. In his misfortune he was lucky, because he was unhurt, but how he had soiled himself from head to foot can only be imagined.

Standing there, Andreuccio started to call the boy, who by now was already relating to his mistress what had happened. She immediately went for the money and, finding it, made it hers. She then locked the door by the alley and, ignoring Andreuccio's cries, took no further interest in him. Andreuccio, realizing too late what had happened, was finally able to find a way out of the alley and turning the corner found himself in front of the house.

He knocked at the door, shouting, *"Ohimè lasso!* In such a brief time I have lost *cinquecento fiorini d'oro ed una sorella!"*

He knocked so hard and called out so loud that a few people came to their windows, awakened by his shouts, among them was a servant of the woman in whose house he had come to such grief. *"Chi picchia là giú!* Who's there?" – *"O non mi conosci tu? Io sono Andreuccio,* Madam Fiordaliso's brother." – "Good man, I don't know what you're talking about. I think you've had too much to drink." – *"Non sai che io mi dico?* Well, if Sicilian folks forget their relatives so quickly, no matter, but at least return me my clothes." – "I think you're dreaming." And shutting the windows she returned inside. At this point Andreuccio became very angry. He picked up a stone and pounded on the door with more fury than ever, causing much nuisance to the neighbours, who complained from their windows. This commotion seemed to rouse, from within his "sister's" house, an evil-looking man he had not met. Bursting from the window, he gruffly threatened Andreuccio with a good beating. The neighbours, who knew him well, counselled Andreuccio, *"Buon uomo, vatti con Dio; non volere stanotte essere ucciso costí;* good man, if you hold your life dear, go with God … and quickly."

So Andreuccio left, to find his way back to the inn. But as he could not stand the stench emanating from his body, he resolved to wend his way by the sea where he could wash himself.

Now, as he was walking he noticed two men holding a lantern coming towards him. Fearing them, as this was the middle of the night, Andreuccio took shelter in a deserted house. Well, this was the very place where the two men were headed and soon they were inside. They set down some iron tools and examined them, talking to each other as they went about their business. Suddenly one of the men said, sniffing the air, "What's this? *Io sento il maggior puzzo che mai mi paresse sentire,* what is this stench?" and holding up the light he discovered Andreuccio and asked him what he was doing there in such a filthy state. Andreuccio told them what had happened to him. – "For sure it must have been the house of Scarabone Buttafuoco. Well, you

should consider yourself lucky that you fell, for otherwise *co'
denari avresti la persona perduta*, along with your money they would
have also taken your life. This way, you lost your money, but at
least you're still alive!"

Then, after consulting with each other, they said, "You know,
we feel sorry for you, losing all that money … if you want to
come with us *ci pare esser molto certi che* you will gain not only
what you've lost, but more."

Andreuccio, who was by now in a state of utter despair, decided
to join them.

On this very day the Archbishop of Naples, Messer Filippo
Minutolo, had been buried with valuable jewels and a fine ring
on his finger, a ruby worth more than *cinquecento fiorini d'oro*.
The two men were headed there to divest him of his precious
jewels, holding them to being more useful to them in this life
than to the Archbishop, wherever he might be. Would Andreuccio
care to join them? Being more greedy than cautious, Andreuccio
agreed to go along.

On the way there Andreuccio still emanated a very foul odour.
One of the men said, *"Non potremmo noi trovare modo che costui
si lavasse un poco?"* – "Why, yes," said the other, "it can be done.
We could get him to wash at the well nearby." And so they
stopped *al pozzo*, at the well. But as they could not find the
bucket which was usually attached to the rope they resolved to
tie Andreuccio and lower him into the well where he could wash
himself. Then, when ready, Andreuccio could pull on the rope
and they'd lift him up.

Everything went according to plan. But just as Andreuccio was
ready to be raised, he pulled in vain: an approaching company
of patrols had frightened his "cohorts," who ran off, abandoning
him at the bottom of the well.

It was such a hot night. The company of patrols had come to
the well to quench their thirst. They laid aside their arms and
shields and pulled on the rope, certain that it bore the bucket
full of water. You can imagine their terror on seeing hands and
arms reaching out from the well. They let go of the rope at once
and fled as fast as they could. Luckily, Andreuccio had taken a
good hold on the rim, for he could have easily fallen back to
the bottom of the well and died on the spot. Andreuccio looked
for his companions, but could not find them; instead he was

bewildered by the arms and shields lined up on the ground. He wandered off, still uncertain where he should go. As he was walking he once again ran into the two men, who were coming back to fetch him. This time they were surprised to see him and asked him how he had managed to come out of the well. Andreuccio told them that someone, he did not know who, had pulled him out and once out of the well all he saw were shields and arms lying about. The men saw clearly what had happened and started laughing – "*Ma certo*, the company of patrols … *avranno avuto paura* and so they fled."

Without further ado, as it was *già mezzanotte*, they went into the church, where they easily found the tomb. It was a monument, very large and beautifully finished in marble. With their tools they lifted the lid, which was very heavy, and propped it up so that a man could go inside.

But who? "*Chi entrerà?*" – "*Non io*" – "*Né io*" – "*Allora Andreuccio*" – "*Questo non farò io*, nor I!" – "If you don't go in we will kill you," one of the men said, while the other threatened him with the iron bars. Fearing for his life, Andreuccio climbed in, and as he went in he thought to himself, "*Costoro mi ci fanno entrare per ingannarmi*. When I've handed everything up to them and I'm busy climbing out of the tomb, they'll have time to run away with everything and I'll be left with nothing." Andreuccio decided to think of himself first and remembering *l'anello*, the ruby, found it and put it on his finger, then handed over whatever else he could find of value to the men above, declaring there was nothing left. "*Ma l'anello, cerca l'anello*" – "*Eh, nol trovo, non c'è.*" Andreuccio insisted he could not find it. The two men understood Andreuccio's trick, but being more shrewd than he, seized the opportunity, pulled out the prop that supported the lid, and fled, leaving Andreuccio locked inside the tomb. You can imagine in what state poor Andreuccio was left! Why, he tried over and over again to lift up the lid, but in vain. Desperate and exhausted he fainted over the dead archbishop (and if anyone had seen them at that moment, he would have had a hard time determining which one of the two was the corpse).

When Andreuccio came to himself he started to cry desperately, convinced that his time had come: either he would die in there, or, if found, he would be hanged as a thief. These most serious and painful thoughts were interrupted by the clatter of people walking and talking in the church, people approaching closer to the tomb. Andreuccio quickly understood why these people were here: they were moved by the same intention that had prompted Andreuccio to come here, that is to seize the jewels and the archbishop's fine ring. Now Andreuccio was really terrified.

They opened the tomb and propped up the lid. Then they started arguing as to who should go in. After a long discussion, one among them, a priest, said: "*Che paura avete voi?* Are you afraid to be eaten? *I morti non mangiono gli uomini.* I will go in." So saying, he threw his legs in to go down feet first. Andreuccio from below, stood up, then took the man by one leg and pulled with all his might. The priest screamed at the top of his lungs and fled from the tomb and so did everyone else: they all ran away in a panic as if followed by thousands of devils. Andreuccio was free to come out and at last he was out of the church. After much wandering he found himself perchance in front of his inn, where his friends had been anxiously waiting for him. When he told them all his adventures of the night, they advised him to leave Naples at once. Andreuccio followed their advice. He returned to Perugia, having invested his money not in horses as he had originally planned, but in a ring *l'anello*, a ruby, worth more than *cinquecento fiorini d'oro*.


## Mariella Bertelli

*I particularly enjoy telling the story of Andreuccio da Perugia, because it moves the listener though a maze of adventures, in a pattern very similar to the one found in folktales. Andreuccio resembles simple Jack, Joha, or the typical folk hero, naively involved in adventures that somehow, in an incredible succession of events, resolve in success — fame, wealth, or happiness. In writing the* Decameron, *in 1348, Giovanni Boccaccio was drawing from the oral tradition of his time, an aspect that comes alive so vividly through the realistic details, the imagery, the fascination with bodily functions and with death. These are the elements that I focus on when translating these stories, while adopting the archaic language for contemporary use. The retention of original Italian words helps the linguistic transition — it is the natural way of keeping the original rhythm and texture of the story.*

# Tales from the Negro Leagues

You know, sailors are a group of people who spend a large amount of time together and so they have a rich folklore. As do the men who work in lumber camps. All sorts of songs and stories about logging. What about today? Is there a group of people today that spend a lot of time together and have a rich folklore? There is, you know! Strange source, you might think. Baseball players!

Of course I like baseball, but it's true … baseball players spend an inordinate amount of time together. They may be in big cities but they spend a lot of time on the ball field. They have a rich folklore – lots of stories. I don't know if they have many songs but they do have lots of stories. I'd like to tell you some.

I'd like to tell you some stories from the Negro League, as it was called. As you know, unfortunately there was a time when there was segregation – segregation in baseball. The Major Leagues were for white ballplayers. They played their games and the games were written up in newspapers, broadcast on radio, records were kept … And then you had the Negro Leagues where the players were black. They played the game, too – at least as well as the white players and possibly even better. But those games didn't get written up so much, or put on the radio. But the stories – lots of good stories! They live on in an oral tradition. Let me tell you some of those stories from the Negro Leagues.

In the Negro Leagues the owners were black, the managers were black, the players were black, the fans were black.

Only the ball was white.

Did you ever hear of a fellow called Cool Papa Bell? Now Cool Papa Bell was a great ballplayer. He was fast. Now when I say he was fast, what I mean to imply is that he was fast. Cool Papa Bell once was standing in the batter's box. The pitcher threw the ball and Bell hit a line drive right back through the pitcher's box and Cool Papa Bell was called out at second base by the umpire for being hit by his own batted ball. Now that's fast!

Now in those days the rookies roomed with the veteran players, and of course there was not much money, so the hotel room would not be a great hotel room. Now when Cool Papa Bell was a rookie, he and this veteran were getting into bed in the middle of an old room with no other furniture. There was only one light, in the middle of the ceiling, hanging down from a long cord. The light switch was by the door. The veteran told Cool Papa Bell to turn the light out. Now Cool Papa Bell was fast. He was so fast he turned out the light switch and was back in bed before the light turned off! He was fast.

There was a pitcher then called Satchel Paige. Some of you may have heard of old Satch? Yep ... Old Satch was fast, too. When he threw the ball, it was fast. He, himself, was rather slow, but he could throw that ball fast.

He could throw so fast that when he threw the ball through a rainstorm the ball wouldn't even get wet. He could throw it so fast that sometimes he would stand up there, act like he was going to throw the ball. The catcher would pound his mitt as if he had caught the ball and the umpire would call *"Strike!"* And the batter would say, "Jeeze Old Satch is fast today – I never even saw that pitch."

They used to call him "The Barber." He'd throw a ball so hard close to the batter's face that he shaved the beard off his face when the ball went by. That's why they called him "The Barber."

Old Satch was a bit of a philosopher, too, and when someone asked him the secret of his success, he said, "Don't look back; something might be gaining on you."

Old Satch used to advertise himself as "The World's Greatest Pitcher – guaranteed to strike out the first nine men." After he struck out the first nine batters he often would deliberately load the bases. Bases on balls to three batters in a row. Bases loaded. Nobody out. Then Old Satch, he'd turn around, wave the outfielders to come sit in the dugout. When the outfield was sitting in the dugout, he'd proceed to strike out the next three batters in a row!

Remember I told you about the catcher pounding his mitt when Satchel Paige was throwing the ball? That catcher's name was Josh Gibson. Josh Gibson could hit the ball. Let me tell you, he could hit the ball! He could hit the ball! He could hit that ball so hard that people called him the Black Babe Ruth. But people who really knew their baseball called Babe Ruth the white Josh Gibson!

Josh Gibson hit the ball out of Yankee Stadium. Now nobody else has ever hit the ball out of Yankee Stadium. Babe Ruth never did that. Mickey Mantle never did that. Reggie Jackson never did that. Josh Gibson did that. Two hundred thousand people saw Josh Gibson hit the ball out of Yankee Stadium. Of course in those days, Yankee Stadium only held sixty thousand people but there have been at least two hundred thousand people say, "I was there the day Josh Gibson hit the ball out of Yankee Stadium!"

He played for a team called the Pittsburgh Grays. One time Pittsburgh and Philly were having a home and home series – the first game in Pittsburgh and the second one in Philadelphia. Now the games were played in those days in the afternoon. They didn't have any lights in the ball park. Now the game was tied, and it went on and on, and it got darker and darker. Finally Philadelphia went ahead 2–0. In the bottom of the inning, the home half of the inning, Pittsburgh loaded the bases. There were two out and Josh Gibson came to the plate.

It was getting dark.

The pitcher wound up and he threw the ball. Josh Gibson hit the ball. Oh did he hit that ball. Godawmighty, did he hit that ball! It went up into the sky. It was getting dark. That ball went up.

It didn't come down!

It got really dark.

The umpires looked at each other ...

Well, they had to call it a home run. What else could they do? So Pittsburgh won the game.

Now I told you this was a home and home series. Next afternoon they were at Philadelphia. This was a bright sunny afternoon – you don't have to worry about the game being called on account of darkness. Well, it's in Philadelphia, so Philadelphia takes to the field. Pittsburgh Grays, they're gonna go to bat. They got their batter in the batter's box, there. Suddenly the crowd started saying, "Look at the centre fielder!"

Everybody looks at the centre fielder – this guy must be crazy – he's running around in circles, looking up at the sky. Everybody else looks up at the sky – there's a little dot up there – little dot gets bigger. The centre fielder is running around in circles, but ever narrower circles. He gets himself right under that thing that's coming down. It's a ball! It's coming down and he catches it. The force of it knocks him right over but he manages to hold onto the ball.

The umpire, quick as a wink calls, "Josh Gibson, you're out yesterday in Pittsburgh – Philadelphia wins the game!"


### Lorne Brown

*Well, as you might gather, I'm a baseball fan. Oh yes, I follow the Blue Jays with interest; but it's the game of baseball that really catches my fancy. To me, baseball has all the ingredients of a folktale. There is rhythm; there is tradition; there is the great use of the number three (or multiples thereof: three strikes, three outs, nine innings, ninety feet to each base, sixty feet six inches to the pitcher's mound – why, even the greatest hero of them all, Babe Ruth, wore number three). The game has heroes (our side) and villains (their side). There are mythic heroes like Babe Ruth and Walter Johnson, tricksters like Satchel Paige, tragic figures like Shoeless Joe Jackson. There is ritual; there is symbolism; even Life and Death are found in the nine innings, for when a player is removed from the game he can't return – for all intents and purposes he is dead. Hence the ritual of the manager's coming to the mound with all due solemnity, usually superstitiously avoiding the chalk lines ("Step on a crack, break your mother's back"), to take the tired and faltering pitcher out of the game and bring in New Life in the form of a relief pitcher.*

*Baseball is a timeless game, as stories are timeless. The very pace of the game – high action punctuated by moments of inaction – invites discussion and commentary. Baseball is the most literary of sports.*

*For my stories of the Negro Leagues I found the following books most useful and entertaining:* The Illustrated Book of Baseball Folk-lore, *by Tristram Coffin (New York: Seabury Press 1975);* Donald Honig's Baseball When the Grass Was Real *(New York: Berkley 1977); and* Josh Gibson, A Life in the Negro Leagues, *by William Brashler (New York: Harper and Row 1978).*

❧

# The First Train and the First Bagel in Chelm

The Council of all the Wise Men of Chelm had been meeting for days now, busy pondering the situation. They were pulling their long beards and scratching their high foreheads.

It was true. A train of nine shiny red cars had come to Chelm. Everyone had seen it. It was true that an engineer sitting inside the train had pulled a chain causing smoke to puff out and that an assistant sitting beside him had pushed a button causing steam to hiss out. They had all seen it, not once but three times. It was true. A dispatcher inside the station house had rung the big bell three times because they had all heard it. And they also heard the long shrieking whistle.

Now, Yakov, who drove a horse and wagon, was a man of experience. He checked the whole train, front to back, and said that he had found absolutely no sign of a haystack. The people of Chelm believed him. What's more, he said that he could not find even one single horse. Yakov stood there on the platform, legs astride and hands on his hips, and spoke with conviction.

"I don't care what these scientists say. If there are no horses, there will be no pulling. And, without pulling this train will not go!"

And, after the first two bells, it is true that the train did not go. Yakov shouted out brazenly:

"Let them puff smoke, blow whistles and ring bells as much as they want. *No horses, no pulling. No pulling, no going.*"

But then it happened … after the third whistle. The wheels began to turn, the train moved and disappeared over the horizon before anyone could even blink an eye.

Yakov remained unimpressed.

"So they got this thing started! Big Deal! They won't get it to stop when they want."

But they did get it to stop. Every day at exactly midday and seven in the evening, it arrived in Chelm. The people in Chelm were amazed at this new thing called a train. Up until now, they had always thought that they knew about everything in the world. Yet here was a thing called a train which could move by itself with no horses pulling. It really was something. What should they do about this new thing? They decided to call a meeting of the Council of Wise Men. Schlemiel the Fool, leader of the wise men, began speaking.

"Today in Chelm something happened. A train moved all by itself with no horses pulling. Whether this is science or whether this is magic, I don't know. But I do know that there must be some things out there in the world that we here in Chelm do not know. It is true that sometimes a Litvak or a stranger comes to Chelm and they don't know too much. Still, it is possible that there are things out there that we should know here in Chelm. Now, when I was a young boy and my grandfather was the leader, I remember a time when they sent a delegation to Warsaw to see if there was something to learn. Now I think the time has come again to send another group of our wisest men from Chelm here to find out what is new in the world."

So the Council decided to send three of their very best minds to search around the big city of Vilna. They chose Hershel the horse-keeper, Yossel the *yarmulke*-maker, and Leibel the *lockshen*-man. When the three arrived in Vilna, it was such a big city that they decided to divide it into three. Each of them would thoroughly examine his section of town. Then, a few days later, they would meet together again at the same place.

So the time passed. When they came back together, they each had a story to tell the other two. Hershel the horse-keeper began.

"In the first place," he sighed, "I did not find one new thing here in Vilna. And, in the second place, they haven't got the brains of our best Helmite goat. Let me tell you what happened to me. I was standing in the town square with other wagon-drivers and horse-keepers. One of the men was bragging that he just bought a new horse that could run so fast that it could leave Vilna at midnight and be in Baronovich by three in the morning. 'You're a liar,' someone else called out, 'and the grandson of a braggart. It is more than thirty-six miles from Vilna to Baronovich. No horse can run that fast.' 'Who's a liar and a braggart?' asked the first man. 'I should bust you in the nose for that but I don't want to dirty my hands with your blood and snot. I say, if I leave Vilna right after the midnight train, I will reach Baronovich by three a.m. and I will prove it. Ride with me!'

"It was then that I intervened. 'Let us assume that you are telling the truth,' I said to the first man, 'and that you *could* arrive in Baronovich by three in the morning. Tell me, what would you do there in the middle of the night?' Someone shouted that they'd bet a bottle that I came from Chelm. 'Of course I'm from Chelm,' I said, 'and you have not answered my question.' They just stood there laughing at me. But do you think what I asked was funny?"

"Well, a similar thing happened to me," said Yossel the *yarmulke*-maker. "I was standing outside of a cap-maker's shop looking at all the hats displayed in the window. There was one I liked very much. Now, as I stood there, the owner came outside. He was very friendly and polite and asked me which cap I liked. I showed him and he said, 'You should buy it! It's not very expensive.' I told him I would like to but that I couldn't. I took the measurement of my head before I left home but I forgot the paper back in Chelm. Well, then the shopkeeper invited me to come into the shop and repeat my story to the workers. You should have heard the laughter. I found myself wondering what all these fools in Vilna were laughing about."

Liebel spoke. "Well, the problem with you two is that you talk to these people as if they were logical like us Chelmites. I know better, since I have also visited Pinsk. First, I listen to people. Then if I don't agree, I don't say anything. I never argue. Sometimes I'm ready to scream out, '*You fools, you idiots, you imbeciles!*' But what's the use of arguing?"

"Listen to this. I was standing in the bakery and I heard one man say to another, 'Do you remember Benjamin, the son of Leibke, the shoemaker? Well, he left Vilna fifteen years ago to move to London, England. When he left, he was wearing a single pair of old, torn pants. Now, they say he has a million.' 'Some people have such good luck,' said another. I looked at them. Were they crazy? He left in one pair of old, torn pants and now he has a million. What will he do with a million worthless old pants! But what is the use of arguing with minds like that?

"Anyway, I didn't have time to argue. I found something very interesting. Look at this," said Leibel, and he took something that looked like a doughnut out from a brown paper bag.

"What is this?" asked Hershel.

"It's called a bagel," said Leibel.

"This is really something new," said Yossel.

"New or old, it's very delicious," said Leibel. "I used to be young and now I am old but I have never tasted anything as delicious as this bagel. Try one," he said to the others.

So they each began eating bagels until they had made a whole meal of it, each one eating nine bagels and drinking four cups of tea. They all agreed that the bagels were something new and very tasty. So the next day all three of them returned to the bakery.

When they arrived at the bakery, fresh bagels were coming out of the ovens. They began tasting them until each one had eaten a whole dozen bagels and they all agreed that the bagels tasted better when they were warm and crispy from the oven.

So, they asked the baker if he would show them how to make bagels. He began showing them how he mixed the dough, how he kneaded it, and how he rolled it into the round shapes joining the ends together. Then he explained how he boiled them in a large pot of water and baked them in the brick oven.

Hershel asked Leibel if he understood what the baker had said.

Leibel said that he did but that it would be good if the baker could repeat everything once more. He understood most of it but he didn't know how the baker got the holes.

The baker then asked if the three were from Chelm. When they said yes, he answered:

"Well, then you must understand all that I have said. And, concerning the holes, that is simple. I got a huge supply of holes from my father, who was also a bagel baker, who in turn got them from his father, who got them from his father, and so on all the way back to our father Abraham, I suppose."

"So how can we get some holes?" asked the Chelmites.

"Well, I could sell you some holes with the bagels. You look like strong men. If each of you takes eight strings of bagels with two dozen on each string, that is sixteen bagels each. That is forty-eight dozen bagels all together, which means that you will have a total of 576 holes. That should be enough to start off with. You should remind people to be careful not to destroy the holes when they are eating the bagels and then you can reuse them."

So the three men each bought eight strings of bagels and wore them around their necks like necklaces. They also bought extras to stuff into their pockets to eat along the way home.

So that is how Hershel, Yossel, and Leibel walked back to Chelm with the burden of the bagels weighing them down. After three days of walking from Vilna to Chelm, they could see their beloved town from a hill overlooking the place. They were very tired and their necks were very sore and chafed from carrying the strings of bagels.

"Friends," said Hershel, "do you remember a few years ago when we chopped down the big tree up here on the hill? Do you remember that it was so heavy that we had to roll it down the hill? Well, these bagels are round just like the tree. I think that we should roll these bagels down the hill. It would be much easier than carrying them."

The other men agreed that was a brilliant idea. So they rolled all the bagels down the hill.

Well, you can just imagine what happened! First of all, the bagels all got dirty and many didn't roll very far at all. And those bagels that did reach the bottom of the hill were eaten by the dogs and goats of Chelm. And do you think that dogs and goats have the sense to save their holes? Not at all!

But, a problem is a challenge to the wise men of Chelm. They would figure out how to get some new holes. It took them many months but finally someone came up with a good idea. They drew a circle on a board, a picture of a hole. Then the baker used this picture and began making bagels around the hole.

And that is the story of how they learned to make bagels in Chelm, the town of the wisest people of all.


### Leslie Robbins

*Chelm is a village with a definite place in the history of the Jewish people. It is a town full of those wise fools of our world, so they say. Thus, in Jewish culture, there are many jokes, anecdotes, and folktales which spread far and wide about the life of the Chelmites. Many of these stories have been put down in print so that nowadays we can get a flavour of Chelm by reading about it.*

*It is from one of these collections that I found the stories about the*

*train and the bagels. It is entitled* More Wise Men of Helm and
Their Merry Tales, *by Solomon Simon, published by Behrman House,
New York, 1965. I have taken the two tales, "The Railroad Comes
to Helm" and "The Holes in the Bagels," and I have adapted them
into my story of "The First Train and the First Bagel in Chelm."
Acknowledgment and thanks must go to the Behrman House for
granting me permission to print my story in this volume.*

 confirming

# If Not Higher

Litvaks! If I was to tell you about Litvaks, we'd be here all night.
We had one once, in Sassov, a real, genuine Litvak. How he got
there, where he came from, nobody knew. The sun goes up one
morning and boomp, there's a Litvak on the doorstep. And not
just any mere Litvak, either, ele a *litvak she-be-litvakim,* a Litvak
par excellence – running around sticking his Litvak nose into
everybody's business, pointing his Litvak beard here and his Litvak
finger there, asking, bugging. You know the kind of Litvak, a
Litvak. "How come, how come, how come?" and every once in
a while, just to keep things interesting he'd put in a "what for."
"What for" this and "what for" that and what for just because
the rebbe wears shoes with silver buckles, white silk stockings,
satin breeches, a long gaberdine, and a wide-brimmed black hat,
how come all you Hasidim have to do the same thing? Go answer
a Litvak. I mean, who in their right minds would even worry
about such a question? "Litvak," we used to tell him, "Az der
rebbe tantst, tantsn ale hasidim mit, when the rebbe dances, everybody wants to cut in."

Of course, this didn't satisfy the Litvak, and he went around
with his questions and his *frages* and his *kashes* and his *shayles* –
his questions, his queries, his interrogations – until everybody was
blue in the face.

He was the kind of Litvak, he was … hmph, I got a perfect
example. One night we're sitting in the *bes-medresh,* the house

of study, just me and the Litvak. It's late at night, we've both been studying hard, and you know what it's like: you sit there and you break your head over the problems you find in the Talmud as to whether this egg which they're talking about, *if* it were here in front of me, this hypothetical egg; and *if* I were hungry, would I be able to take this egg, break it open and eat it, that is, would it be kosher. I mean, questions like this, of the greatest possible moment to a Jew's life. You sit and you worry about these a whole day, it comes the end of the night, you're tired, your head is twisted up in knots. So I said to the Litvak, "Litvak, why don't we close our books and have a drink?" The Litvak seemed to think this was a good idea, so I go over to the shelf where, behind one of the large legal codes, we keep a bottle of vodka. I pull down four or five volumes, find the bottle, but on account of our sins, there's only enough in it for one drink. I tell this to the Litvak. He looks at me with disdain written all over his face, and says to me, "You dumb Polack, you." The Litvak, with their customary *passion* for logic, says to me, "Look. You take the bottle, you pour what's there into a glass, you drink half and I drink half, and we'll both get a little."

For once the Litvak was right. There was no way I could disagree with him, so that's what I did: I poured it into the glass, and since the Litvak of course was a guest, I set the glass down in front of him and wait anxiously for my hit of the drink. Well, the Litvak, he picks up the glass, mumbles a blessing, shuts his eyes, throws back his head, and washes the whole thing down in one gulp. "Litvak!" I said, "Litvak, I thought we were supposed to go halves. You drink half and I drink half. So what'd you drink the whole thing for?" The Litvak, he just looks at me, the pillar of logic, and says, "Nu, do me something. My half was on the bottom."

This is the kind of Litvak he was.

It happened once that it was Elul, the month before the High Holidays, a month of meditation and penance, a month in which the *shoyfer*, the ram's horn, is sounded every day in the synagogue, and Moishe-Leib, the rebbe, he suddenly begins to disappear at nights. Now, normally Moishe-Leib would come into the *bes-medresh* at night, pray the evening service, and then he'd spend the evening hanging around with the boys: kibitzing, praying, studying, telling stories. Taking care of business. Nu, *all of a sudden*, Moishe-Leib comes in, prays, and runs out of the *bes-medresh* like he's on his way to a fire.

To be quite honest, we, the Hasidim, we didn't care that much. Moishe-Leib, he's the rebbe, number one; number two, he's got things to do; and number three, to tell you the truth, we had our own things to do, and we really didn't take much notice, you know. We had to get ready for Rosh-Hashana/Yom Kippur ourselves. But the Litvak ... the Litvak, the way he noticed, you would have thought he was taking attendance: "Monday night, no Moishe-Leib; Tuesday night, no Moishe-Leib; Wednesday night, no Moishe-Leib," et cetera et cetera.

Finally he asked us one day, he said, "Tell me, where does the rebbe go when he disappears at night?" Being as we ourselves didn't know, we couldn't give him much of an answer. We said to him, we said, "Litvak, we don't know." But of course this isn't good enough for a Litvak. The Litvak said, "C'mon, you can tell me. Where does he go at night?" We said, "Litvak, we really don't know. If we knew, we would tell you." He said, "No, I don't believe you. You're holding out on me because I'm a Litvak. Please, just one favour I'm asking of you – tell me where the rebbe goes when he disappears at night." By this time we'd had enough of the Litvak, and just to shut him up we said, "Litvak, when the rebbe disappears at night he goes up to heaven."

Nu, the Litvak he looks down at the floor, he looks up at the ceiling, he walks over to the window of the *bes-medresh*, the study house, he sticks his head out of the window, he looks up to the sky, and he starts calculating. "Ummhmm, OK. It's so far from Sassov to heaven, and from heaven to Sassov it's ... uh ... roughly the same distance, and you've gotta allow him time to hang out, do whatever he's gotta do – uh uh! He can't do it! It's too far to go and come back in one night. You don't even have a train here, he's gonna go to heaven?"

Go answer a Litvak. "Litvak," we told him, "that's the way it is."

Of course, this wasn't good enough for the Litvak, so what do you think he does? One night the Litvak waits until he sees Moishe-Leib running off to *daven minkhe-mayriv*, to pray the afternoon and evening prayers, and the Litvak, who had of course prayed about fifteen hours earlier, he runs up into the rebbe's room and hides himself under the bed, waiting to see what is going to be when the rebbe should come back. The Litvak is lying there under the bed, scarcely breathing because he doesn't want his paunch to rise up and start rocking the mattress, when Moishe-Leib comes in. He goes over to the closet, Moishe-Leib, takes out a pack, hefts it onto his shoulder and walks out of the house.

The Litvak follows at a discreet distance. And he follows Moishe-Leib through the twisting streets of the Jewish quarter and down through the marketplace, across the bridge to the other side of the river into the Christian section, and down past that even to the rickety shacks on the outskirts of the city where the less pleasant Christians lived, and even past that to the Jewish cemetery and on past there to the Christian cemetery, you'll pardon the expression, until pretty soon they weren't in the town at all but had already entered the woods.

Once they get a little ways into the woods, Moishe-Leib stops in a clearing, he puts down the bundle, unwraps it, and begins to take off his clothes. First come the shoes with the silver buckles, and then the silken stockings, the nice satin breeches, the gaberdine, the wide-brimmed hat – he takes them off and replaces them with a pair of filthy, tattered breeches, no socks at all, a shirt that had so many holes in it that it was more hole than shirt, a pair of shoes with cardboard soles, and to top it all off, a battered, defiled straw hat. And he wraps up his other clothes in the pack that he had brought and he puts that over his shoulder, and he bends back down and picks up an axe that he'd also had wrapped up in the pack, and heads off into the forest.

The Litvak thinks this is wonderful. Not only is Moishe-Leib out there in the forest in the middle of the night, but he's walking along and at the top of his lungs, he's singing. And what is he singing? Is he singing the Psalms of David? He's not singing the Psalms of David. Is he singing the Song of Songs which is Solomon's? He's not singing the Song of Songs. Moishe-Leib, the Sassover rebbe, the little tin god of the Hasidim, is singing Russian Army marching songs at the top of his lungs and loving every second of it.

The Litvak, he was already framing the letter to the Vilna Gazette in his head: "The Sassover rebbe goes out at night just before Rosh Hashana; he disappears into the forest, and he turns from a holyman into a highwayman." After all, what's the difference? A couple of syllables?

The Litvak loves it. And meanwhile they're walking along into the forest, going ever deeper and ever deeper, and it's getting darker and colder and Moishe-Leib is singing louder and louder, but he doesn't seem to be killing anybody. In fact, they haven't even come upon anybody for him to rob, despoil, or behead.

Finally, they stop again at a clearing, and Moishe-Leib of Sassov puts down the pack with his clothes in it, takes the axe in both hands, and what do you think he does? Much to the surprise of the Litvak, he chops down a tree. And when the tree is lying on the ground, he cuts off the branches and begins to chop the tree into cords. And he takes the cords of wood, and he binds them up into a nice pack, and he puts that on his back, and he picks up the pack with his clothes in it and he puts that on his back and he picks up his axe, whips it over his shoulder and continues on his way, ever deeper into the forest.

By now the Litvak is not thinking so much highwayman – not only has Moishe-Leib already used the axe in a legitimate sort of a fashion, but – they're getting farther and farther into the woods, the night is getting darker and darker, the woods are getting lonelier and lonelier, and the Litvak, to be quite honest, is starting to get pretty scared  So scared that he would have turned tail and run home and forgotten all about his letter to the Vilna Gazette, except he figured he'd rather at least be close to somebody like Moishe-Leib – and remember, Moishe-Leib who was out in the middle of the woods dressed like a peasant, is also built like a peasant: six foot five, a good three hundred pounds, and with an axe over his shoulder. The Litvak figures that if he's going to be safe anywhere, it's going to be close to Moishe-Leib, and damn the consequences if he should get caught. There are worse things than staying alive.

And on and on they go, deeper into the forest, till finally they pull up outside a shack – shack's not even the right word – some kind of hovel in a tiny clearing, barely illuminated from within – you could see through an oilcloth window the flickering of what looked like a filthy and sputtering kerosene lamp. And Moishe-Leib goes up to the door, and he gives it a kick, and says in a gruff, peasant's Polish, he says, "Lady, lady in there, you want any wood?" From the distance at which he's standing, the Litvak can just barely discern, barely make out a tired old voice, as weak and attenuated as our exile, saying, "No, no, I don't want any wood. Go away." And Moishe-Leib says again, he says, "Look lady, it's my last load, I got no use for it, I don't wanna carry it home. I tell you what, I'll let you have it for free." And again the voice responds in its Yiddish-accented Polish, saying, "Even for free, I don't want it. I couldn't make the fire. I'm sick here in bed. Just go on, I don't need the wood." And Moishe-Leib begins to holler and curse in Polish; he lifts back his foot and kicks the door of the hovel right in, and marches inside.

The Litvak, soon as this happens, he runs around to the back of the hovel, and there, fortunately, there's another tiny – "window" is not it, hole in the wall – covered with another piece of oilcloth. The Litvak gets up against it, and he wipes against it with his sleeve until he can see in, and he sticks his nose through it, and he looks down inside and there's Moishe-Leib, the Sassover rebbe, on his knees before the oven, loading it with the wood that he had cut before. And while Moishe-Leib is doing this, the Litvak can see that his lips are moving, and it's obvious he's not talking to the old lady, so the Litvak he peers even closer. Finally, figuring nobody can see him anyway, he lifts up a corner of the oilcloth there, sticks his ear in, and he can hear, just faintly, that Moishe-Leib under his breath is muttering the prayers that are said at midnight lamenting the destruction of Jerusalem and begging God to send His redeemer and rebuild His Temple speedily and in our day.

The next day I go into the *bes-medresh* and sitting there is the Litvak, resplendent in shoes with silver buckles, white stockings, satin breeches, a long, long capote and a wide-brimmed black hat. I couldn't find any grease stains, so I knew it had to be the Litvak. I looked at him and I said, "So. Now, Litvak, tell me" – I still didn't know what had happened, but obviously it was something – I said, "nu, Litvak, tell me. Now when we tell you that when the rebbe disappears at night, when Moishe-Leib is nowhere to be found – not in the *bes-medresh*, and not in his house, not anywhere in the precincts of Sassov – now do you believe us when we tell you that he goes up to heaven?" And the Litvak just looks at me and says, "If not higher."

## Michael Wex

*This is, more or less, the version I heard from my grandfather – a conflation of I.L. Peretz's story with the original folktale about Moishe-Leib of Sassov, with the addition of a dollop of prairie Yiddish humour. Try living in Lethbridge without Yiddish humour.*

# Is It True?
## An Interlude with Alice Kane

"I cannot tell what the truth may be / I tell the tale as 'twas told to me." This was one of mother's verses, a grown-up cop-out we thought, as an answer to the question: "Is it true?"

Some years ago, at Harbourfront, after I had told the story of Tsar Saltan to a big, dark roomful of people, a little girl with her parents came up and, very politely, thanked me. Then she asked, very quickly, "Is it true?" Her parents tried to hurry her away but she waited while I did my best to answer.

I told her that I thought it was true, not in the same way as the date of my birth or that I had oatmeal for breakfast. It was true because it taught a truth – the truth that in the end evil is shown up and truth is made clear. She thanked me again, and went off with her parents, apparently satisfied.

I think quite often of that little girl and of all the children and grown-ups whom I have known who asked that question; but most of all one little girl, long, long ago – and that was me. I had many questions: "Mammy, why does Santa Claus write just like you?" "How could all those animals live together in the Ark?" "Why does Captain Moore say we must never whistle on board ship?" "Why does Katy think that Bloody Mary was a better Queen than Good Queen Bess?"

About many things grown-ups were consistently evasive and we just had to wait and learn and work them out. For instance:

Far and few, far and few
Are the lands where the Jumblies live,
Their heads are green and their hands are blue
And they went to sea in a sieve.

We knew this was not literally true, but what made it funny was the matter-of-fact, truthful way it was told. We never really believed that Daddy was once a little girl, but we chose to believe in this and the torments she suffered at the hands of a naughty boy named Hugh Kane. We clung to belief in Santa Claus long after we had solved the mystery of the handwriting, and we even joined in the adult conspiracy to keep the little ones from knowing.

But fairy tales! These were different. Why were they singled out for a different, more urgent questioning, and why are grown-ups so evasive?

All my life it seems to me that the greatest truths, the truths by which I live, the truths that give me hope and courage and joy and a brightness almost beyond bearing, are enclosed in the fabric of a fairy tale. It is here I learn that the youngest son (clumsy, shy, like me) very often wins what his clever brothers miss. It is here I find that truth prevails and becomes apparent in the end. It is here I learn to laugh at the pompous, silly wife of the kindly little fisherman and at the Emperor who had nothing on.

All down the ages soldiers on the march, mothers working in the house, children by the fire, scholars and storytellers and wise men and fools have taken new comfort and laughed and looked ahead and asked that same question – "Is it true?"

Hans Andersen tells you to go and look in the museum, for the pea is still there if nobody has stolen it. In another tale he says: "And this is true for I read it in the newspaper – but you can't depend on them." Neither of these is very reassuring in one's search for truth. Dick Whittington is a little better. All the places are real and it happened in the reign of Henry V – as true as history and history, as my father assured me, is not as true as all that.

According to the openings these tales begin:

"When my father was a little boy and before *his* father was born ..." Or – "Once on a year and a day ..." Or – "There was, there was, and yet there was not." The settings are equally doubtful:

"Down by the iron forge at Enniscorth."

"East of the sun and west of the moon."

"On an island in the Nile above the first cataract."

There seems to be no way to measure or prove the truth of fairy tales. We have only the word of all the generations in every land who went – believing – before us. And our own instincts, and our longing for it to be true. That, and the tales themselves, and experience. Experience, of course, is the real teacher.

As I look back on a long life, eighty-two years of it, I am overwhelmed by the constant, steady proof in that life of the truth of fairy tales.

Life is not easy. It holds sorrow and pain and disappointment and long, grey periods of failure; but always (just as it happened to Cinderella or Jack or Dick Whittington or the good little Russian girl), if we meet the trouble squarely and come to terms with it and do the best we can, unfailingly we find that the clouds lift and the Beast becomes a Prince and new paths open and new gifts appear. And, as the fairy tale says, "If they didn't live happy ever after it's none of your business, no nor mine either."

Long ago I used to tell stories every Friday to a class of little boys at a downtown school. They loved Billy Beg and Lazy Jack and Little Fool Ivan and the Steadfast Tin Soldier. Sometimes they interrupted the story to advise the hero or cheer him on or warn the Wicked Baron that his doom was sealed: "You old fool! She's got the ring!" But as the story ended they sat still and listened to the verse that closed it: "The wedding lasted seven days and seven nights and the last was better than the first. I was there. They gave me brogues of porridge and breeches of clay, a piece of pie for telling a lie, and here I come slithering home today!" And that is true, true as true can be. You'd better believe it – for success and joy and laughter and hope, birds singing and clouds lifting after rain, depend on your yielding to that joyful belief.


*Alice Kane*

*Toronto, 1989*


ᕦᕤ

# The Hare and the Lioness

A Hare was once passing by a cave, and in the cave a Lioness had just given birth to her first child. The Hare looked at her and asked, "How many children have you?"

"One," said the Lioness.

"Oh, pitiful," said the Hare, "pitiful! I have seven; and the last time I had nine!"

"Yes," said the Lioness, "it's true. I have only one child. But the one I have is a Lion."

෩

# A Second Language

A mother Mouse was walking down the road with her little ones around her, and suddenly an enormous Cat appeared. The little mice screamed and tried to hide behind their mother. But the mother turned around bravely, and she faced that Cat, and she said to it, "BOW WOW!" And, as the Cat ran away, she looked at her children and she told them, "Let that be a lesson to you. Never underestimate the value of a second language."

෩

# The Corpse Watchers

There was a poor widow woman once who had three daughters. And one day the eldest came to her and said, "Mother, bake me a bannock and cut me a collop, for I'm off to seek my fortune."

So the mother prepared the bread and meat, and then she said to the girl, "Would you like the whole of this with my curse, or will you take the half of it with my blessing?"

And the girl looked at the food and she said, "Och, mother, there's little enough as it is. Curse or no curse, I'll take it all."

So she took it all and went on her way. And whether her mother cursed her or not I don't know. But she did not give her her blessing. The girl walked until she was tired and hungry, and then she sat down by the side of the road to take her dinner, when suddenly an old woman appeared, all dressed in rags, and begged for some of the food.

But the girl said to her, "I've little enough for myself. Devil a bit will you get from me." And the old woman turned away, sorrowful.

The girl walked on, and towards evening she came to a farmhouse, where she asked for lodging for the night. And the farm woman told her yes, she could have lodging there. But she said to her, "If you could watch the corpse of my son, who's in the next room, I'd give you in the morning a spadeful of gold and a shovelful of silver." And the girl said yes, she thought she could do that. So the woman showed her into the next room. And there under the table was the corpse of a young man.

So the girl sat there until the dead of night, when suddenly the corpse got up from under the table and came over to where she was sitting and said to her, "All alone, fair maid?" And she was so frightened, she couldn't answer. And the corpse repeated, "All alone, fair maid?" And she opened her mouth, but no sound came. And he said to her a third time, "All alone, fair maid?" And still she could make no sound. So he touched her, and she turned into a grey flagstone on the floor.

Well, back at home the second daughter came to the mother

and she said, "Bake me a bannock and cut me a collop, for I'm off to seek my fortune." And it happened to her just as it had to her older sister. She took the whole of the food without her mother's blessing, and she refused a share of it to the older woman on the road. And in the night at the farmhouse she couldn't speak or answer the corpse. And she too was turned into a grey flagstone on the hearth.

And then some time later the youngest daughter came to her mother and she said, "Mother, bake me a bannock and cut me a collop, for I'm off to seek my fortune."

And the mother prepared the bread and the meat and she said to her, "Will you have the whole of it with my curse? Or will you take the half of it with my blessing?"

And the girl said, "Oh, mother, your blessing please." So she took half the food and her mother blessed her, and she went on her way. And when she was tired and hungry she too sat down by the roadside to take her dinner. And the old woman appeared to her, and asked her for food. And the girl said, "I haven't much, but what I have you're welcome to share."

So the two of them took the dinner together. And the old woman turned away joyfully, but she said to the girl, "I'll watch over you. I won't leave you."

She too came to the farmhouse at evening and asked for lodging. And the woman said to her, "If you could watch my son overnight – his corpse is in the next room – I'd give you in the morning a spadeful of gold, and a shovelful of silver."

And the girl said yes, she thought she could do that. So the woman showed her into the next room, sat her down by the fire where the dog and the cat were already sitting, and she gave her apples and nuts and left her.

She sat there, and she looked at the corpse under the table, and she thought what a pity it was that so handsome a young man should be dead. And she roasted the apples, and she cracked the nuts.

In the middle of the night the corpse wakened up and came over to her and said, "All alone, fair maid?"

But she tossed her head and she said, "All alone I'm not! I've Douse my dog and Pussy my cat, I've apples to roast and nuts to crack, and all alone I'm not!"

"Humph!" said the corpse, "a girl of courage you are. But you couldn't follow me where I have to go."

"Oh yes I could," she said, "for I promised your mother I'd take care of you."

"Ah," said he, "but I have to go through the quaking bog. I have to go through the flaming forest. I have to go through the pit of terror. I have to climb the hill of glass. I have to dive into the Dead Sea. You couldn't follow me."

"Oh yes I could," said she. He tried to persuade her to stay, but she was as stiff as he was stout. And when he went out through the window she went out after him.

He walked till he came to the green hills, and he knocked upon the green hills and he cried, "Open, open, green hills, and let the light of the green hills through."

And she said, "And his lady after him." The green hills opened and let them through. There before them was the quaking bog. As the girl looked, the corpse was already hopping from hillock to hillock across the quaking bog. And she didn't know how she was going to do it.

Suddenly at her side she saw the old woman of the road – only much nicer dressed. She touched the girl's shoes with the wand that she was carrying, and they spread out several inches all round. And she was able to hop across the bog too.

When she got to the other side, there before her was the flaming forest, and the corpse already part-way through. But there waiting for her too was the old woman, with a heavy cloak, all damp. She put it around her shoulders, and the girl ran through the flaming forest, and not a hair of her head was singed.

And in front of her now was the pit of terror. She could see blue lights. She could see snakes and toads. She could see many fearsome things, but she could hear nothing, because the old woman was waiting for her, and plugged her ears with wax. So she came safely through, not hearing the dreadful cries. And there in front of her was the glass mountain, and the corpse, already climbing up. But the old woman was there too, and she touched the girl's shoes and made them sticky. And she went running up the glass mountain as fast as he did.

When she got to the top there he was waiting for her. He turned and faced her and he said, "Go home now. Go home and tell my mother how far you have followed me."

But she said, "No. I follow you wherever you have to go."

But he said to her, "You can't do this. Come and look." And

he showed her down below them – a quarter of a mile below – the Dead Sea. "I have to dive into that," he said.

But she said, "I'll come too." And before there was time for another word, he dived right down into the Dead Sea, head first. She jumped in after him without waiting a second.

At first, she was stupefied. But then she hit the water and her senses came back to her. And as she went down the water became green like the sky above her, until she found herself in a beautiful meadow full of flowers. And she was so sleepy she could hardly keep her eyes open. And she fell asleep with her head against the side of the corpse.

She didn't know how long she slept, but when she awakened she was in a bed back in the farmhouse. There watching her was the corpse – only he wasn't a corpse now – and his mother. They told her how she had saved him. They told her how a wicked witch had seen him and wanted to marry him, and he would have none of her. So she had turned him into a corpse hanging between life and death, until a girl could be found who would do just what he had done that night, and would break the spell and save him.

Now they asked her if there was anything she wanted from them. And she said yes, she wanted her sisters back. So they were turned back into their own shapes again, and they went home to their mother. I'd like to think they were better, but I doubt it very much.

As for the girl, the youngest one, she married the young man. And if they didn't live happy ever afterwards, that may we do.


### Alice Kane

*"The Hare and the Lioness" is an old fable.*

*"A Second Language" I read about twenty-five or thirty years ago in a trade magazine in a dentist's office.*

*"The Corpse Watchers" is retold from the Patrick Kennedy story of that name.*

# The Dun Horse

Once upon a time in the Ukraine, a land blessed by God and beloved by her people, there lived a rich farmer with three sons. The farmer's wife had died, and it fell to the farmer alone to raise his sons. The two elder sons were vain and selfish. They liked only to dress themselves in finery. The youngest, called Ivan the Fool by his father and brothers, was a dreamer. He liked to spend his days lying on the large clay stove, and dream his dreams. And when he wasn't dreaming, he was out gathering mushrooms in the birch forest for a soup his father loved so well.

As the farmer grew older he gave to his elder sons all authority over the farm. Those two became pampered and spoiled, full of arrogance; and they placed upon Ivan the Fool all the menial, dirty work of the farm. Ivan did his tasks as best he could, for he loved his father and brothers. The grander and finer the brothers became, the more tattered and dishevelled grew Ivan. But of this, the father said and did nothing.

One day the father became ill, and he called his sons to his bedside. "My sons, I am old and I fear I am dying," he said. "When I am in the ground, bring to my grave white bread three nights in succession."

The sons, their eyes glistening with tears, all gave their assent to their father's last wish. That very night the old father died; and when the *Panichidas* were sung and the Requiem Mass celebrated, he was buried beside his wife on a green knoll in the midst of the birch forest. Now, that same night the eldest son should have gone to the grave as his father had asked. But, because he was either lazy or afraid, he went instead to Ivan the Fool.

"Ivan, go in my place to our father's grave," he said. "And if you do this I will buy you a *medinyk* – a honey-cake – of such sweetness the likes of which you have never tasted."

Ivan agreed. He went and baked the white bread. At dusk he set off for the grave on the green knoll. Quietly he walked through the birch forest. The shadows lengthened and deepened. The light of the moon shone palely like a reflection from a shining skull. The birches stood stark and white against the black shadows like skeletal hands thrust up from the earth. Ivan was fearful, but he pressed on slowly. At last, he stood at the foot of his father's grave. Ivan knelt and he prayed for the soul of his father and he sang the *Vychnya Pommiat* – the Hymn of Everlasting Memory. When he was done he lay upon the grave and soaked the cold, soft earth with his tears, and waited for what would happen.

The night was still.

At midnight the grave opened. His father arose – a grey, shimmering shade with dull, dead eyes. He spoke: "Who is there? Is it you, my eldest son? Tell me how the world fares. Do the dogs bark; do the wolves howl?"

"Yes father, it is I, your son," said Ivan the Fool. "But all is quiet in the world. Here is your bread – take it and eat it." The father ate the bread and slipped again beneath the now warm earth. Ivan the Fool slept on the grave and dreamed strange dreams.

In the morning Ivan awoke and descended the green knoll; and, as he walked through the bare birches, he saw among the gold and brown leaves small, white mushrooms growing in the rich forest soil. Ivan filled his cap with the mushrooms and made his way home. When he came to his father's house, his eldest brother was waiting for him.

"Did you see our father?"

"I did."

"Did he eat of the bread?"

"He ate all he needed."

Now, the next night the second brother should have gone to the grave; but, because he was either lazy or afraid, he went instead to Ivan the Fool. "Ivan, go to our father's grave in my stead," he said, "and if you do this, I will give you my belt of red Araby leather the likes of which you could never buy."

Ivan agreed, and he went and baked the bread. As the sun set, he set out for the grave on the green knoll. The air was cold in the birch forest, and the wind blew strongly. The branches of the trees seemed to clutch at Ivan's dirty khaftan like bony fingers. Ivan trembled with fear, pulled the khaftan tighter about him, and pressed on.

At last he stood at the foot of the grave. He knelt upon the cold earth and prayed for his father's soul, and sang again the *Vychnya Pommiat* – the Hymn of Everlasting Memory. Ivan lay upon the grave and soaked the broken earth with his tears and waited.

As before, at midnight the grave opened and his father arose, grey and ghostly, his eyes dull like tarnished coins. The father spoke: "Who is there? Is it you my second son? Tell me how the world fares. Do the dogs bark; do the wolves howl?"

"Yes father, it is I, your son," said Ivan the Fool. "But all is quiet in the world. Here is your bread – take it and eat it." The father ate the bread and again sank back into the now warm earth.

Ivan slept on the grave and dreamed his dreams. At dawn Ivan awoke and descended the green knoll to the birch forest. As Ivan walked he saw again mushrooms sprung from the black earth. Small and white they were, like little knucklebones. They grew in such profusion Ivan the Fool filled his cap and the deep pockets of his khaftan.

When Ivan arrived at his father's house, his second brother was waiting for him. "Did you see our father?"

"I did."

"Did he eat of the bread?"

"He ate all he needed."

The third night drew nigh and Ivan the Fool went to his brothers. "Brothers, will you both go to our father's grave this last night?"

"Ivan, Ivan," said the brothers, laughing, "you know the way so well; go yet again."

Ivan baked the bread and set off in the dark. The birches shone in the new moon's light; their remaining leaves lit the forest with a golden lantern glow. Ivan walked slowly to his father's grave that night.

It was late when Ivan reached the crest of the knoll. As before he knelt upon the earth, prayed for his father's soul, and sang for the last time the *Vychnya Pommiat* – the Hymn of Everlasting Memory. Ivan lay upon the earth to await his father. At midnight, just as it was on the previous nights, the grave opened and his father arose – pale and tattered, his unseeing eyes like two round, grey stones.

The father spoke: "Who is there? Is it you, Ivan, my youngest son – heart of my heart? Tell me how the world fares. Do the dogs bark; do the wolves howl?"

"Yes, father, it is I, Ivan the Fool, your youngest son. But all is quiet in the world. Here is your bread – take it and eat it."

The father ate the bread. Then Ivan leaped up from the grave and fell prostrate upon the wet grass quivering with fear. He peeked under his arm to look upon his father. The old man, no longer tattered and ragged, was robed in white; his eyes shone like two small suns. The father spoke: "Be not afraid, my son. Because of you I now have eyes to see the 'Light of the World.' You were the only son to come to my grave – you alone heeded my bidding.

"Listen to me, Ivan, and listen well. Go to my first field, that I wrested from the forest. When you are there, say these words:

"Dun Horse, Magic Horse
Horse of power and might,
Come when I call!"

Fear not, Ivan, for a horse will appear – a great dun horse with fire in his eyes and smoke from his nostrils – but fear him not, Ivan. When he gallops to you, climb in his left ear and out his right – and something wondrous will happen to you. Mount the horse, Ivan, for then he will be yours.

"Farewell, my beloved son, your vigil is done."

And then the father was gone.

Ivan's heart was filled with great joy, and he lay upon the warm earth and slept and dreamed his dreams. When the sun rose, Ivan awoke and descended from the green knoll to the birch forest. As he walked he saw all about him mushrooms; mushrooms everywhere, on every patch of black earth. Ivan ran about gathering them. There were so many he filled his cap, his pockets, and his arms. He could not gather them all, so great were their numbers. When Ivan arrived at his father's house, his two brothers were waiting for him.

"Did you see our father?"

"I did."

"Did he eat of the bread?"

"He ate all he needed and bid us that the vigil is ended." But Ivan the Fool said nothing of the horse.

One day a splendid cavalryman came riding to their farm. Oh, he was splendid – all tassels and braids, mounted on a spirited dapple-grey. The three sons raced to the door. The horseman was a messenger of the Tsar, and he proclaimed to the three brothers: "Listen and be attentive! I come from our little father, the Tsar. Hear me and hear me well: Our little father commands all unmarried men of the realm to come to the Tsar's courtyard in the Holy City of Kiev. There you will see a great tower, twelve logs high standing on twelve pillars. At the top of the tower is a small window where the Tsar's lovely Tsarevna will sit waiting for a horseman who can leap with his horse to her sill and kiss the Tsarevna upon her lips. Then, no matter his birth, the Tsar will marry his daughter to the horseman, and give him half the Tsardom as dowry."

Away rode the cavalryman; the stones of the road flew about like rain as he raced down the road.

When Ivan the Fool's brothers heard this news, they rubbed their soft hands with glee and danced about the yard scattering the chickens. They shouted to each other: "Oh, brother – this is truly amazing news! Let us go and try our luck!"

They ran into the house and combed their hair and moustaches, polished their boots, pulled out all their best finery, and preened and petted themselves before the small mirror. Then, they saddled their horses and wound ribbons in the horses' manes and tails. Oh, they looked grand sitting in their saddles!

Poor, tattered, and ragged Ivan the Fool said to them, "Brothers, may I try my luck too?"

The brothers leaned back in their saddles and roared with laughter. "Ivan, you fool, you dolt! What mushrooms have you been eating? Go sit on the stove and dream your dreams." The two brothers tilted their caps at a jaunty angle and away they went, whooping and whistling, with only a pillar of dust to mark their going.

Ivan went back into the house and sat on the clay stove. He thought and he thought. Then he roused himself and ran to his father's first field, now lying fallow and overgrown with weeds. Ivan the Fool leaned on the broken old fence and he called out as his father had told him:

"Dun Horse, Magic Horse,
  Horse of power and might!
  Come when I call!"

At once, a huge horse appeared from across the field. The horse reared and stamped his hooves and the earth trembled. Smoke streamed from his nostrils and flames spurted from his eyes as the horse charged towards Ivan the Fool. The poor lad fell to his knees in abject fear. The horse stopped at the fence and asked most politely, "Master, what is your command?"

Ivan the Fool was soothed by the horse's gentle voice. He stood and stroked the great horse's powerful, arching neck. He took hold of the bridle, and suddenly the dun horse jerked up his head, throwing Ivan the Fool onto his neck. Ivan remembered his father's words. Quickly he climbed in the dun horse's left ear and out its right ear. When Ivan the Fool alighted upon the ground, he was turned into as dashing and handsome a young Tsarevitch as one could ever imagine.

"Up onto my back, my young master," said the dun horse. Away they galloped, tearing the earth as they went. The dun horse flew over hills, valleys, woods, and forests. As they crested the last hill they could see the wooden spires and cupolas of the Holy City of Kiev.

Ivan quietly rode through the back gate of the city, where the muzhiks entered. The dun horse trotted to the Tsar's courtyard; and oh! ... what Ivan the Fool saw there dazzled his eyes.

In the great courtyard swirled all manner of horsemen: Teutons, Cossacks, Tartars, Turks, and even some Muscovites. There were sleek chestnut barbs from Araby, great black horses with huge feathered feet from the North, prancing bays from Tartary, high-stepping greys from the Urals, and shaggy ponies from Siber. The din of their clattering hooves upon the flagstones deafened the huge multitude of people surrounding the square. And then Ivan the Fool saw the tower and his heart sank. It was thick and strong and high. Ivan the Fool looked up and up, and in a small window near the top he saw the Tsarevna. Ivan's eyes opened as round and big as plates. The Tsarevna was a matchless beauty. Her long tresses were as glossy and black as a raven's wing in the sun. Her eyes were deep violet pools. Ivan the Fool's heart now beat in his mouth.

Then, trumpets sounded, drums were beaten, and a captain of the guard called out, "Listen and be attentive! If any horseman can leap with his horse and kiss the lovely Tsarevna upon her lips, to him will be given half the Tsardom as dowry and the beautiful Tsarevna's hand in marriage! Let the horsemen begin!"

So the fine young men began to jump, one after another. But the tower was high and unforgiving. Horses crashed against the pillars. Riders tumbled to the flagstones. Horses tore their legs on the logs. Riders cracked their heads and limbs against the walls. Men moaned and horses screamed piteously. But not one succeeded in even reaching halfway up the tower. Soon the courtyard was well smeared with blood. Many more riders turned away without even trying, including Ivan the Fool's two brothers.

Ivan the Fool quaked with fear when he saw the carnage. The dun horse could feel Ivan quivering, and he spoke firmly: "Fear not, young master, for soon we shall see what we shall do!"

The square cleared. None were left to try the crippling leap. The Tsar and his guard were about to leave, when the muzhiks near the peasants' gate began to shout, "Wait, wait – a young Tsarevitch still stands. He will jump!" The crowd parted and away flew the dun horse. His iron hooves cracked and shattered the flagstones, so fierce was his gallop. The tower's rough logs rushed fast, oh so fast, towards Ivan's terror-filled eyes. Then – up, up, up sailed the dun horse.

The lovely Tsarevna's heart nearly stopped when she saw the handsome young Tsarevitch rising up to her. But so high did the dun horse fly that Ivan began to shake with fear, and he let loose the reins. Down, down, down came the dun horse.

The whole courtyard shook when horse and rider thudded to earth. All the people gasped. Surely the great horse had broken all his legs! But the dun horse shook his silver mane and wheeled back to the peasants' gate and turned again to face the tower. The dun horse spoke quietly: "Courage, courage, young master – be not afraid. Hold tight to the reins and we will see what we can win this day."

The horse charged forward, faster and faster; the tower loomed before Ivan the Fool. The dun horse leapt, his flanks rippling, mane and tail flying. The Tsarevna beckoned the soaring Tsarevitch with her tender eyes. Never had she seen his like! "Oh, rise, rise, dear rider," she cried.

But again, Ivan the Fool's hands began to tremble and the reins fell free. Down, down, down came the dun horse. The huge crowd scrambled back in fear for their lives, so great was the shower of sparks from the horse's iron hooves. Slowly, slowly did the dun horse turn back to the peasants' gate. He squared himself before the tower and spoke to Ivan the Fool: "Fear not, master, fear not! You need only hold tight to the reins. Come, let us win your rightful prize. Look you how the sweet Tsarevna calls to you with her eyes!"

Ivan the Fool took up the reins and wound them thrice about his hands. Then, keeping his eyes on the Tsarevna, he dug his heels into the dun horse's flanks. Away raced the horse, like the wind he flew. Up, up, up leapt steed and rider, both rising like a flame. Ivan the Fool kept his eyes on the Tsarevna. He did not see the blood-splattered logs. He did not tremble. He did not drop the reins. Higher and higher they soared, and then – there she was! Her violet eyes were wide. Ivan the Fool leaned forward and kissed her upon the lips. And as he passed, the Tsarevna struck Ivan the Fool on his forehead with her ring, leaving her mark. Back to the hard flagging crashed Ivan and the horse. Seeing he succeeded, all the people began to shout, to cry, to laugh and throw their caps into the air.

And where was Ivan the Fool? Why, galloping away back to his father's first field. When they returned, Ivan climbed into the horse's right ear and out the left. When he alighted upon the ground, he was a lowly, shabby muzhik once more. Ivan released the dun horse and it disappeared as it ran across the field. Ivan trudged back to the house to warm himself on the clay stove. He bound his forehead with a piece of rag, covering the Tsarevna's mark. Then he lay down to sleep.

Late in the evening Ivan awoke to a tumult of horses neighing and men whooping. His brothers had returned from Kiev. They burst into the house. "Ivan, Ivan, you lump of dirt," cried the eldest, "get up and hear what wonders we have to tell!" "Oh, Ivan, you should have seen him!" shouted the second brother.

"Seen what, my brothers?" asked Ivan.

"Why, the young Tsarevitch on his magnificent stallion," they cried. "Never has the wide, white world seen such a steed and rider."

"What did this Tsarevitch do, my brothers?"

"Oh, Ivan, he soared like a falcon on the back of an eagle," said the eldest. "And he kissed the beautiful Tsarevna!" completed the other. "But then he rode off, and no one knows where," continued the eldest; "Yes, yes," said the second, "and oh, how distressed was the sweet Tsarevna. Her tears fell like rain from the tower. But no one knows where the Tsarevitch can be found."

From the stove Ivan said, "But ... was I not that handsome Tsarevitch?"

The two brothers stared at Ivan the Fool in amazement. "Ivan you fool, is your head an empty pot?" said one. "What mushrooms have you been eating now?" said the other. And they laughed and laughed until they rolled on the floor.

The next day the Tsar summoned all his noblemen, boyars, farmers, and muzhiks, rich or poor, old or young, to a great banquet. Ivan's brothers made ready to attend. Ivan asked them, "Brothers, will you take me with you?" "Ivan, you stay here on your stove and eat your mushrooms and dream your dreams." The two brothers mounted their horses and rode to Kiev.

Shortly after, Ivan set off on foot following his brothers. It was a long walk, and Ivan arrived at the Tsar's palace just in time for the passing of the mead cups at the end of the banquet. A gruff guard set Ivan the Fool down on the floor in the farthest vault of the hall. The music stopped and the Tsarevna began to go from one guest to another, offering each a bowl of mead, and looking to see if anyone had the mark of her ring on his forehead. Slowly she wound her way among the guests, always drawing closer and closer to the poor muzhiks sitting on the floor. Finally she was standing before Ivan the Fool.

The Tsarevna smiled at the piece of Ukrainian clay at her feet. Suddenly her heart beat faster. She looked again at Ivan. He was covered with dirt, his clothes were rent with holes and covered with ragged patches, and his unkempt hair stood up on end. Nonetheless, the lovely Tsarevna asked, "Whose son are you? And why is your forehead bound?"

Softly, Ivan the Fool replied, "Dear lady, I knocked it on a stall."

The Tsarevna reached out and took the rag from Ivan the Fool's head. At once a golden glow shone forth, illuminating the dark vault. The Tsarevna cried out, "My Tsarevitch, my Tsarevitch!" Ivan the Fool quickly covered the mark of the ring. A great hubbub ensued. Down the long hall strode the Tsar of all the Ukraine, flanked by his guards. But when he saw the object of his daughter's ecstasy, his eyes started out from his head. The Tsar began to rant and rage: "This, *this* is her Tsarevitch? This clod of Ukrainian muck! This soot child who looks like he sleeps on stoves! Take her away; she's lost her mind. And take this clump of dirt and separate his head from his shoulders!"

The guards were about to seize Ivan the Fool, when the Tsarevna screamed, "No, no, spare him! I beg you spare him!" Ivan the Fool kissed the Tsar's boots and said, "Oh, Tsar Majesty, let me return to my father's farm. I will not trouble you."

The Tsar relented, and Ivan rushed from the hall to the dark, deserted courtyard. In a strong, clear voice he called out as his father had told him:

"Dun Horse, Magic Horse,
  Horse of power and might!
  Come when I call!"

At once the dun horse appeared and galloped to Ivan the Fool with flames spurting from its eyes and smoke streaming from its nostrils. "Come, young master! In my ears and out – and let us see what you will win tonight!"

Ivan kissed the great horse's neck. He swung up to the dun horse's powerful withers and in a trice climbed in the left ear and out the right, turning again into the handsomest young Tsarevitch ever to be seen. "Come, great horse," said Ivan, "it is time to drink the sweetest mead in the world."

The dun horse clattered into the great hall with Ivan sitting straight and tall in his saddle. All the people cried out in astonishment; and when the Tsarevna saw Ivan she wiped the bitter tears from her eyes and raced to him. Ivan reached down and swung her up on to his saddle. Their joy filled the hall with its sweet warmth. The multitude cheered and laughed. But of all that happy company, no one was happier than the little father, Tsar of all the Ukraine.

The very next day, Ivan and the Tsarevna were wed. When the old Tsar died in peace, Ivan and the Tsarevna ruled that land so blessed by God. And they ruled both wisely and well.

### Ted Potochniak

*I heard this story in bits and pieces over a period of a few days, and I gathered parts from several Slavic variants for my own version. Alice Kane, the finest "Russian" storyteller I have ever heard, gave me the idea of weaving these diverse fragments into a whole. Parts of the beginning come from a man named Bunza, who worked in my Uncle Longin's bakery. I think he may have been one of my uncle's partners. Mr Bunza was a dramatic, vital, larger-than-life figure during my teenage years, and I loved working with him on the evening shift at the bakery. We worked together as a team on the bread-slicing machine. Sliced rye bread was still a very novel product to the Ukrainian community of West Toronto in the late fifties. During the "long" hours of the nightshift (those of you who have been working nighthawks will know what I mean), Mr Bunza would tell me snippets of Slavic lore and old tales. He was a most arresting raconteur because, when he became especially animated in his telling, there was always the distinct possibility that his upper plate would come flying out at you. When he told you a tale you had to be on your toes. Mr Bunza also had a well-deserved reputation as a fine eulogist. He spoke the eulogy at my Uncle Longin's funeral. I have never forgotten it. You can see from the beginnings of this story that Mr Bunza had a very Ukrainian view of death. This story also comes to me wrapped in the sour-sweet redolence of rye bread baking in the ovens.*

എ

# J. Percy Cockatoo

There was once a man who owned a property outback of Biloela. His land was lush and well watered and he was able to run sheep. He had no sons, but he had a daughter, a buxom, strapping lass. Her mother had died when she was no more than a babe and he had brought her up himself as best he could. Now this girl could ride a horse, round up sheep, throw a ram, shear and tail as well as any man, but when it came to doing anything inside the house her brain went soft and her fingers went to thumbs.

The girl was that dozy! If she opened a tin she was like as not to throw away the beans and keep the lid. By the time she'd cooked the mutton she'd burned the potatoes, but what was worse, there was never enough to go around. The extra men brought in to help with the dipping or the shearing complained that if she didn't starve them she poisoned them. They muttered, too, that dozy as she might be, the girl was so high-minded she thought she was too good for any of them. Her father was afraid his daughter would never marry. He feared she had gotten grand ideas from the treasures her poor mother left behind.

Along the shelf above the stove was a row of coronation mugs, seven of them, with pictures of the Royals on them. The girl's great-great-great-gran had bought the first in honour of Queen Victoria's Diamond Jubilee. The second mug had a picture of King Edward VII and his Queen, to mark their coronation. The third had King George and Queen Mary on it. The fourth one, with only one face on it, showed the man who said he didn't want to be king. The girl's grandmother had bought that one. Within the year she had had to buy another, the one with Queen Mum and her husband. When she was just a schoolgirl, the girl's own mother saved her pocket money and bought the sixth mug, to celebrate the wedding of Queen Elizabeth and Prince Philip. Just before she died she bought the seventh mug, the one in honour of the Queen's son, Charles, when they made him Prince of Wales. She bought it special, to give to her new-born daughter.

The girl doted on those porcelain mugs. They were the only things not cracked or broken in all the shambles of her father's house. She doted on the Royals, too. She cut out their public pictures and stuck them on all the walls of the shack. She had pictures of them opening Parliament, pictures of them trooping the colours, riding in coaches, doing walkabouts, pictures of them at christenings and funerals. Why, she could put names to all the faces on the Palace balcony! You would have thought they were her own family, or were about to be. Most of all she doted on Prince Charles: Prince Charles sailing; Prince Charles skiing; Prince Charles playing polo; Prince Charles in the kilt, walking on the moors. The day the news came that Prince Charles was going to marry Lady Di that dozy girl went into her room and closed the door. When she came out three days later her eyes were red, her face was swollen, and she said she would never marry.

Her father went quite white when he heard the announcement. He had no intention of spending the rest of his life eating burnt dinners. His plan was to sell up and retire to the coast as soon as his daughter could be decently settled. So he was glad as could be when the stock and station agent phoned to tell him that a well-to-do cattle baron was interested in looking over his property with prospects of buying. He agreed to let the man fly his helicopter out to the station on a day his daughter would be out in the bush mustering till sundown. He didn't say a word to the girl.

The farmer was pleased when he saw the man. Not only was he wealthy but he was young and handsome and he seemed to like the property. "I tell you what," said the farmer, "I'll make a package deal with you. I'll throw in my daughter with all the equipment as long as you marry her fair and square. She's young and strong and as pretty as her mum, though I've took care never to tell her that."

"Thank you kindly," said the cattle baron, "but 'struth. Every farmer for miles around seems to have a daughter he wants me to marry. I have always had in mind to marry someone special. What's so special about your daughter?"

The farmer thought fast. He didn't want to say what the girl did best was cutting off sheep tails. He had a glimmer that it didn't sound attractive enough. He was a desperate man, that farmer. He lied like a trooper. "What she does special," he said, "is to sniff out water. Why, in seven years she's found seven sources, one for every cup on the shelf."

Water is worth more than gold out back. The cattle baron was knocked for a loop. "How does she do that?" he asked.

"Just put her in a room, give her a map and she'll put her nose to it. She'll mark the spot by next mornin'," said the farmer. "Takes after her dear mother, she does. *There* was a woman with a nose for water! Modest and delicate with it, though. They doesn't like to do it with some'un watchin'."

"By all the stars of the Southern Cross," said the cattle baron, "your daughter's the one I want to marry. Now look ye here," he said, "if I marry your daughter, for fifty-one weeks of the first year I'll give her all the food she likes to eat and all the clothes she likes to wear and all the company she likes to keep, but the fifty-second week I'll lock her in a room with a map every evenin'. Every mornin' of that week I'll come get the map, then I'll fly out in my chopper and check the source. As long as I find new water every day for seven days your daughter won't have a thing to worry about and, what's more, I'll never ask her to do it again."

"And if she don't find you seven sources in seven days?" asked the farmer.

"Here comes the chopper to chop off her head," said the cattle baron, and he drew his finger in a line across his throat.

The farmer felt real fussed about his daughter having her head chopped off, but he got to thinking what a grand wedding it would be and he got to thinking, by way of contrast, about years and years of scorched potatoes. He told himself that maybe the cattle baron was just fooling or maybe he'd forget or maybe he'd change his mind. A lot can happen in a year, he told himself. "By gum, you've got a bargain," he said to the cattle baron, and they shook hands on it.

Soon after sundown, when the girl came home from mustering, she learned that she had been betrothed to the cattle baron while she was out counting sheep. Moreover, her father had told a pack of lies in his boasting way and she was liable to lose her head. She stormed and raged at her father and went into the kitchen where she banged the pots and pans around something awful. Then she went into her room and banged the door. What was she to do? She didn't have enough money to buy her father out because he'd never paid her for all the years she'd worked like hired help. She knew she didn't want to spend the rest of her life cooped up in a high-rise unit with her father. So she got to figuring.

The girl had read in the *Weekly* that a baron was almost as good as a prince. What's more, this particular baron's name was Charlie. As for getting her head chopped off, there's an old saying and she paid heed to it: "Don't roll up your pants legs till you come to the creek." Next morning she came out of her room and told her father she'd marry the man.

So there was a grand wedding and the farmer retired to a unit on the coast. He spent his days playing bowls and meeting his mates for a stroll along the tide line. His daughter moved to her husband's biggest homestead to live the life he'd promised her. The only things she took with her were the clothes upon her back and the seven coronation mugs that had belonged to her mother.

At her new house that dozy girl had a kitchen full of every

gadget you could mention, with a cook hired from the nearest town and extra help laid on for parties. When she and Charlie gave big barbecues they invited guests from miles around. People flew in with their light planes and choppers. Later on these same people invited Charlie and his bride back to their places for dances and dinners. When the girl ran up big bills on the radio telephone Charlie never complained. And when she had ordered all the clothes she wanted from the catalogue he flew her into the city where she could buy more. Mrs Anderson, a fine local seamstress, came to live in the house. She altered the hems, did the washing and ironing, and embroidered a complete layette for the new baby who was expected.

And so it came to be that when the year was almost over the girl gave birth to a little daughter. She was a peach of a child. When Charlie said she was like a little princess the doting mother thought immediately of Prince Charles and Princess Diana's baby son who was born about the same time. She was convinced that one day he would be the perfect match for her own child.

So it went for fifty-one weeks. But on the first day of the fifty-second week Charlie said, "Well, my dear, the time has come for you to keep your father's promise." As soon as they had finished supper he led her though the yard and down a path to a room underneath the water-tank stand where she had never been before. The only furniture in the room was a bunk bed, a stool, and a table. On a shelf above the table, arranged in a row, were the seven coronation mugs.

"I'll give you the map, I'll give you a lamp and a magic marker," said Charlie, "and leave you to your own divinin'. In the mornin' I'll come by and pick up the map, fly off in my chopper, and check out the source. If I find a new source every day of the seven you'll have nothing to worry about my dear."

"And if I don't?" asked the girl.

"A bargain's a bargain. I'll have to chop off your head," said Charlie. Then he kissed her goodnight, went out, and locked the door.

The girl sat down on the stool and put her head down on the table. She cried something awful. After a while, when it was dark, she blew her nose, wiped her eyes, and lit the lamp. First thing she saw was the coronation mugs. She lifted them down off the shelf, one by one, and set them around on the table like she used to do when she was a wee girl playing house. Just looking at those well-known faces she didn't feel so bad. They were like her own family.

As she sat there, staring at the Royals and those Royals staring back at her, she heard a scraping scuffling noise low down. She lifted up the lamp so she could scan the better. A small thin lizard-like creature scrambled in through the space between the worn earth floor and the bottom of the door. When he stood himself up to his full height she saw that he had a long tail and that he was dressed like a dandy. A high starched frill encircled his neck, he wore a mustard-coloured doublet, and gold velvet hose clad his spindly legs.

"What you doin' here?" he asked.

"What's that to you?" said she.

"Never you mind," he said, "but tell me what you're doin' here."

"Will that do me any good if I do?" asked she.

"Maybe yes and maybe no," said the creature, and he twirled his tail round fast as a windmill in a dry spell.

"Well," says she, "that won't do harm if that don't do good," and she upped and told about the seven water sources and her father's boasting and everything.

"I'll tell you what I'll do for you," said the creature, "I'll creep under the door every night and take the map, and every morning, before dawn, I'll bring it back with a new source marked on it. Just for you," he said, and his eyes glinted.

"What's your pay?" she asked.

The creature looked real mean and calculating at her. "Every mornin' I'll give you three guesses to guess my name, and if you haven't guessed it before the week's up your baby will be my pay," he said. "And if you have your head chopped off I'll take your baby anyway."

Well, what could the girl do? It was all six of one and half a dozen of the other. She made up her mind that come what may she would guess that name before the game was over. "'Struth," she said, "your pay's too high but I agree." And she took the creature's claw-like hand to bind the bargain.

Next morning before dawn there was that scratching sound low down again and in came the creature carrying the map. "Here's our map all ready for you," he said. "x marks the spot." He looked at her out of the corners of his eyes. "What's my name?" he asked.

The girl looked round the room and her eye lighted on the mugs. "Is it Edward?" she asked.

"Missed," hissed the creature and twirled his tail.

"Is it George?"

"Missed again," he hissed, and he twirled his tail till it hummed like a spinning wheel.

"Is it Charles?"

"Missed, missed, missed," he hissed. The frill around his neck stood straight up and his tail hummed even louder. Then he scuttled out.

Hardly had he left than her husband was unlocking the door. "I've brought you your breakfast and your dinner," he said, "and now I'll take the map. I'll bring your supper this evenin' and let you know if I found water and whether or no I have to take your head off." Then he gave her a kiss, went out, and locked the door.

All day long the girl sat on the stool staring at the mugs and trying to think up names. She thought of Royal names and history names, Bible names and film star names, sports names and names she had read in novels and story books. She was so busy thinking of names that she never had time to be scared about having her head took off. Towards nightfall she heard the key in the lock and her husband came in with a tray bearing her supper.

"I'm glad to tell you, my dear," he said, "that I found the water source just where you'd marked it and I don't have to take your head off this night. I'll pick up the map again tomorrow morning after you've made your X on it." Then he wished her sweet dreams and away he went. When it was dark the creature came to collect the map and early next morning he was back with it marked with the magic marker.

"What's my name, you dozy girl?" he asked. The girl had a whole list of names but just when she was ready to open her mouth her eye fell on the mug with a picture of Queen Victoria on it.

"Is it Albert?" she asked.

"Missed," he hissed, and he twirled his tail.

"Is it Gladstone?"

"Wrong, wrong, second time wrong," he jeered, and he twirled his tail a little faster.

"Is it Dizzy?" she asked.

"Missed, missed, missed," he hissed and his tail was twirling so fast that the girl felt her head spin.

So it went. Every evening the map and food were brought and every night when it was dark that frilled-neck dandy came and took the map. He brought it back every morning with an x marked on it, and left just in time, so Charlie never knew he existed. Charlie collected the map, kissed his wife goodbye, and went off in his chopper. All day the girl sat looking at the mugs. She even got to talking to them. She told those Royals all about the pickle she was in and sometimes it seemed to her they were helping her to guess the names. She reckoned she had twenty-one guesses, but she was using them up fast.

On the last evening when Charlie unlocked the door he said, "Well, my dear, here's the map. I don't see but what you'll mark it right once again just as you have before so I thought you could come up to the house and eat on the veranda, it's such a nice night. I've been missing you and so has the baby besides. Bring anything you might need with you."

The girl looked around the room, wondering what on earth she could possibly want from there, then she grabbed one of the mugs. Charlie held open the door for her and together they went up the path to the house. First she took a peek at her baby, then she went and had a shower and got herself all dressed so she looked pretty as a picture. Then she went into the nursery and got the baby dressed and put her in the pram so she could wheel her out to the veranda.

The cook had spread a fancy tablecloth with best dishes and candlelight and wine, and beer for Charlie. The girl insisted on pouring the beer herself. She poured it into the porcelain mug she had brought back with her, the one with a picture of Prince Charles on it.

Well, Charlie hadn't swallowed but a mouthful or so, when he stops and sits staring down into the depths of the mug, then he begins to laugh.

"What is it?" she asks.

"'Struth," he says, "you'll never believe it, but I was out in the bush lookin' for the place you'd marked on the map when I heard a kind of sort of hummin' sound. I crept forward and came to the edge of a gully. I was looking straight down into a billabong, a pool of dead water with an old gum tree leaning over it. I saw somethin' caperin' about. At first I thought it was a bird, a cockatoo, because it had a sort of ruff around its neck. Then I saw it was more like a lizard, the one whose picture is on a two-cent piece. I must have been sun-struck because I could swear to you that it really was a little man togged out all old-fashioned and he was spinning his tail – his tail, mind you – so fast it made that humming sound. More than that he was singin' a ditty. I never thought of it till now, when I was starin' down into my beer mug."

"What was he singin'?" she asks.

"Don't bother to ask," Charlie says. "It makes no sense."

"Sense or nonsense," she says, "tell me what he was singin'."

"All right. Just for you," says Charlie, and he clears his throat.

"Tell Charlie the Duffer
That he never knew
'Twas me who found water,
J. Percy Cockatoo."

Well, when the girl heard she could have jumped out of her skin for joy, but she didn't say a word except that it was time for her to be getting back to the room under the tank stand.

"Oh, please don't go," says Charlie, "I thought you would spend the night with me. You've marked the map right each time so I trust you'll do it again."

But the girl wanted to get back to the water tank in a hurry. She was afraid the creature would come and go and she not be there. She couldn't bear to leave her babe, though, so she wheeled the pram down the path with her. No sooner had she got back to the room and lit the lamp when the creature came scrabbling in under the door. When he saw the pram his eyes glittered and he held out his claw-like hands.

"Give her me," he says. "Might as well give her me now 'cause you'll never guess my name."

"I have until mornin'," says the girl. "First you mark the map and then I have three more guesses."

"I'll mark the map now," says the creature, and he makes an x with the magic marker. "Now give her me."

"First the three guesses," says the girl.

"'Tain't no use," says the creature, and he twirls his tail.

"Maybe 'taint but maybe 'tis," says the girl.

"Then what's my name?" says he.

"Is it Tuppence?" she asks.

"Missed by a long shot," he hisses.

"Is it Chlamydosaurus kingii?" she asks.

"Missed by a mile. Take care, girl. One more miss and your little princess is mine." The frill stood straight up around the creature's neck and his tail twitched so that the girl felt right creepy. But then she remembered that she had bobbed a lot of tails in her time.

Well, she backed up a step or two and she looked at that creature and she laughed out and, says she, pointing her finger at it:

"I don't have to be feared of you,
   Your true name's J. Percy Cockatoo."

Well, when that heard her it hummed and hissed and roared like a tea kettle, getting louder and louder till it blew up into a thousand million bits. She knew she had spoke the truth: she would never have to fear it more.

She put the mugs in the pram and she put the map in the pram, and she blew out the lamp. Then she pushed the pram up the path to the house. She told Charlie that she'd changed her mind and wanted to spend the night with him after all. Of course Charlie was delighted.

They put a mosquito net over the pram so the baby could sleep beside them in peace and they drew a mosquito net, like a veil, over their own big bed. And there we shall leave them.

## Joan Bodger and Meg Philp

*One Friday morning at breakfast, while I gave a little lecture on the hidden-name motif, Meg Philp, who was visiting from Australia, switched on her tape-recorder. I pointed out that such tales as "Rumpelstiltskin," "Tom Tit Tot," and "How Crab Got a Hard (Shell)" are actually sexual initiation stories. It's not so important that children get the pun as it is that they apprehend that there is a mystery connected with marriage or (in the Anansi story about Crab) with the Great Goddess. The other message is that even the doziest of us deserves the very best.*

*With the tape still running, we concocted a modern Australian hidden-name tale over the coffee cups. That night, together, we told the story at One Thousand and One Friday Nights of Storytelling. Even in the telling, as we bounced off each other's words and images, the story grew and changed into pretty much the version printed here.*

❧

# Lord of the Deep

Violet was an orphan. Her father had died shortly after his wife, leaving his daughter well off – the owner of valuable property – and in the care of foster-parents (who had their eyes on Violet's fortune).

Try as they could, her foster-parents could find no fault with Violet. She was good-natured, did her chores cheerfully, and gave no cause for conflict.

In that village the people got their water from a nearby river, which was muddy and turbulent most of the time. One of Violet's chores was to fetch water every day; and she alone returned home with her buckets filled with clear, fresh water. Her family wondered about this. They were pleased to have clean water, and for a long time raised no questions.

Day after day, Violet would go to the river, along the path that led from the house, through the bushes to the river-bank. There she'd put her bucket down at the edge. There she would stand and sing –

"Lim, Lim, Lim, Lord of the Deep,
Lim, Lim, Lim, Lord of the Deep,
It's Vio Vio Violet
Come for to fetch pure water."

And as she sang, the river would churn, the water would swirl, and up, up from the deep would rise a huge fish. To the river-bank he would swim, take the handle of the bucket in his mouth, and down to the bottom of the river he'd go. He then returned and placed the bucket on the bank. Violet would take it home – a bucket of fresh, clear water.

Pleased as they were to have fresh water, Violet's guardians became envious. They could not understand how she could obtain what no other villager could.

One day, when Violet went to fetch water, her brother was sent to watch her. He followed her stealthily as she went along the path, through the bushes, to the river-bank. From behind the bushes he watched as she put the bucket at the edge of the river-bank, straightened herself up, and sang beautifully –

"Lim, Lim, Lim, Lord of the Deep,
Lim, Lim, Lim, Lord of the Deep
It's Vio Vio Violet, come for
To fetch pure water."

He watched in amazement as the river churned, the water swirled, and up, up from the deep rose a huge fish. He watched as the fish swan to the river-bank, took the handle of the bucket into his mouth, and disappeared down into the deep, deep river. He stared in disbelief as the fish returned shortly, and placed the bucket on the bank, and Violet picked up the bucket of clear, fresh water and took it home.

The next day Violet was sent on an errand to a neighbouring village. That errand took a long time, and she returned home in time for supper.

There was fish for supper. Violet sat at the table, but somehow she could not eat. A strange sadness came upon her. As if in a dream, she got up from the table, walked out of the house, along the path, through the bushes, to the bank of the river.

There she stood, looking at the churning, swirling river. In the foam she saw flecks of blood. Violet knew that her friend was no more.

Sadly Violet sang –

"Lim, Lim, Lim, Lord of the Deep,
Lim, Lim, Lim, Lord of the Deep,

It's Vio Vio Violet, no more
To fetch pure water –
No more, no more, to fetch pure water."

The river churned even more violently than before, and swirled until it rose to reach the river bank.

Violet stood there and cried. She cried and cried until her tears made a pool, in which she stood; and she was swept away into the river.

If you go to that little village in the island of Trinidad, and stand on the bank of that muddy river, and listen carefully, you can still hear that sweet voice singing above the sound of the waves:

"Lim, Lim, Lim, Lord of the Deep,
 Lim, Lim, Lim, Lord of the Deep,
 It's Vio Vio Violet –
 No more to fetch pure water,
 No more to fetch pure water."


## Rita Cox

*Stories have always been a favourite pastime for me. When I grew up in Trinidad everybody told stories, proverbs, fables. They were used for fun, as cautionary tales, to illustrate a point, in the classroom, in church. Children told stories to each other on moonlight nights. We heard tales of magic, we heard the story of our people, and we heard stories of animals and strange and wonderful people. We celebrated and laughed with Anansi; we shivered with fear at the wrath of Papa Bois, at the wickedness and deception of La Diablesse and Lagahoo (Loup Garou), at the lure of the Doens (spirits of unbaptized babies), and at the evil of the Soucouyant; and we marvelled at the haunting tales of the fairymaids, mermaids, and other magic creatures.*

*I've heard many versions of "Lord of the Deep." This is my own adaptation, which is greatly influenced by a retelling by the great Trinidadian baritone Edric Connor. His rendition of the haunting refrain in this story captured my imagination at an early age.*

# Makonde and Moyomiti

Makonde had built himself a fine hut. The beams stood straight and strong, the doorpost was beautifully carved and the roof tightly thatched to keep out the rain. But it was silent and empty. There was no one to laugh or shout or squabble or sing. There were no children to chortle or cry or run to greet him when he came home – not even a wife to pound maize in the mortar, to cook dinner for him and listen to his tales.

Makonde decided it was time to marry. He watched the village girls as they walked to the river to fill their calabashes with water, but not one of them was quite the wife he dreamed of – he knew her so well, this wife of his dreams – he knew just how every plait of her hair would feel, the exact shape of every feature of her face – so well that he could even find her in a block of wood – and so he could, for Makonde was a woodcarver, a fine artist indeed.

Tired of searching for a wife, he walked far into the forest until he found the most graceful young tree that grew there. He cut down the tree, stripped away the leaves and branches and bark, and began to carve a wife. His fingers flew as he chipped and scraped away the wood that concealed her shape, and he sang as he worked, calling his love to come forth from her hiding place in the tree:

"*Mke wangu – njoo.*
*Njo na mimi.*
*Njo mapenzi.*

*Moyo ya mimi*
*Moyo ya miti*
*Njo na mimi – njoo.*

*Mke wangu nakuchora*
*Mke wangu nakuchora*
*Moyomiti – njoo nami.*

*Moyo ya mimi*
*Moyo ya miti*
*Njoo na mimi – njoo.*

Come, my wife
Come to life
My love – njoo.

Heart of mine
Heart of a tree
Come to me.

O wife I am carving
O heart of a tree
Come to me.

Heart of mine
Heart of a tree
Come to me."

And so he called her Moyomiti, heart of a tree.

He had never before carved so skilfully, so joyfully, and soon the heart of the tree had become the woman he had been dreaming of, the wife he had been searching for – so perfect and so beautiful – yet so still and so wooden.

Makonde carried his wooden bride to his hut, took her inside and propped her against the doorpost, and left her there, mistress of the house – the wife of his dreams. His heart, too, felt wooden as he looked at her, for his hands could not make all that he had dreamed.

He left his house and his wife, and went to visit the Mganga, the old medicine-maker who was priest and healer. She listened to his story, and then she sold him, at great price, one very small but perfect *lulumizi* – an oyster shell. For three days and three nights, Makonde stayed in the dark hut of the medicine woman and wept into that oyster shell. He filled it with all his sorrow and longing and loneliness and dreams and desires. And when the sun rose on the third morning, he had done, and the Mganga took the *lulumizi* shell and shut it and sealed it and sent him home with it.

Makonde took the shell home and fastened it in the hair of his carved wife of wood. And he waited and watched, and nothing happened. He sang to her again, calling her:

"*Mke wangu nimekuchora.*
*Mke wangu nimekuchora.*
*Moyomiti – njoo nami.*

*Moyo ya mimi*
*Moyo ya miti*
*Njo na mimi – njoo.*

O wife I have carved
O heart of a tree
Come to me.

Heart of mine
Heart of a tree
Come to me."

He looked into her eyes, and they started to shine a little, yes, and then to smile, and her cheeks smiled with her eyes and her mouth laughed, and her limbs began to move. She was alive – he felt the warmth of her skin and the drumbeat of her heart.

"Moyomiti, heart of mine, you are my wife, for I have found you in the heart of a tree."

And he gave her food and she prepared it and they fed each other as was the custom for bride and groom, and so they were wed.

Makonde was happy. His wife was all that he had dreamed of. He wanted to give her a gift as sweet as his joy and so he went away to fetch honey from some hives far in the forest. Moyomiti was happy too, for life was good to her and she loved the sun.

While Makonde was away, she had time to enjoy the sunshine outside their hut. She was there when four men came by, thirsty from their travels, and asked for water. They watched Moyomiti as she fetched a calabash and poured out water, for never had they seen such a beautiful woman before. And when they left, they decided that it might profit them well to tell their chief that here in the forest was hidden a woman whose beauty was worth a great price.

When Makonde returned, his wife told him of the four men who had asked for water and he was afraid. The next time he went away, he ordered her to stay inside the hut and close the door. She obeyed her lord and master at first, but it was so dark inside the hut, and she longed for the sun and heard the birds calling her and so she went out, just for a little while. The same four men came back and seized Moyomiti and carried her away to their chief and though she cried out, there was no one to hear.

When Makonde returned, he could not find his wife anywhere. He went into the forest again, and cut down another tree, a strong and sturdy one. He could not sing as he carved it – he could not even speak of what was in his heart. He carved a drum, and when he had stretched a goatskin over it, it gave him voice. It cried out his pain, thundered his anger, whispered of the love he had lost. With this drum, he danced through one village after another singing of the wife he had carved and lost; but wherever he searched he could not find Moyomiti, the heart of a tree.

News of his drumming and dancing spread from market to market. At each village, crowds followed him and danced and sang with him, and when they tired of dancing they asked him questions and told him stories of beautiful women. They said that they had heard that the most beautiful of all was the new wife of the chief who lived in the valley below, but none had seen her, for she was kept hidden in his palace.

Makonde took up his drum and made his way to that valley. People soon gathered to hear him, for never had he danced and drummed so wildly. Round and round the village huts he danced, ever nearing the greatest hut of all, the chief's palace. He called and sang:

"*Mke wangu nimekuchora*
*Mke wangu nimekuchora*
*Moyomiti – njoo nami.*

*Moyo ya mimi*
*Moyo ya miti*
*Njo na mimi – njoo.*

O wife I have carved

O heart of a tree
Come to me.

Heart of mine
Heart of a tree
Come to me."

And his wife heard him, and came to the door. She reached out to him, but four strong men pulled her back. Makonde's hand touched her face, and as they took her from him, she just managed to remove the *lulumizi* shell from her hair. Holding it tightly, he slipped away silently into the hills.

The guards carried Moyomiti back into the palace, and the chief rewarded them well for saving his prized possession. For she was indeed a work of art. The chief praised her beauty, but did not notice the wooden stare of her eyes. Her body stiffened and soon there was only a beautifully carved wooden figure leaning against the doorpost. When she was no longer of interest, she was put outside. The sun shone upon her and the rains fell. Moyomiti reached out her roots to the earth and her arms to the sun.

Many years passed. The chief died and his hut fell in ruins, but the tree still stands, spreading its leafy branches in the sun. Children sit in the shade of this tree. They laugh and sing and listen as the elders tell them old stories. They still tell the story of Makonde and Moyomiti. I heard it there, and now I have told it to you.

### *Beverley Grace*

*When I became fluent in Swahili, I enjoyed visiting the roadside sculpture markets where families of Makonde artists gathered to carve and polish and sell their sculptures. Tourists often asked me to translate for them as they bargained for these valuable souvenirs, and usually asked what these beautiful and mysterious forms were supposed to be. The Makonde artists always smiled and said, "These are the spirits of our ancestors."*

*This story echoes the creation myth of the Makonde people of East*

*Africa. They say that the first man carved his wife from a tree, and Makonde men still carve female figures in memory of this first mother of their people. Makonde woodcarvers are known world-wide for the fine quality of their ebony sculptures. Some of these are natural forms of traditional figures, ceremonial masks, or "people trees" showing many generations of men, women, and children intertwined around heavy totem poles; others are graceful, strangely elongated, surrealistic modern figures.*

*I have lived with this story for many years – first hearing it from my students in Tanzania; gradually understanding it as I heard different versions done through dance, drama, and storytelling; finally telling it myself in Canada as it fed on my memories, visions, and dreams, and grew into my own story.*

ↄ

# The Singular Sister

There were sixteen brothers and sixteen sisters. That would have been perfect except that one of the sisters was singular. She was the sort who would get up and say, I'd like some ice-cream, and then go down to the sea and catch a fish instead. She wouldn't catch that fish in an ordinary net, no, she would use a little net she had knotted herself out of wildflower stems, and the poor fish would come out with wet daisies flopping all over it. She wouldn't eat the fish in the ordinary way, with potatoes her brothers had grown and ketchup her sisters had made and sold to each other at the store. No, she would gather things from the woods, perfectly ordinary things that turned strange when she cooked them with the fish, and the intriguing fragrance infused the whole village.

It was a very disturbing situation until the seventeenth sister arrived. Then all the brothers married all the sisters except the singular sister, who settled herself in a cave on a hill some distance from the village. When they went for long walks they noticed her gathering sticks and branches, not for firewood, but to use as a kind of ornament over the entrance to the cave. They noticed her painting the entrance deep pink. But all the brothers had married all the sisters except the singular sister, and they decided to forget her.

Until the sixteen couples had children, and it was handy to have someone help around the house and knit extra scarves, as long as she wasn't the one who chose the colours. In the daytime she tied a kerchief over her hair and made her way down the hill to the village. In bad weather the men fetched her and walked with her in silence. But as they walked her back up the hill at night they asked, What do you eat? Do you think when you knit? And before the singular sister could untie her hair, with seeds and ribbons all threaded through it, the men walked down the hill much more quickly than they had walked up.

Women would gladly let their sister babysit. First, over coffee, they would talk to her at great length about their children, then return from the hairdresser as late as they pleased. But when the children began to intersperse their songs with animal cries and even the boys asked for kerchiefs to wear, the women mended their ways. However, the scarves she had knitted they still washed carelessly, and kept in bottom drawers.

At night in bed the women's thoughts would stray to their sister in the cave: what crazy thing was she making up now? And they would feel resentful, for after a day's work they deserved to sleep. They often dreamed of pulling up the deep pink clover that grew thick around their houses. Sometimes they dreamed of pulling up the cave. But by daylight that was all forgotten, for they kept themselves busy. The men by day, at work in the fields, would watch the deep pink clover clustering around them and bending over in the breeze. Reminded of their sister in her cave, they would feel troubled. Fleetingly they would think of pulling up the clover, or even the cave, but at night they slept soundly, for they were happy.

And so there was a balance: her sisters forgot her by day, and her brothers by night. Until, one day, there was an eclipse of the sun. The sky darkened and a strange wind came up. The corn in the fields and the trees in the woods curled inward to shield themselves. The coloured fish in the sea huddled together. The birds made eerie cries. The women with their brooms and frying-pans ran into the village square, thinking, Here's our chance! It's night! The men with their hoes and sickles ran into the square thinking, Here's our chance! It's day! And they all marched towards her hill, chanting, Away with her! Away with her! Away with her! But before they had gone very far, the sky lightened. The men returned sheepishly to the fields and the women went home. That was just as well, for it is known that men and women can never really agree. And who would have minded the children?

The wind was always sharper and the grass more tender further up the hill. There were plants along the way no one had ever seen before. Men confronted her: How can you live alone with babies locked inside you? What do your other brothers ask you? When they came home their wives said, Isn't it dark enough for you down here? The women painted their houses deep pink. The men mistook it for trendy purple.

When the next generation of children was expected, all the brothers and sisters decided again to forget their singular sister. But this time they did it right. Together they weeded out all the clover from the fields and around the houses. Together they searched out all the scarves she had knitted and burned them in a pile at the edge of the village. When they went for long walks, as they still occasionally did, it was more difficult to catch sight of her cave, for the paint seemed to have faded. One twilight the brothers and sisters all found themselves on their sister's hill. The caves all looked the same, and not mysterious.

Everyone in the village became very busy. The men created honours for themselves and the women created fine clothes to wear to banquets. The men painted the houses white or brown. When they took the new generation of children on a historical tour of the caves on the hill, they chose vaccination day, and the weather was always bad. The children worked hard in school, and never, ever, looked out over the sea.


*Marvyne Jenoff*


*I wrote this piece in the late seventies and improved it for telling more recently when my ear had been trained by regular attendance at One Thousand and One Nights.*

*I have always been intrigued by the position of the single person, the eccentric, in society. This story deals with the fate and the importance of the eccentric, and the fragility of social restraints. It is a signature piece for me.*

ॐ

# Aschenpöttel

Once upon a time the wife of a rich man fell ill, and, as she knew that her end was drawing near, she called her only daughter to her bedside and said, "Be good and pious and the good God will always protect you and I will look down from heaven and be near you." Thereupon she closed her eyes and departed. Every day the child went to her mother's grave and wept and prayed and she remained pious and good. When the winter came, the snow spread a white sheet over the grave, and by the time the spring's sun had drawn it off again, the man had taken another wife.

The wife brought with her into the household two daughters who were beautiful and fair of face, but they were vile and black of heart, and now began a bad time for the poor stepchild. "Is the stupid goose to sit and eat in the parlour with us? She who wants to eat bread must earn it. Out with the kitchen wench!"

They took her pretty clothes away from her, gave her an old grey bedgown and heavy wooden shoes. "Just look at the proud princess. How decked out she is!" They laughed and they shoved her into the kitchen. There she had to do hard work from morning to night. She had to do the cooking and the cleaning. And by evening when she had done a full day's work she was tired. But she had no bed to go to. And so on that account she had to lie on the hearth amongst the ashes. And as she always looked dusty and dirty, her two stepsisters took to calling her Aschenpöttel. "Aschen – Aschen – Aschenpöttel!"

Now, it came time for the father to go to the fair and he asked his two stepdaughters what he should bring back for them.

"Beautiful dresses," they said, "pearls and jewels!" "And you, Aschenpöttel, what will you have?"

"Father, bring for me the first branch that knocks against your hat on your way home." The father went to the fair and he bought beautiful dresses and pearls and jewels for his two step-daughters. But as he was riding home through a green glade, a hazel branch brushed against his hat and knocked it off. And then the father remembered what Aschenpöttel had asked for. He broke off the branch from the hazel tree and when he returned home he gave his two stepdaughters the things that they had asked for and to Aschenpöttel he gave the branch from the hazel tree.

Aschenpöttel thanked her father and then she went out into the garden. She planted the hazel branch on her mother's grave and then she wept so much that her tears fell down upon it and watered it and it grew. It grew into a handsome tree. And a little white bird always came on the tree and if ever Aschenpöttel expressed a wish, the bird would throw down to her what she asked for.

Now, the King of that country gave orders that there should be a festival that would last for three days, a festival to which all the beautiful maidens in the country were to be invited in order that his own son might choose himself a bride. And when the two stepsisters heard that they too were to appear among the number, they were delighted and they called Aschenpöttel and they said, "Comb our hair, fasten our buckles, and polish our shoes. We are going to the festival at the King's palace!"

Aschenpöttel obeyed, but wept, for she too would have liked to go with them to the festival, and asked her stepmother to allow her to do so. But her stepmother said, "No. You are much too dirty. You may not go with us."

But Aschenpöttel kept on asking and at last the stepmother said, "I will empty the lentils amongst the ashes for you and if you can pick them out again in one hour, then you may go with us." And when the stepmother had emptied the lentils amongst the ashes and had gone away, Aschenpöttel went into the kitchen and she called through the window,

"You tame pigeons, you turtle doves,
And all you birds beneath the sky,
Come and help me to pick,

The good into the pot,
The bad into the crop."

Then two white pigeons came in by the kitchen window and afterwards the turtle doves and at last all the birds beneath the sky came whirring and crowding in and alighted amongst the ashes. And the doves nodded with their heads and began: pick-peck, pick-peck, pick-peck and the other birds also: pick-peck, pick-peck, pick-peck, and before one hour was over they had picked all the good lentils and put them into the pot and had all flown out again.

Aschenpöttel was glad, for she knew that now she would be able to go to the festival, and she took the pot of lentils to her stepmother, who said, "You may not go with us. You are much too dirty. We should be ashamed of you." But Aschenpöttel went on asking and the stepmother said, "I will empty two dishes of lentils amongst the ashes for you and if you can pick them out again in one hour, then you may go with us." After the stepmother had emptied the lentils amongst the ashes and gone away, Aschenpöttel stood in the kitchen and called through the open window,

"You tame pigeons, you turtle doves,
And all you birds beneath the sky,
Come and help me to pick,
The good into the pot,
The bad into the crop."

Then two white pigeons came in by the kitchen window and afterwards the turtle doves and at last all the birds beneath the sky came whirring and crowding in and alighted amongst the ashes. And the doves nodded with their heads and began: pick-peck, pick-peck, pick-peck and the other birds also: pick-peck, pick-peck, pick-peck, and before one hour was over they had picked all the good lentils and put them into the pot and had all flown out again.

Aschenpöttel was delighted. Now she knew she would be able to go to the festival and she took the two pots to her stepmother, but her stepmother said, "All this will not help. You are much too dirty. We should only be ashamed of you." And she turned

her back on Aschenpöttel and she hurried away to the festival
with her own two proud daughters.

Now that Aschenpöttel was all alone, she went out into the
garden and stood under the hazel tree and sang,

"Shiver and quiver,
  My little tree,
  Silver and gold,
  Throw down over me."

And the bird threw down to her a gown of silver and gold
and the slippers were made of silk. Aschenpöttel put on these
clothes with all speed and then she hurried off to the festival.
No one recognized her. They thought she must be some foreign
princess, she was so beautiful. The King's Son took her by the
hand and danced with her. They danced and they danced. They
danced until it was evening and then Aschenpöttel wanted to
go home. The King's Son wanted to follow her for he wanted
to see into whose house she went. But she sprang away from
him and she ran until she came to the pigeon house. She clambered
inside so nimbly the King's Son did not know where she was
gone. And he waited until her father came. Then he said, "The
beautiful maiden I was dancing with has escaped from me and I
have reason to believe that she is in your pigeon house." The
father thought to himself, "I wonder if that could be Aschenpöttel."
And they brought him an axe and a pickaxe that he might hew
the pigeon house to pieces. But there was no one inside. They
went into the kitchen, and there was Aschenpöttel in the grey
bedgown and a dim little oil lamp was burning on the mantelpiece.

On the second day of the festival when everyone was gone,
Aschenpöttel went into the garden and stood under the hazel
tree and sang,

"Shiver and quiver,
  My little tree,
  Silver and gold,
  Throw down over me."

This time the bird threw down to her a gown that was more
beautiful even than on the previous day. And when she went to

the festival in these clothes, everyone was astonished at her beauty. The King's Son took her by the hand and danced with her. They danced and they danced until it was evening and then Aschenpöttel wanted to go home. But the King's Son was anxious to follow her. He wanted to see into whose house she went. But she sprang away from him and she ran. She ran until she came to the garden behind her house. In the garden, there was a beautiful pear tree on which hung the most magnificent pears. She climbed so nimbly amongst the branches the King's Son was not sure where she was gone. He waited until her father came home and said, "The beautiful maiden I have been dancing with has escaped from me once more and I have reason to believe that she is in your pear tree."

The father thought, "I wonder if that could be Aschenpöttel." They had to bring him an axe in order for him to cut the pear tree down. But no one was on it. For you see, Aschenpöttel had jumped down from the other side of the tree. And she had taken her beautiful clothes back to the bird on the hazel tree and there she had exchanged them for her own grey bedgown and heavy wooden shoes. And then she had seated herself as before on the hearth amongst the ashes.

On the third and last day of the festival when everyone was gone and Aschenpöttel was all alone, she stood under the hazel tree once more and she sang,

"Shiver and quiver,
My little tree,
Silver and gold,
Throw down over me."

And this time the bird threw down to her a gown that was more beautiful than any she had yet seen. And the slippers were golden.

When she went to the festival, no one could speak for astonishment. The King's Son had been waiting for her. He took her by the hand and he danced with her and if anyone else asked her to dance he said, "No, this is my partner."

They danced and they danced. They danced until it was evening and then Aschenpöttel wanted to go home. But the King's Son this time had employed a ruse. He had caused the entire staircase to be smeared with pitch and there when Aschenpöttel ran down did her left slipper remain stuck. The King's son picked it up and it was small and dainty and all golden. "No one shall be my wife but she whose foot this golden slipper fits," he said. And the next day he took it to the house where he thought he had seen Aschenpöttel run. And he asked the stepmother if she had any daughters. Then were the two stepsisters glad, for they had pretty feet. They wanted to try the shoe on. The elder took the shoe into her chamber and her mother stood near by. She put her foot into the shoe, but her toe was too long. Her mother gave her a knife and said, "Cut off the toe. When you are Queen, you will have no more need to go on foot."

The maiden cut off the toe, forced her foot into the shoe, swallowed the pain, and went out to the King's Son, who took her on his horse as his bride and rode away with her. But they had to ride through the garden. And when they passed under the hazel tree there were two pigeons who sat on it and cried,

"Turn and peep, turn and peep,
   There's blood within that shoe,
That shoe it is too small for her,
   The true bride waits for you."

The King's Son looked down and he saw how the blood was running out of her shoe and he turned the horse around and he took the false bride home. He asked the stepmother if she had any other daughters. Now the younger stepsister wanted to try the shoe on. She went into the chamber and her mother stood near by. She got her toe safely into the shoe, but her heel was too large. Her mother gave her a knife and said, "Cut a bit off the heel, for when you are Queen, you will have no more need to go on foot."

The maiden cut a bit off the heel, forced her foot into the shoe, swallowed the pain, and went out to the King's Son, who took her on his horse as his bride and rode away with her.

But when they passed under the hazel tree the two pigeons sat on it and cried,

"Turn and peep, turn and peep,
   There's blood within that shoe,

That shoe it is too small for her,
The true bride waits for you."

The King's Son looked down and he saw how the blood was
staining her white stockings quite red. He turned the horse around
and took the false bride home and said, "Do you have any other
daughters?"

"No," said the stepmother. But the father, who stood near by,
said, "There is a stunted kitchen wench that my late wife left
behind."

The stepmother said, "She cannot possibly be the bride. She
is much too dirty." But the King's Son insisted that she be called.
Aschenpöttel first washed her hands and her face clean. Then
she went up to the King's Son and bowed down before him, and
he gave her the golden slipper. She seated herself upon a stool,
drew her foot out of the heavy wooden shoe, and put it into
the slipper, which fitted like a glove. And when she rose up, the
King's Son looked into her face and he recognized the beautiful
maiden with whom he had been dancing and said, "This is the
true bride!"

Then were the stepmother and stepsisters angry and they became
pale with rage. But the King's Son took Aschenpöttel on his
horse as his bride and rode away with her. As they passed under
the hazel tree, two pigeons sat on it and cried,

"Turn and peep, turn and peep,
No blood is in that shoe
That shoe it is just right for her,
The true bride rides with you."

And when they had finished singing that they flew down and
they alighted upon Aschenpöttel's shoulders and they have
remained by her side from that day to this.

### Lynda Howes

*For me, "Aschenpöttel," with its poetry, simplicity and timelessness,
is a deeply satisfying story to hear and to tell. My main source is*

*the nineteenth-century translation by Margaret Hunt of the story by
the brothers Grimm.*

જી

# Schlange Hausfreund
## (Snake Housefriend)

An old couple once lived hard by a forest off which they made
their living, he as woodcutter and she as gatherer of herbs and
such. Yet they remained quite poor despite their hard work.

The man helped fell trees, cart logs, sawing and splitting them,
and gathered also the wood for their own use, which he took
home in a wheelbarrow once or twice a week. They were allowed
only dry wood; fresh still-greening wood was protected by law
and anyone removing it would be registered for forest violation
and punished – a wise law, for without it the greening forests
would have long since disappeared. Now when the woodcutter
came to the forest one day, how happy he was to see from quite
a distance that a big dry branch of an oak tree had broken off
in the night's storm. He wanted to cut it up immediately and
cart it home. Yet approaching closer, the man was surprised to
see a large snake reaching out from the tree to the branch,
wherefore he gave it a wide berth and gathered other wood.

The next day he returned to the forest intending to take the
branch with him, but there the snake had wound itself around
the very branch, lifting its head on its slender neck matter-of-factly,
as if, quite unafraid, it wished to make his acquaintance. How
easily the man could have killed it, severing its head with but
one heave of the sharp hatchet that he carried with him! However,
this man was one of the few country people who in their simple
wisdom would think it sinful to needlessly kill a creature of God's,
out of wickedness or lust for murder, as so many do out of
ignorance or, what is worse, sheer spite. He rather gave up the
branch, and gathered lesser kindling.

When the man got home with his then mere faggot-bundle he said to his wife, who met him helpfully, as he threw down the wood, "Alas, I couldn't bring the branch again of which I told you yesterday, for the snake had wound itself right around it."

"Oh you and that snake!" said the wife. "I'm glad I wasn't there; it would have scared me out of my wits!"

Barely were the words out of her mouth when she screamed and jumped back in horror, for suddenly slithering out of the bundle was the snake – scaring the woman nearly to death!

"Oh come now, dear wife!" cried the husband. "Calm yourself; it is not a poisonous snake, just a harmless *Unke* that feeds on frogs and mice. The kind of snake which, it is said, brings luck into one's house. Who knows, maybe this one brings ours. It's about time, for poverty has been with us long enough. You know the old sayings, about people who have buried their treasure being turned into snakes to guard their glistening gold? Who knows but this may be such a one; let us therefore not harm it."

The wife was still too shaken to say anything to her husband, because of that ancient grudge, said to exist between snake and womankind; the snake, however, went at once to the hut and there met the family cat and said, "Good day!" The cat arched its back and spat; the snake hissed and bared its fangs, which convinced the cat not to risk getting on enemy footing.

"What do you eat?" asked the snake.

"I eat mice," answered the cat.

"I eat mice too," said the snake. This peculiar similarity reassured the cat, who now asked the snake, "What do you drink?"

"I drink milk, when I can get it!" answered the snake.

"Well! I drink milk too," said the cat. "We're really quite suited together."

On that the cat and the snake established peace and friendship, and the woman gradually got used to the snake. When she gave the cat milk, the snake, who needed very little, drank out of the same dish. As for a working agreement on catching mice, this too they settled amicably, snake in barn and cellar, cat in attic and hut.

In the little woodhut blessings came with the old couple's reception of the snake: the man's daily wages increased, and the berries, edible mushrooms, and healing herbs the woman gathered in the forest fetched more money in the nearby town market where she sold them. And they lived their lives in peace and contentment that served them better than any sudden wealth could have done. Evenings, after work, the old people would sit – before the door in summer and in winter around their warm stove – the woman spinning and the cat beside her spinning too (though, alas, without any yarn), and the snake would join them, coming up by runways that the mice had made. And so the man and the woman would listen to the animals tell each other stories, in which cats or snakes always had leading roles. The snake especially, being quite old, could tell many stories from her own experiences as well as from those of her mother and grandmother.

"I don't know if you know the story of that woman," the snake said one evening to the cat, "who carried a snake at her breast for a long time?"

"No, I don't know that one; I would be very thankful for you telling it to me," answered the cat, stroking her head with her right paw, whereupon the snake told the following tale.

## Die Schlangenamme  (The Snake's Wet-Nurse)

There was once a poor woman, said the snake, who went to the meadow one morning to cut grass, and carried with her her small child, whom she still breast-fed. She laid the child, after she had nursed it and it had fallen asleep, gently on the grass, where she bedded it softly and painstakingly in the shade of an old willow that was hollow. In the trunk of the tree there lived a snake.

The woman tended diligently to her work until the hour of noonday, when she laid down her scythe and went to nourish her dear child while she too enjoyed her midday meal. She took the child to her breast and hummed a lullaby, and as the day was very hot and the hard work of grass-mowing had tired the woman, she too fell asleep, and the child let go of her breast and fell softly asleep in her arms.

All this the small snake saw, who lived in the hollow trunk of the old willow, because she had crept out to sun herself and to bask in the heat of noon; and, as we snakes gladly drink milk, she sidled quietly up and attached herself to the young mother's breast and drank with great pleasure the sweet mother's milk. But great was the fright of that woman as she wakened from her slumber and realized what uninvited guest she nourished. Then the old enmity between woman and snake awakened at its keenest. But the snake bided too well there where she was, and the woman dared not exert force to remove her, for right at the first attempt the snake held on so tight that it hurt, and the young mother had to acknowledge that the snake would bite her if she did violence to her.

This left the woman just the one breast for her child, and the other the snake commandeered, who didn't leave off while the milk worked wonders towards her growth; and the child wasn't harmed in the least for having the snake as its nursing companion; it flourished likewise and grew in competition with the snake. The woman could have been quite contented, for where snakes live, luck and blessings enter in, had it not been for her senseless assumption and fear that the snake would bite her – as if we snakes had a sting in our mouths. And people also hold us for ugly while they think themselves handsome, and are so dull-witted they cannot comprehend that in all of creation there is nothing to surpass the perfect beauty of a snake: curvaceous fullness, free of unsightly ugly hair and bristles, grace in every gesture, vigour in the faultless undulations of our bodies that are unmarred by angular clawed limb or stilt legs.

Since the woman continued languishing, and the snake continued to nourish itself on her, the child had to be weaned. But the snake would not let herself be weaned; she grew and grew, and the woman had to fashion a carrying bag, in which she carried the heavy snake body, while the mouth of the snake remained firmly attached to her breast. Unfortunately, the woman now had the mockery of her neighbours to contend with, who gave her the nickname Schlangenamme (Snake Wet-Nurse).

The woman had already carried the snake for ten months when a stranger chanced to come to the village, who heard this story of which all the world spoke, and went to the woman and saw the guest, and her languishing body, and her distress that the snake did not let go of her, and he said to her, "Woman, I will free you of this snake, if you will trust and follow me to the woods, and not be afraid when you see yet more of the snakes. That no harm will come to you, of this I assure you."

This man was a snake-charmer. The woman followed him trustingly to the nearby woods, in which he made a circle with his wand in a clearing, and on a small pipe shrilly piped. Soon there came swishing, rustling sounds through grassy foliage and bushes and from all directions so many snakes appeared, big and little, that the woman became anxious and afraid and wanted to jump out of the circle; but the charmer motioned her to stand calm and blew again, and all the snakes began lifting their heads and raising their upper halves candle-straight in the air, and to dance; and the snake at the woman's breast became restless and gently began moving her body, her head letting go of the breast, and quickly she slipped from the pouch, slid down to the ground and glided towards the other snakes and danced with them, while the charmer played happy tunes on his pipe.

Then the woman felt at once released, and was quite happy. She could work unhindered again, was no longer the object of her fellow villagers' scorn (who had been wondering what sin she had committed to do such penance as carrying around a snake), and raised with tender love and care her lively child.

When the child was several years old, it ran along with the neighbourhood children to look for berries in the woods. It was evening already, and the children had not yet returned. The mother sat by the door, working and looking up from time to time towards the entrance to the woods. Suddenly she heard the children screaming from thence and saw the bunch bursting out of the woods towards the village; but her own small child, who could not yet run as fast as the others, was not among them. A boy yelled out, "A wolf! A wolf!" and a second one, "A bear! A huge bear!" and a third, "A snake, a horrible snake!" to the mother's heartbreak, and she jumped up and ran to the nearby woods.

In vain she asked the children, who rushed terror-stricken past her, about her own child. Not a one seemed to hear as they fled by. Barely past them, the woman saw a big wolf still making a few remarkable leaps; it then collapsed before her very eyes, all four of its legs stretched out. Full of fear she hurried past the wolf and reached the edge of the woods, to a horrible sight. A fiercely bellowing bear reared itself, though not against the woman, but in combat with a huge snake, which had coiled itself tightly about him and was choking him – one moment she had seen him rearing and the next he slumped to the ground, and right beside the spot where he fell, still twitching, oh miracle! there lay, quite unmolested and sweetly slumbering, the child of the woman, over whom she fell with a joyful cry.

Now the snake uncoiled itself from the neck and body of the bear and cold shudders coursed through the woman anew – for she knew this snake. The snake, however, said to her: "You need not be afraid of me. We snakes are not false and ungrateful, as you people imagine and proclaim, who stamp us as symbols of your own hate. It is you who nursed me to such size and strength that I was able to overcome both wolf and bear, who posed threats to your child. I have repaid Good with Good! Farewell!" she said, and slithered into the bushes.

## Klare-Mond (Clear Moon)

With pleasure the cat listened to the storytelling of her friend the snake, and when it had ended she said, No animal species has to bear so much human ingratitude as we poor cats. As these people make of you snakes symbols of falsehood, ingratitude, and malevolence, so they do of us too; wherefore we do well to hold together in friendship with one another. So it goes, that "false" cat, cat "falseness," and other such honourary titles, do we receive. One of their numerous vices, thievery, they have, after our God-given calling and survival instinct to catch mice, named "mousing," which is downright shameful of them; and finally they've made up false tales that their wicked witches and devil's paramours can transform themselves into such noble and beautiful creatures as cats. This then has led many people to take each cat as a witch, through which unholy naïveté many thousands of our species have met the most gruesome death. I could tell you such tales until the end of my life, in which we are said to have played roles; and still I would not finish.

I will tell you only one such tale, one that is not so gruesome with details of paw- or head-severing as so many others, but one in which rather our gift for wonderful singing and our joy in contemplating the beautiful starry heavens are featured. I firmly believe that the Sirens of old were no other than singing cats who lived in the sea, and therefore were the true sea-cats, while the insidious people appended to this now-extinct lovely animal species their hideous hoax of a name – "mermaid."

It is common knowledge among us that the night-glow in our eyes is nothing but starlight, which we absorb from our first eye-opening. That is also why we see by night, and there is for us, the most privileged of creatures of the entire world, no darkness; and when we slink through the night we never do so in the dark, and it would be in equally poor taste of the people to take us as symbols of spiritual darkness, as they do with owls, who share with us that blessing of perfect round-the-clock vision. Far be it from me to praise myself and my species. I need in truth no self-praise. Here goes my tale:

There once lived a man who had a nice spacious deck on his house, from where he could enjoy the beautiful view over the city in which he lived, and far beyond. Adjacent to this deck was the man's summer bedroom, leading out through a glass door to lovely potted flowers, shrubs, and a belvedere of ashwood.

One glorious summer night, when the moon shone bright and full and the sky was thick with stars, the man awoke to heavenly sounds coming from quite nearby. He rose from his bed and looked out through the window on to the deck. There he saw to his great surprise a large gathering of beautiful women, dressed in whites, in bright and darker colours, all most handsome to behold. They sat around the table that usually stood on the deck and sang a round-song with the loveliest voices, that went:

"We're drinking here much sweeter wine
Than Burgundy wine,
Than Champagne wine,
We're drinking the clear clear moonshine."

Meanwhile this gentle company did not disdain partaking of more solid foods; leastwise the man saw this apparently all-female group indulge also in earthly wine and delicacies. He could not imagine, since he was a bachelor, and apart from aged servants, lived here alone, who these maidens and women were, and where in all the world they came from, and why they were specifically up here.

It occurred to him it might be a lovely dream; but against that argued his feeling so wide awake, and so it finally dawned on him: I am the master of this house and therefore have the right to join them, and so will hear right away what rare occasion brings them up here to me. So he unlatched the glass door and stepped out to them in all calmness and friendly greeting.

They rose at his glance from all their seats, and a quite young and well-behaved maiden in a snow-white dress, with blond hair and a rose-red mouth and soft, tiny hands, approached him and said, "Excuse us, noble sir, for the privilege we have taken this wondrously ecstatic May night to celebrate on your deck, and pray, take it not amiss if perhaps our singing disturbed your slumber. Please join us, be seated, have cookies, have wine!"

The man was at a loss for words; this dainty little maiden's charming chatter gave him no chance at response. He settled himself in at the round table, accepted a glass of champagne with no reluctance, and as he now drank with them, they sang the round-song somewhat differently:

"We're drinking the most treasured wine,
Burgundy wine!
Champagne wine!
And the clear, clear moonshine."

The white-clad maiden snuggled up with such great trustfulness, like a young daughter with her father whom she loves, and offered him now too of the cookies; he took one and found it rather unpalatable, something was missing, and so he said, "Honourable ladies! Might I ask you, in God's name, for a bit of salt?"

Barely were these words spoken when suddenly, for the man, in the place of the lovely singing a wild cacophony of caterwauling sounded, for the plebeians' ears are totally closed to our subtle melodies and incomparable harmony, and they've no innate sense for it; so too he saw the entire company changed to cats, among them his own, who had just been that lovely white maiden, who'd had her own birthday celebration this day. The man saw only cats streaking out in all directions, jumping from the deck to neighbouring roofs, quickly clearing the balustrade and away, and before he realized, everything, even the wine glasses, plates, cookies, and wine, had vanished, save that bit of cookie that he still held in his hand, and was nothing but a piece of stale cracker. His own cat had escaped through the window of the glass door into his bedchamber, into which he too now angrily returned, grabbing a Spanish cane to repay her hospitality with ingratitude. When the man poked around under the bed with his stick the white cat screamed and spat frightfully, sprang out from under the bed and again through the window of the glass door, so that now two panes lay shattered on the floor, out onto the deck, onto a roof, never to return. The man kept telling his friends, over and over, of this adventure with the cats, including the singing, and then swore destruction of all cats, so they laughed much at him, and mockingly called him Klare-Mond and Katzen-Herodus (Cat-Herod) to his very end.

# Siebenhaut (Sevenskin)

When the cat had finished its storytelling, the wife of the wood-cutter, who had listened attentively, spoke up and said, "I know enough such stories too. Whether they are all true I couldn't say. And as for your story, my good snake, about a woman who nursed one of your relatives at her breast and raised her, I know an even nicer one, about a woman who actually delivered a snake and had to nurse it as her child." Then the cat and snake were eager to hear this story, and begged the woman to tell it to them.

There was once a Count, hereupon began the woman, who was very rich and also had a very beautiful and loving wife who loved him with tenderness; but they had no child, which made him love her a good deal less than she him, and he was anyway of somewhat rude and rough habits even though he might not really mean it. So he'd call his wife, who tried through friendliness, modesty, and her quiet ways to keep him good-humoured, an eelskin, a flatter-cat, a smooth snake, and the like; and oftentimes the woman would cry about it, and say, "You perjure yourself, that you liken me to a snake; may God not punish you for that one day!" At this the Count only laughed. Then it happened in a year and a day that prospects for a child came this couple's way, and the Count became in his behaviour as if transformed, and couldn't show enough kindness to his wife; but fate laid a heavy hand on both – the Countess delivered, instead of a child, a snake into the world.

The Count was beside himself with rage and fury, and the wife almost frightened to death. "Are you now a snake, snakemother, or are you not?" he bellowed. "A witch you are, a devil's paramour, a false cat! Die you shall and your snake brat that you have borne along with you!" However, with imploring and praying the Countess got it to where he would not have her and the snake killed, and the shudder with which she viewed the snake became tempered with mother love. The Count now hardly bothered her, and no longer regarded her as his marriage partner; she was not allowed out of her separate quarters, and except for the most necessary servant, no one was allowed to see her.

The Countess in her seclusion laid the snake to her breast and nourished it with her milk, and slowly got used to it and loved it as a child. And she had an oft-recurring dream: the snake was a fine boy, and had taken on a snake form because she had so often been terrified and wept when her husband called her "snake." Therefore she tended the snake faithfully and well, and finally saw with pleasure how it grew and thrived, and how it would rest quietly on her lap, or raise its slender neck with its delicate head and its intelligent, sparkling eyes up to her mouth and make as if kissing, whereby tremors of joy coursed through her, when the snake put its quick little tongue between her lips for a moment, or slithered and circled in dance on the floor like a happy child at play.

Monotonously enough did time pass for the imprisoned Countess. Twenty years had passed and the snake had fully grown, and she thought seriously about her death and what would happen to the snake. Then one evening the snake, who had not spoken a single word in all these years, opened its mouth and said, to the utter surprise of the Countess, "Most honourable mother! I have now passed my twentieth birthday and wish to marry. You would put me in great indebtedness if you could procure me a bride, no matter of what class, as long as she be steadfast and brave."

The Countess promised to fulfil her son's wish, and sent out messengers. However, far and wide the responses all came back negative and some even mocked. Slender suitors, they said, would be welcome, but snakes as suitors are hardly the order of the day. Such a union is too uneven; a gold snake ring around the finger one could accept, also a gold snake as a bracelet, but a snake around the whole body – that is unbearable. This saddened the Countess, and since no marriage partner could be found the son repeated his request, so the Countess bethought her of the hen-girl, a young fresh maiden, and tried to talk her into this match.

The girl, however, said, "What use to me is a snakelet? Such a one only feeds and works not! Surely I'd find a suitor who had hands and feet!" But the Countess showed the hen-girl that working would be out of the question. If she married the Count's son she would be rich, and could walk about in gold raiment. If she were wise like the snakes she'd take the snake, and if she'd rather stay with the hens, she was a goose.

Good advice is well taken, so the saying goes, and the hen-girl said she wanted to think it over and sleep on it. Good advice comes overnight. And it came too. After her artless bedtime prayer, the maiden fell asleep and began to dream. In her dream an angel appeared and whispered to her, "Take him, take him, you won't get a better! You are chosen to release him!" And whispered to her how to proceed on the wedding night. All this the girl noted well, and in the morning brought the Countess her decision to accept her very heart's proposal.

This gave the mother of the snake great joy, and she made all the preparations for – quite understandably – a most private wedding. When at last the young couple were together, the snake said to his bride, "Now you undress!"

"No!" said the bride. "You undress yourself first!" Then the snake hooped a circle, caught itself on the back with its fangs, and slipped out of its skin. It had a much lovelier skin beneath the old skin; the old had been brown and the new was green.

The snake said, "I hope! Now you undress"

"No, you undress!" cried the bride.

The snake repeated the ritual moulting as before, slipped out of the green skin sky blue, and said, "I trust! Now you undress!"

"No, you undress yourself!" cried the bride, for that was the secret that the angel had confided in her in her dream.

Again the snake obeyed, and raised with that the fondest hopes of the day, to become a good and yielding husband. The blue skin fell from him, and a new rosy red appeared, and the snake said, "I love you, and now you undress!"

"No, you undress yourself!" said the bride.

"You demand a lot, my child!" answered the snake, but moulted for the fourth time and was now all silver. "My heart is clean, like silver! Undress yourself now!" said the snake.

But the bride again refused, repeating, "No, undress yourself!"

With that the snake sloughed off its silver skin, and crawled out a gloriously shiny gold, and said, "My heart is true, like gold! Now, finally, undress yourself!"

"No! You undress yourself!" said the bride for the sixth time and again the snake obeyed, and came out of the gold skin, which it threw off, emerging like a living rainbow in all colours, glistening and glowing, that hardly eye could stand to see.

"With me and you be peace!" said the snake. "But I beg you, do now undress yourself!"

"No! You undress yourself!" said the bride, unrelentingly.

Then the snake reared high, and in what skin did it now appear? You guess!

"That I can't guess," said the snake. "I moult but once a year."

"And I even less," added the cat. "I never moult, I only shed hair."

"Pah! In a human skin!" replied the storyteller.

And transformed itself at once into a human, and that into a beautiful youth, and he took the bride in his arms, kissed her, and cried, "Thank you, you have released me!"

And that was what the angel had whispered to the bride in her dream. Seven times she must refuse his request, and turn it back on him. Now he stood before her as the most loving earl, as the handsomest knight, and she sank lovestruck to his bosom.

That the Countess was most happy about this and that her husband made amends is self-evident.

So they'd tell always one round the other, the occupants of the forest hut, first the woman, then the man, or the snake or the cat; and the two old people enjoyed this life together, they lived to a ripe old age and died one soon after the other. Then the cat died, and the snake left the little house in which she had been so happy.

## Marta Goertzen

*Walking in my neighbourhood park, Lessard, earlier than usual one summer morning, soon after dawn, I met a woman gathering mushrooms. She waved at me in greeting. "Good mushrooms today after* the rain last night. Almost like in my old country home ..." Did she still go there sometimes? "Oh no! No go back. Anyway, the woods all gone, the woods that were our life. The war, you know; now here is home" – setting down her basket as she kneeled and picked the next mushroom with her deft hand.

On that very day I walked in the other direction, to the Book Barrel, another favourite haunt, where the proprietor, a genius at sensing what kind of book one might be looking for, handed me the beautifully bound Sämtliche Märchen of Ludwig Bechstein. I soon realized, indeed, this was for me. In it I found the very setting of how the poor people lived off the woods, as the woman gathering mushrooms had so vividly described to me.

The stories so fascinated me I truly didn't wait to get home: on a conveniently located bench I sat reading – and couldn't believe how quickly the afternoon had passed. Here was another treasure trove, I felt, that my sixteenth-century peacenik Mennonite ancestors had left behind while fleeing from country to country for their lives and for the sake of their religious conscience. This truly felt like coming upon some long-lost family treasure.

To those who say Bechstein is somewhat didactic, I say: Well he should be! For even during my Canadian prairie Mennonite village childhood in the 1920s and 1930s there were still some people killing snakes and equating them with evil.

I am publishing my translation with the kind permission of Winkler Verlag (Munich).

❧

# The Peasant's Tale

This story is about a peasant lad who works hard all day long and barely has enough to eat. From time to time he finds himself at the foot of this vast marble staircase, that reaches up into the sky like a huge tidal wave. He paces back and forth, and every once in a while stops and angrily shakes his fist at whatever it is at the top of the stairs.

One day he was pacing back and forth and he turned around and bumped into the Devil himself, standing there. "Oh, good day," said the Devil. The Devil's always polite. They exchanged a few words. Finally the Devil said, "Who are you?"

And the peasant explained, "I am a peasant among peasants, and these whom you see here" – and he pointed towards the town – "are my brothers and sisters. See the rags that they wear, and hear the pitiful cries of hunger and pain that they emit. And see the hovels that they are forced to live in, barely strong enough to keep out the wind. If I could but get to the top of these stairs, where the oppressors and exploiters of my people live, what terrible vengeance I would wreak on them!"

"Well," the Devil said, "I happen to have some influence around here. Maybe we could make some arrangement."

"Oh, if only we could," the man said.

He, the Devil, said, "Well, sure." And the man started to go up the stairs.

But the Devil said, "Wait a minute, wait a minute. There's a price for everything."

"But," the peasant said, "what could I possibly give you? I have nothing."

"Well," he said, "let me see. You could give me your eyes."

"My eyes? What good would I be without eyes?"

"Oh, don't worry," said the Devil, "I'll replace them with eyes that are much better than the ones you have!"

So the bargain was struck. The exchange was made. And the man started up the stairs. But after he had gone up a few stairs the Devil stopped him and said, "Wait a minute! You've only paid till here. To go up higher you must pay more. But before we go, tell me who you are."

"I," he said, "am a peasant among peasants. And these whom you see" – and he pointed down the stairs to the village – "are my brothers and sisters. See the hovels, hear their cries ... But where did they get those lovely clothes to wear?"

"No matter," said the Devil. "On our way. But first you must pay me."

"Well, what do I have?"

"You have your ears."

"My ears? What good would I be without ears?"

"Oh, how quickly they forget! I'll give you ears much better than the ones you already have!" So the deal was made, and up the stairs they went.

After they'd gone surprisingly few stairs the Devil stopped him and said, "Wait a minute. You've only paid till here. To go higher you must pay more. But before we strike up a bargain, tell me who you are."

"I am a peasant among peasants. And these, whom you see there, are my brothers and my sisters. But who taught them to sing those lovely songs?"

"No matter," said the Devil. "On we go." So on they went. And at every few steps there was another exchange made, until finally there was only one step left. And the Devil said, "Wait a minute. There's only one step left, but it has its price too."

"Oh, what could that possibly be?" he said. "What have I got left?"

"Your heart."

"My heart? But what good would I be without my heart?"

"Oh," said the Devil, "I'll give you a heart much better than the one you already have. Don't you remember?"

"All right." And the deal was made.

So the step was taken, and he was about to leap on to his work when the Devil stopped him and said, "Wait a minute! Before you go, tell me who you are!"

He drew himself up proudly and said, "I am a prince among princes," and he pointed to the castle and said, "and these are my brothers."


*Jack Nissenson*

*I've been telling this story for a few years now and not everyone catches on right away. I know I did not when I first read it in a left-wing youth newspaper during the early fifties. Whether you sell yourself to the Devil a bit at a time or all at once, the end result is the same.*

# A Duppy Tale

Once there was a boy who lived with his parents in a small house at the edge of a graveyard. One day he ran into the house and asked his mother if he could go out with his friends to shoot rocks at birds.

His mother said: "No."

The boy begged and pleaded, and pleaded and begged. "Please," he cried, "the other boys are already outside playing. They will leave me here if I don't come out soon. Please, let me go."

"All right! All right! Go out with your friends if you want and shoot birds," said his mother. "But, do not go into the graveyard and shoot birds there. If you do you are sure to hit Simon Tutu, King of the Duppy Birds. Then you will be in trouble and I do not want to lose you."

The boy promised he would not go anywhere near the graveyard. And off he ran to join his friends. All afternoon the boys ran about shooting rocks at birds. They did not hit any. But as the afternoon wore on, they drew closer and closer to the graveyard. They were not far from the entrance when the boy peered inside and saw, sitting on a branch in the crown of a tree, a beautiful and enormous bird. He could not resist.

Forgetting all about his mother's warning, or perhaps choosing to pay no attention to what she had said, the boy slipped into the graveyard. Quietly yet quickly, he drew a rock from his pocket and fitted it to his slingshot. He steadied himself, pulling the sling way back, took aim, and let the rock fly.

Direct hit. The bird flew into the air with a screech, then fell to the ground dead.

Proudly, the boy ran over to take a look at the bird. But when he knelt down to pick it up, the bird began to sing:

"Why ya shoota me for?
Why ya shoota me for?
Mea Simon Tutu,
Why ya shoota me for?"

The boy was terrified and knew he was in trouble. He turned
to run away, but got no farther than turning around when the
bird sang again:

"Ya betta hurry me home,
Ya betta hurry me home.
Mea Simon Tutu
Why ya shoota me for?"

To the boy's surprise, his hands reached for the bird and picked
it up. His legs ran him home. As soon as he got there, the bird
began to sing again:

"Ya betta pluck me now,
Ya betta pluck me now.
Mea Simon Tutu,
Why ya shoota me for?"

The boy hesitated, but not for long. Soon he pulled one feather
from the bird, then another. One by one at first, then handfuls
at a time until he had plucked the bird bald. Just as he was
finishing the task, that bird started to sing again:

"Ya betta gut me now,
Ya betta gut me now.
Mea Simon Tutu
Why ya shoota me for?"

The boy's eyes grew wide and his mouth hung open. He did
not want to gut the bird, but this was a Duppy, a ghost who
was singing orders. The boy got a knife from the kitchen. He
slit the bird open and cleaned it out. He had not finished cleaning
the knife, when the bird began to sing:

"Ya betta roast me now,
Ya betta roast me now.
Mea Simon Tutu,
Why ya shoota me for?"

Beads of sweat formed at his brow and his face turned white

as he carried the bird into the kitchen. Carefully, he placed it inside a roasting pot, put the pot in the oven and turned the oven up as high as it would go.

After a while the kitchen was filled with a wonderful smell and the boy felt his muscles relax. But then he heard a sound coming from the oven. It was the bird, singing again:

"Ya betta eat me now,
Ya betta eat me now.
Mea Simon Tutu,
Why ya shoota me for?"

Quickly, the boy turned off the oven and pulled out the pot. He reached inside. The bird was hot and it smelled so good. He broke off a small piece of meat and brought it to his mouth, knowing he should not eat it. He paused, and at that very moment the bird began to sing again:

"Ya betta chew me now,
Ya betta chew me now.
Mea Simon Tutu,
Why ya shoota me for?"

The boy bit off a small piece of meat and began to chew it. Oh, it tasted wonderful! Yet he knew if he swallowed it something terrible would happen. But he had no time to think about it, for the bird started to sing again:

"Ya betta swallow me now,
Ya betta swallow me now.
Mea Simon Tutu,
Why ya shoota me for?"

So the boy swallowed. It tasted so good that he ate up the rest of the bird.

He sat down on a stool, feeling relieved. There was no more bird. There was no more singing. And his stomach was full.

But ... After a while, his stomach began to ache. Suddenly his pants felt too tight. He loosened his belt, but it didn't do any good. For his stomach was growing. It grew bigger and bigger and bigger until: POP. His stomach burst open.

Then from out of the boy flew the bird, whole again. It flew right back to the graveyard and landed on the same branch at the top of the same tree. Then it sang:

"Why ya shoota me for?
Why ya shoota me for?
Mea Simon Tutu,
Why ya shoota me for?"

### Ray Gordezky

One day in 1983 I was telling stories to a group of grade six students. I ended the session by asking the young people if they had a story to tell. Kwesi Thomas, a small, bright-eyed boy from Jamaica, walked up to the front of the room. Kwesi was not supposed to be at the storytelling session. He was doing poorly in his schoolwork, and some teachers complained about his behaviour. But the enrichment teacher decided to include him in the storytelling session because he had won the school's public-speaking contest the year before. She hoped the storytelling would give him some motivation to change.

Kwesi came to the front and said he had a story. He began telling his story in the rhythmic patois of his native country. The other students were smiling. They loved to hear him speak "Jamaican," as they called it. He was not long into his story before he had us all laughing and chanting the Duppy Bird's words. When he finished, we asked him to tell it again. After the other students left, I had him tell the story one more time. By coincidence, I had my tape-recorder with me.

That was in 1983, and I have been telling Kwesi's story ever since. Kwesi is now in grade eleven. I have been told he is one of their top students in dramatic arts and music.

ↄ

# The Tale of Crooker

A lonely traveller made his way over a moorland bridle path towards the town of Cromford in Derbyshire. It was summer, but a chilly wind was beginning to pick up as evening came on. The traveller turned onto a footpath that led towards the Cromford road. The path cut steeply down the hillside and then began to level off. The night was drawing in and the traveller could no longer see clearly. Suddenly an old woman stepped out from behind a boulder. "Where would any man be going at this time of day?" she asked. The traveller remained silent. "I see you are wise enough to keep your own counsel. You'll need more help than that, if you meet Crooker." The old woman proffered a small posy of St John's Wort. In the fading light it seemed to the traveller that the old woman was dressed all in green, but he took the posy since he sensed that she meant well. "If you meet Crooker, show him these. I wish you well. You freed a bird once from a fowler's net. I know that bird. Be on your way." The traveller turned to go and then turned back to thank her and to ask, "Who is Crooker?" But the old woman had already melted into the gathering dusk.

The traveller continued on his way. His footsteps quickened, as the light faded and the sun sank behind the hills. His hand tightened on the posy that the old woman had given him. Suddenly he started at the sound of a low voice. "Are you headed alone towards the Cromford road at this time of day?" He stopped and saw another woman dressed in green standing in his path. She held a posy of primroses out towards him. "My old mother lies sick in bed in Cromford. I am her only son. I must get there as soon as I can," said the traveller. "You freed a rabbit from a hunter's snare once. I know that rabbit. Take these and show them to Crooker if you meet him. Be on your way and hurry." Before the man could thank her, she too disappeared into the deep shadows cast by the hedges along the roadside.

The traveller's unease was growing as he hurried on. He came to the junction of two roads and turned onto the Cromford road, and as he did, his path was blocked once more by a third old woman dressed in green. "This is a wicked time to be travelling this road," she said. "Who is Crooker?" the traveller blurted out. "If you must take this road, stay well away from the Darrent River where it runs close by the road. And try to be on the Cromford bridge before the moon is up overhead. Take these." She offered him a posy of daisies. "I see you have some good help already. You freed a vixen and her cub once from a trap. I know that vixen and I wish you well." She too was gone into the thickening dusk and shadows as the man raised his hand and wished her "Good night."

A wind moved the clouds slowly across the night sky. Here and there a star glimmered through. The traveller's steps were hastened now by urgency and by fear. He clasped the three posies in his hands, trying to squeeze comfort from them as he hurried along the road. He looked back over his shoulder from time to time and he saw through the clouds that the moon was beginning to rise. Then he began to hear the sound of the Darrent running and tumbling over rocks and pebbles. He stayed well over to the right away from the river. He could see the moon now reflected off its rippling surface. He passed a group of trees that grew alongside the bank and then he saw one tree that grew apart from the others. It was a great, huge, old tree, twisted and gnarled with long-reaching branches. The man quickened his pace and he hurried past it. His heart was pounding in his chest, and as the wind stirred through the tree, it seemed to him those branches were like arms stretching and bending towards him.

He was almost running now. The sound of the river was growing louder. In its rushing he thought he heard a voice cry, "Hungry!" Then on the road before him he saw a long thin shadow cast by the moon, which was still behind him, but rising higher in the sky. The shadow grew longer, clawing after him. He threw the posy of daisies over his shoulder. The voice from the river called, "Give!" He heard a splash and saw that he had escaped beyond the shadow's grasp. He stumbled on, and again the shadow began to reach out over his shoulder, ahead of him onto the road. The rushing Darrent roared in his ears and the voice called, "Hungry!" The traveller threw the primroses over his shoulder. "Give!" cried the voice and again he heard a splash, and the shadow halted and receded. But before he could feel relief or catch his breath, the shadow was grabbing and clawing at him again. The river roared, "Hungry!" again, as he half stumbled, half ran towards the bridge. He turned and flung the last posy, of St John's Wort, over his shoulder at the tree. It screeched and stopped. The man fell onto the Cromford bridge and the Darrent ran quietly over its rocks and stones once more.

The people in the town heard and looked at each other. "Darrent and Crooker have been out tonight. There'll be another for the graveyard in the morning," they said, and they remembered how, the last time they'd heard Darrent roar, an old travelling woman had been found a ways down the river with her neck broken. In the morning the townspeople sought out the priest and went down to the bridge. There they found the traveller asleep. The sun was shining on the river and the Darrent flowed placidly over its rocks and stones.

*Maggie Fehlberg*

*I'm from Swinton in South Yorkshire. Walking in Derbyshire was part of my childhood. I have adapted this story from one collected by the English folklorist Ruth L. Tongue. Her version is printed in* A Dictionary of British Folk-Tales in the English Language, *ed. Katherine M. Briggs (London: Routledge and Kegan Paul 1970).*

ɔ

# Ownself

There was once a house on the moor. The old straight track ran by that house so close, so close that one corner of it had been sheared off, then cobbled up again all askew. Some folk said that the track was a fairy path and that the house had been built too close to it.

One day a woman came along that track dragging a small child, a boy, behind her. When she came to the house she stood looking at it, then she walked around the house three times, careful not to go widdershins; that is, the wrong way round, against the sun. Only then did she touch the latch, creak open the door, step over the sill, set her bundle down on the clay floor.

The house had a hearth and a sleeping loft. That night she kindled a fire and she and the boy slept on beds of bracken that she had brought in from the moor. Every night after that, as soon as dark came, she banked the fire and called the boy to follow her up the ladder. At night bog lights danced in the hollows near the house and even played about the rotted window sills. The wind wuthered and clawed at the very stones and rattled in the chimney.

The woman did not much like the house. She was afraid of it, but she stayed there season after season, year after year. No one else wanted to live in the house, that was for sure, nor did anyone come to claim rent or fee. It was a roof over her head and a place to keep the boy. She never bothered to scratch out a garden. Perhaps she thought it would call attention to herself and to the boy, although whom she was afraid of she would never say. She took the boy with her when she went foraging on the moor, gathering roots and berries and rosehips, seeking out green herbs to keep off sickness. She taught the boy how to gull for trout, how to set a snare. Aye, when I think on it, they ate like queen and prince, smacking their lips over hare and partridge while honest folk were shaking out the last mouldy turnip from the bottom of the basket.

The boy was never allowed, except at a distance, to see or be seen by another being of their own kind. Whenever the woman spied someone coming along the old straight track she hurried and harried him up into the loft and told him to stay there, with the quilts drawn over his head, until she told him he could come down again. Most often, though, during the day, they were out on the moor. Sometimes they went up to the mawn pools to cut peat, or to Warren Bank to search for rabbits, or to a certain spring to gather cress. The boy knew where the wild ponies roamed; he had climbed the hidden waterfall; he called his respect to Old Brock the badger in his sett, and he played with the fox cubs by their den. But he had never played with another child.

Over time the woman managed to find the wherewithal to fashion a plain board table for her and the boy, and a couple of wooden stools besides. Sometimes, after their supper and before dark had come, she would take from her skirt a pack of greasy cards and spread them out on the table. She peered over them, mumbled, reshuffled, dealt new patterns. Whenever the boy crept close to steal a glimpse she waved him off. As the boy grew older, however, he learned to wait until she was asleep, then he would search in the folds of the skirt as it hung on a peg and look at the pictures on the cards by means of the moonlight that shone through a window near his bed.

He gazed in wonder. Here is the moor, and there is a spring, and here a woman, naked, dripping water from it. And here is a traveller with his bundle on a stick, sensible enough, about to step off a crag. He must be mazed. A small animal, the likes of which the boy has never seen, is biting the man on the leg. And here is a man dressed all in black, riding a huge black pony. But there is something strange about his face: the flesh on it is ravaged, eaten away. It looks like the head the boy found when he and the woman were digging in the mawn pool. On that day the woman had hurried him home when the shadows were still short. She had spent the rest of the day in bed.

She had also drunk more than usual from her bottle. He liked it when she drank because then she told him stories. The process was mysterious and a little frightening to him. It was as though she reached into his thoughts and dreams and spun out a filament from which she wove a web and caught his mind-pictures in its toils. His pictures were not unlike the ones on the cards. The difference was that the people and creatures in the stories moved about, talked, touched each other, felt yearnings and longings that wrenched his heart yet left him hungry for more.

When the boy was going on seven years of age the woman found he had a will of his own and, what's more, he was getting too big to harry about. She could not frighten him up the ladder into the loft. He told her he would not go. He wanted to stay by the hearth and play his game.

For the boy had made a game for himself. He took the clay from the floor and ashes from the fireplace. He spat on them and mixed them, then spat on the mixture again so as to make it pliable enough to mold into little figures. He turned the hearth into a moor and he pinched out sheep and ponies, badger and hedgehog, the vixen and her cubs. Clumsily he attempted the likenesses of people, too, and set them down upon his moor. He even took chips from the wood pile and stuck them together with clay, setting it way off in the shadows. He told himself it was the house on the moor, the house in which he and the woman lived.

In vain the woman called to him at night. She begged and pleaded, threatened, warned. It was not so much that the boy was stubborn. He was caught up in the spell of the game. The woman found she must climb the ladder by herself. The boy would come to bed only in his own good time. Angrily, resignedly, she left him to his fate.

One night as the boy was playing with his game the logs of the fire crashed and fell in upon themselves. As he turned to look he saw a flame child step out from the coals. Tiny, she was. Atop her head she wore a pointed cap of palest mauve. Her hair was the colour of the copper kettle spun into thread. Her eyes were blue-green, her lips like strawberries, her cheeks like the wild rose. She wore a flame-coloured dress that flickered at the hem as she stepped out of the embers and came tripping towards him. He had never seen a creature like her.

"Who are you?" he asked.

"Ownself," she replied. "Who are you?" Her voice was thin and high, like the trickle of a rill or the trill of a bird. "Ownself," he said. His voice sounded gruff in his own ears.

"What're you doin'?" she asked.

"Playin' my game," he said.

"Pooh!" she said, "I know a better game than that." She knelt down on her hands and knees and blew upon the little figures. In a moment they had taken on a life of their own, walking or running or crawling about, engaged in their own pursuits. She had set a whole world a-wagging. The boy soon learned that if he knelt down and breathed upon the figures he, too, could make them work his will. He had only to think of a story and they were there to act it out. He and the flame child played till dawn, then she stepped back into the coals and he pulled himself up the ladder to the loft.

The next thing he knew, the woman was shouting at him and shaking him. "Get up, get up! We are going out on the moor,"

she said. "Hurry now. I don't know what makes you so lazy." All
that day he found her looking at him suspiciously and once she
felt his forehead and made him eat some borage leaves. He barely
noticed her though, for all he could think of was the wonderful
game. At last they turned homeward. He ate his supper under
duress, scolded by the woman, who swore he was sick. She ordered
him to bed. She even took a stick to him, but he was not to
be budged. She left him by the hearth, convinced that he was
burning with fever, but she was too afraid to stay with him. She
did not like the sounds in the chimney or the light that flickered
on the window ledges.

As soon as he heard the woman's snores the boy crept up the
ladder, felt in the folds of her hung-up skirt, and took out the
pack of playing cards. Then he descended to the hearth and
reached behind the woodpile, where he had hidden the figures
made of clay and ash and his own spit. He took out the wood-chip
house, too, and put it in its usual place in a shadow by the
chimney. He arranged the figures all about on his make-believe
moor, then he knelt down and blew upon them. Just as he had
feared, nothing happened. He thought up stories in his head, but
still the animals he had fashioned and the clumsily made people
sulked lumpishly on the hearth. The boy took a stick and stirred
the fire, but nothing happened. At last he sat down by the fire
and put his head on his knees. He sighed a great sigh. For the
first time in his life he knew he was lonely.

"Ownself," he implored. It was hardly more than a whisper.
"Ownself, where are you? I want you."

Something rattled in the chimney. By the time the boy had
lifted his head the flame child was stepping out of the coals. Her
eyes gleamed and it seemed to the boy that her lips and cheeks
were brighter than ever. "What's the matter, Ownself?" Her voice
was mocking. "Can't you play the game?" She bent down and
blew on the figures. Instantly it was as it had been. Men and
women, children and creatures moved about on the moor, coming
and going and meeting in patterns that grew more complex and
interwoven as the boy and the flame child were caught up in
the game.

As the night wore on the boy took out the pack of cards.
Proudly he laid them out in the light from the fire. "What do
you have there, Ownself? asked the flame child, and she crept

under his elbow to take a look. He had thought to make her envious, to let her see that he owned something she didn't own. He was half prepared to grab up the cards and hold them to his chest if she tried to wrest them from him. But by an act of will she seemed to be able to make the beautiful creatures who lived in the cards rise up and out of their own accord, to intermingle with his own creations, made from clay and ash and spit.

In fear and amazement he watched as the traveller still headed for the crag edge. But now the precipice was real and the young man, so silly and yet so lovable, could be killed or hurt in the fall. And over here the skull-faced rider bore down upon the naked lady! She, all unknowing, dipped water from the spring, her back turned towards impending disaster. The boy did not know whether to cry out and warn her or to change the story in his head. But now he found it was no longer his story. The flame child had taken it over. He feared that terrible things were about to happen.

The boy stepped back into the shadow and in doing so kicked against the wood-chip house. When he went to pick it up the flame child was on him in an instant. "What's this?" she asked, and she scooped it out of his hand to look at it. She put her eye to a chink and called out, "If you could see what I see!" The boy ran after her, feeling clumsy for the first time in his life.

"Give it to me," he panted. "It's ownself's!"

"Ownself's!" echoed the flame child. "Ownself owns it and everything in it," she said. "Body and soul," she said.

The boy made a lunge and pulled the chip house away from her. He put his eye to the chink and saw that inside the space was lighted by the light from a tiny hearth. Against one wall was a ladder going up to a loft. There was a table and two stools and, silhouetted in front of the fire, two tiny figures, two children: a boy and a flame child.

Just then the firelight failed, both in the toy house and in the larger room surrounding the boy. In the darkness the flame child danced up to him again, took the toy out of his hand, and pirouetted away across the hearth. As she did so the fire flared up suddenly and a coal rolled out to touch her foot and burn it.

"Oh, oh, oh!" she screamed, her voice a piercing wail, keen as wind through a keyhole.

There was a rattling in the chimney and a harsh voice called out, "Who's that?"

"Ownself," answered the flame child, sniffling.

"Who be troubling you?" asked the voice.

"Ownself," said the flame child, and she pointed to the boy. When she saw him tremble she stuck out her tongue at him, a little flicker of flame that came and went so quickly he could not be sure what he saw.

"Then quit your fashing," said the voice in the chimney. "If it's nought but ownself troubling ownself there's nothing to fash about." A long white arm with soot smuts on it reached down the chimney, caught the flame child by the scruff of her neck and pulled her, wailing, up and up and out of sight. A log cracked and a trail of sparks flew after her.

The boy did not wait to see what would happen next. He dashed across the room to the ladder and climbed up into the loft. He leaped into his pile of straw and sweet-smelling bracken and pulled the quilt up over his head, closing his eyes tight. A long time went by before the blood stopped pounding in his ears and the beating in his heart slowed down. At last, since he couldn't sleep anyway, he lowered the quilt, let out a long breath and peered into the moonlit darkness. "She's just something in my head," he told himself. "She's just something made up of bits and pieces, shadows and shine. If I don't think of her she isn't. She won't be or have been."

With a sigh of relief he lay down to sleep. Then he sat up again. Bolt upright. "What if ownself, the woman, the house on the moor, the great moor itself, are just a passing fancy in the mind of a flickering flame child?"

So he sat until he was too weary to ponder more, while the bog lights beckoned in the hollows and the silver moon rolled across the sky.

*Joan Bodger*

*The "original" of this tale comes from Joseph Jacobs's* More English Fairy Tales. *According to his notes, Mrs Balfour (that indefatigable folklorist) was told it by a woman of North Sunderland. There are*

*other versions, all from the north country, but Jacobs contends that
the ultimate source is the Polyphemos incident in the* Odyssey.

*At best the story is fragmentary and lends itself to sea change. I
never much liked Jacobs's cautionary ending. Somehow, over forty
years, this sage-and-butterfly motif crept into my telling. My long
walks on the Welsh moors inform my images, as do incidents in my
own life.*

☙

# The Piper's Tale

I'll tell you the story of Willie Johnstone the Piper. Now, Willie
Johnstone was a tinker-man and he made his living travelling
this way and that way, making baskets from the willow, or carving
clothes-pegs, or doing a bit of hawking; this and that, and he'd
work for the farmers now and again. But the main way he made
his living was playing the bagpipes.

Och, he was a grand piper, was Willie Johnstone! There wasn't
a games or gathering the length and breadth of Scotland that
Willie Johnstone wasn't winning the cups and medals. There
wasn't a competition that he didn't come first in. He was known
the length and breadth of the country as just about the best
piper there was.

Willie was a married man. He was a young man and he had
a young wife, Maggie was her name; and she was an Argyllshire
woman. They had two children, oh, two bonny wee bairns they
were, a boy and a girl. They were a happy family, happy as they
could be. They didn't always eat well and they weren't always as
warm as they might have been, because they lived in a wee tent
most of the year, you see. And they travelled about Perthshire
doing this and doing that, earning their living the best way they
could.

Anyway, it was coming up for the salmon-fishing season, and
all the gentry and all them with money would be going to the

town of Pitlochry for salmon fishing. Oh, there are some good, good fishing waters around the town of Pitlochry. And they decided they'd go down to the town of Pitlochry, Willie to play his pipes around the houses and the hotels, and Maggie to do a bit of hawking, to sell her baskets and her clothes-pegs and the other things she made.

So they hitched up their little cart, they hitched up their shelty, their little Highland shelty, to the cart, and they took it away up the back-road, round up the back of Pitlochry. They got to the top of the hill yonder, and they put up their wee bow-tent, and Maggie made a fire and a little pot of stew for the children, you see, and they put the children down to sleep and away they went, down into the town of Pitlochry.

They got down there, and Maggie went her way with her baskets and her clothes-pegs; and away Willie went to the hotels where all the gentry would be staying. Och, he expected to make a good thing that night, for he was well known among the gentry; particularly those that were army-men, you see, oh they could tell a good piper when they heard one.

Anyway, Maggie, she did a good thing, she did a good thing that night; she'd made a few pennies at the doors. There were always people willing to buy her baskets and her scrubbers. Away she went, back up again. It was getting late, and she went back up to the town of Pitlochry. And there was no sign, no sign at all of Willie Johnstone. "Och," she says, "he'll have made a shilling or two playing his pipes, and he'll be having a drink before coming back to sleep." So, away she went up to the camp.

Now she was walking up the back road yonder, and she thought she'd like a smoke of her pipe, you see. So she sat down at the bank at the side of the road and she put her hand into the big pocket in the back of her apron, and she pulled out her pipe and pulled out her bit of tobacco, and she filled her pipe. She was looking around inside her big pocket to see if she could find some matches. But she didn't have a match; she couldn't find a match there at all. And she happened to look around behind her into the field, you see. There on this little knoll in the middle of the field was this little cottage.

Now, it was a cottage in the Highland manner, a little black house in the Highland manner, not common around there at all. "I don't remember seeing that on my way down," she says. "Oh well, I wasn't in mind to be thinking about things like that." So she decided to go and ask for a light for her pipe, you see.

Away she went, and she knocked on the door. The door opened, and there was an old hag of a woman, with her hair hanging in rat's-tails and not a tooth in her mouth but a few blackened stumps, and every crack and crinkle in her face was filled with the dirt of ages. "Och, what do you want here?" said the old woman.

"Oh, I'm just a poor tinker-body; I would like just a light for my pipe, a wee brand from your fire to light my pipe."

"I suppose I can give you that," she says. And Maggie went in and took a little branch from the fire and lit her pipe, and away she went up to the camp.

There was still no sign of Willie Johnstone.

"Oh, he's got himself in trouble down there in Pitlochry," she says, "and he'll be spending a night in the cells again. I'll see about that in the morning." So she made some supper for the children, put the children down to sleep, and the next morning, first thing, away she goes down into the town of Pitlochry and straight to the police station she goes. "Have you got my Willie in there?" she says.

"Och, no. Willie was here last night and he had a drink or two, but he didn't get into any trouble. We had no reason to lock him up last night."

So she asked here and she asked there around the town. They'd all seen Willie last night, and they'd all listened to his piping, you see, and they'd had a few drams with him; but no, they didn't know where he was now. So she stayed there for two or three days, just waiting to see if Willie would come back. But no, after two or three days, he hadn't come back.

Now it was getting on for time to go down to the potato harvest in the Lowlands. She'd better get down or she wouldn't get a job, you see. So she packed up the camp, and tethered up the shelty, and away she went down to the Lowlands, thinking that Willie would catch up with her. Well, Willie didn't catch up with her there either. Nor for many a long year after that. Och, for twenty years or more she'd never seen Willie Johnstone, her husband.

By this time the children had grown up and they were away their own road. They had married and they were away their own road, and it was a poor old Maggie by this time, you see. Doing the best she could now – but folks wouldn't buy the baskets or the scrubbers or the clothes-pegs she'd made. They'd rather go down to the stores and buy something made of plastic, you see;

it was much easier. It was a poor old Maggie, following her wee shelty around, trying to make her living the best she could.

And one day she found herself near the town of Pitlochry. Oh, the memories that that brought back! So she went up the back road of the town, up to the hill there, and she set up her camp. She tied up her little shelty and she put up her little bow-tent, and away she went down into the town of Pitlochry.

But things were as bad there as anywhere else. She didn't sell a thing. The only thing they would give here were a few bones and scraps to feed herself. With those few scraps she walked back up the road.

Now, she sat down on the bank by the side of the road, and she thought she'd have a smoke of her pipe, you see. So she put her hand in the big pocket at the back of her apron and pulled out her wee pipe; and she pulled out her tobacco and she filled her pipe. But she looked around and och, she didn't have a match on her! What would she do? The poor old soul couldn't have a smoke of her pipe.

Now she happened to glance around her into the field, and there in the middle of the field was this little knoll, and on that knoll was a little house. It was a little cottage in the Highland fashion, not common around that part of Scotland at all. "Now, I can't remember seeing that on my way down," she says, "but och, I wasn't thinking about things like that at all." So she decided to go there and ask for a light for her pipe. She knocked at the door and this old hag of a woman opened it – and her hair was hanging there in rat's-tails, and there wasn't a tooth in her mouth but a few blackened stumps, and the wrinkles and cracks in her face were filled with the grime of an age.

"Och, get away, get away! I have no time for the likes of you tonight," she says.

"Oh, just a light for my pipe, Missus, that's all I'm asking; a light for my pipe for a poor old tinker-body."

"No! I have company tonight," she says, "and I have no time for the likes of you. Go on, get away with you! *Get away with you!*"

"For a poor old tinker-body like myself, a poor old soul like myself, just a light for my pipe – that's all I'm asking."

"Och, well, I suppose I can give you that." Now Maggie was bending down at the fireplace to take a little brand of burning wood to light the pipe. There was a door at the other side of the room, you see; and it was open just a crack, and the light was shining through it. And she thought she heard the sound of bagpipes. She listened. It was the sound of bagpipes. And oh, she recognized that playing! That was the playing of her man, Willie Johnstone!

She made a dash for that door and she threw that door wide open. And it wasn't a little Highland cottage at all. It was a hall, a big hall – with chandeliers hanging, and tapestries hanging from the wall; and all these wee folk, inches-high they were. And they were dancing and they were reeling and they were whooping! And there playing the music for them was Willie Johnstone, her husband, himself no more than inches-tall.

She made a grab for him. She grabbed him by the arm and she pulled him out of that place. Now the old woman, she grabbed the other arm and was pulling him back – and they were pulling this way and that way and this way and that way; and for all the love she had in her for her man, she gave one great pull and pulled him right past the threshold-stone of the house!

The house disappeared.

There was Willie Johnstone standing there, up to his full height. And not a day or a minute older was he than the last time she had seen him. She fell at his feet crying, "Oh Willie! Oh Willie Johnstone my man! Where have you been all these years?"

"Get away from me!" he says, and he lifted his foot and gave her a kick. I have a wife and a family up at the top of the hill there, and I've got to get up to them!" And away he strode off over the fields.

She lay there sobbing. Oh, she was breaking her heart! Then the realization came to her; he had been taken by the fairies. For they have no music of their own, you see, and they have to have human musicians to play for their dancing – for they're awful fond of their dancing. And among the fairies there is no time. And he wasn't a day or a minute older than the time they had taken him.

And that's the story of Willie Johnstone the Piper.


## Jim Strickland

*I came to stories by listening to traditional storytellers. I didn't delib-erately go out seeking traditional storytellers. I was looking for something else entirely. I was looking for songs, and I went to where there were a lot of singers around. My introduction to stories happened on a Sunday morning at a very nice festival. We'd had a grand night on Saturday. It was quite memorable, so I'm told. Sunday morning we crawled out of our sleeping-bags. Nothing was happening at all. I was trailing my tongue along the sidewalk. We went into the first hotel that opened, many hours after we started looking. We were in there settling down for our first pint of the day. One of the best ballad singers I'd ever heard was a woman named Jeanie Robertson, and she happened to come downstairs. We followed her into the lounge and demanded that she sing; not really demanded – requested … grovelled. She was very reluctant to sing but she agreed to tell a story. I had never heard a traditional storyteller. I was absolutely and totally spellbound. Jeanie was a tinker. They have a similar life to the gypsies, but they're not Romany. They're probably very old Celtic peoples. I can't say that I heard her story. I saw the story. That's the extent of her power as a storyteller. You saw it all happening. I wasn't aware that I had listened to her language. Another experience like that was another tinker, a man called Davie Stewart. A much more flamboyant storyteller, and you were much more aware of his presence. You weren't only aware of the story. But again the experience was much more seeing it than just passively listening to it. The story of Willie Johnstone was his story.*

❧

# Tam Lin

Up on the highest moors, where the heather meets the sky, there is an old, lonely, broken well. Neither summer's heat nor winter's chill change its dark waters. Roses grow about and over it, but no one comes near. Passing shepherds leave it to one side, and if a maiden should find herself there, she leaves a gift of flowers or the bracelet from her wrist and flees away – for this is a magic well, the well of Carterhaugh.

And nae maid comes to Carterhaugh
And a maid returns again.

But this is a story of a maiden who heeded not those warnings, and left more than a token by that well.

Her name was Janet, the only daughter of a clan chieftain in his hall. She was wild and windblown as the hawks in the sky, with eyes like the ocean blue and hair as fine and gold as wheat in summer. Ever since childhood she had been warned of the well and its danger. But one day while sewing in her chamber, she grew fretful and bored, and so wandered to the castle garden and through the gate down by the river Ettrick, and away up across the moors till her feet stood at last on the grey stones of the well of Carterhaugh.

She looked out across the moors, across the wild rolling hills and way off to the sea, listening to the wind and the curlews calling. There seemed no danger there at all, for no one was near. Then she turned and broke a rose from the bush that grew across the well, and as she did, three petals fell from her hand to the water. And as they fell, a voice came from behind her.

"Lady Janet, let them be!"

For a moment, Janet never moved. Then she turned to see a tall man gazing at her, dressed in grey and pale of face – pale as the snow. But his eyes were green, and they laughed at her.

"Why do you pick the roses?" said he. "Why do you pick the roses and break the tree? And why have you come here without leave?"

"The roses belong to no one," said she.

"Nay, Janet," he replied, "they belong to someone and may not be taken without his leave. What will you give me in return?"

Then Janet remembered what she had been told as a girl, and the warnings given about the lonely well and those one might find there.

"Then I am at fault, sir, and you have me at your will. You seem to know me well, and yet I know you not. What is your name?"

"My name is Tam Lin," said he, and he bowed to her.

And as he bowed, he smiled, and as he smiled her heart grew bolder.

He's ta'en her by the milk-white hand,
And by the grass-green sleeve,

He's led her to the fairy ground
At her he's asked nae leave.

For a while they lay together on the fern, and when she arose,
Janet looked at him with a new longing in her heart.

"I am afraid to leave you," she said, and as she spoke she felt
his hand grow cold in hers.

"I am afraid," she cried again, but he turned her to face her
father's hall and, lo, his hand was gone from hers, and she was
alone again on the moor with the wind and the birds.

Janet returned to her home, but her heart was left behind her
on the moors and great was her sorrow, for they who love the
Faery Kind are given no such gift in return.

So Janet sang again with the harp in her father's hall at night
when the torches were lit, and sewed at her seam, and played
again at ball with her maids in the garden. But all was not well.
As the weeks wore on towards autumn her face grew pale, and
her smiles were few and cold.

Then some began to guess what it was that ailed her, and one
old knight spoke out against her, crying that they should all be
blamed for her shame. But she laughed at him in scorn.

"Call me as you will, I care not. I never will bring shame on
you. My love is no earthly knight, but proud and fair, and I shall
have none but him."

Then came her brother to her, and his eyes were hard.

"Look you find yourself a husband, Janet," he cried, "lest our
father should know your secret, and cast you out for shame."

His voice grew lower as he leaned near.

"Or hie you again to Carterhaugh. There grows a rose there
will put an end to your shame."

And so he left her weeping.

Janet has kilted her green kirtle
A little abune her knee,
And she has braided her yellow hair
A little above her bree,
And she's awa' to Carterhaugh
As fast as she can hie.

Summer had gone and the blooms had faded from the roses

on the bush, but she tore off the last dying blossom with shaking hands. The petals fell on the dark water.

There beside her, once again, stood Tam Lin.

"Lady Janet, pull no more," cried he. "Why do you pick my roses and break the tree?" And he took the last blossom from her hand.

"Oh, Tam Lin," she cried, "my family will have me wed. The child in me cries for a father's name."

And she wept bitterly.

"And now you would harm the child?" asked Tam Lin, standing dark and tall before her.

"Oh, Tam Lin," she cried again, "my heart is for none but you. Help me end my sorrow."

"I cannot wed you, Janet," said he, "for my heart is no longer mine to give. It belongs to them – the Faery Kind."

"Oh, Tam Lin," she cried at last, "did ever you hear a church bell, did ever a priest say a prayer for you? For if not, I am lost!"

Then Tam Lin's face grew long, and his voice came hard.

"Once long ago," he said, "I was the son of Roxburgh, and well could I hawk and well could I ride, and few who saw me could not say, There goes a proper man! But one day as I hunted, a fell cold wind came upon me, so that I was weak and chilled, and I came from my horse and lay on Faery ground. Thus they captured me, and held me for their own. Now there is no way for me to return."

"But why should they have need of you?" cried Janet.

"O my dearest," he replied, "they keep me for themselves and for the tithe they must pay. Have ye not heard, Janet, that once in every seven years they must give up one of themselves to the Dark Land, as rent and tithe for their title here on earth? This is why they keep me, Janet, for this is the year that I must go, for them, to the gates of hell and pass through for ever."

Janet spoke no word, but lay on the fern and cried bitterly.

"But you might save me, Janet, if you are strong," said Tam Lin. "Tonight is Hallowe'en. Tonight the Lordly people will pass by here to take me to my new master. Here, when the moon rises, you may save me, if you will."

"Tell me, tell me," said Janet. "I shall not be afraid!"

Tam Lin raised her to her feet, and his hands were as ice.

"Tonight, as the moon rises, Janet, you must hide here by the well. Along the path of the moonlight, you will see the hosts of

Faery pass. At midnight they will come, and I shall be among them."

"But how shall I know you from all of that company?" cried Janet. "How shall I win you from them?"

"Many and fair will there be, but pay them no heed. Look for the three knights. The first will be riding a horse as black as midnight, the second a horse of brown, and the third a horse as white as snow. Let the first pass by, pay no heed to the second, but the third, the third, Janet, with a gold star on his brow and a glove on his right hand, run to him and pull him from his horse. Hold him fast, Janet – for it will be me. They will not let me go lightly. They will know I am gone and try to wrest me from you, but they may not lay hands on you. Rather they will change me, horribly, but *do not let me go!* Remember always it is I, the father of your child, and when at last I am my own shape again, cover me with your cloak, and so I will be won. Hold me fast, do not let me go, and when the morning sun touches us, I will be free."

Janet looked at him, standing cold and alone, and held him close.

"I shall do it, Tam Lin," she said, "though I am deathly afraid."

Then he kissed her, once for love, once for sorrow, and once more for all. Then he turned her to face her father's hall, and his hand was gone from hers, and she was alone once more.

All that night Janet waited, crouched in her cloak by the cold well-curb, and, as she waited, the moon rose.

By its light, a great silver road was formed, leading from the far hills to a dark unknown behind her. And as she watched, and as she waited, the hosts of Faery rode.

The first to pass was the King, carried on a high steed like a gust of cloud, clad in mail of silver and steel, his eyes hollow, so that the moon shone through. Fell was his glance, so that Janet cowered in terror and let him pass. Then came the Queen of Faery with her ladies about her, and their passing was like the wind over the winter ice, fair and cold, and the air was filled with the flutterings of veils and hair, and the whispers of many tongues. Still Janet waited.

Then came three knights, the first all in black and mounted on a black steed. His eyes were like coal, and his voice crying like the steel on the grindstone, and Janet let him pass. The next, dressed all in brown, and his horse of brown, eyes of fire and voice as a hunting eagle, and Janet let him pass. Then came the third, riding a milk-white steed, with eyes of green, and on his brow a star of gold, and on his right hand, a glove.

Up sprang Janet and ran to his horse and pulled him down, and instantly, the light about them was quenched, as one might snuff a candle flame.

A shrill voice cried, "Tam Lin, he's away! She's taken away the bonniest knight in all my company!"

"The Queen of Faery," cried Tam Lin, as Janet held him. "Hide me, Janet!"

Screams of rage swelled about them in the dark, and a great wind arose, chilling them with its icy breath. She clung to Tam Lin, but he struggled in her arms, and suddenly it was no longer Tam Lin that she held, but a writhing adder that struck and bit at her till the blood ran red from her hands. Janet screamed and wept, but held it fast, and then the serpent was gone, and in its place a raging lion with milky teeth and tearing claws that lashed her face so that it ran red with blood, but still she clung and wept, so that the lion was gone and in her arms she held a bar of white-hot iron that burned her to the very heart. She gripped it tight till it seemed she must die with the pain, and then in her arms was Tam Lin again, a naked man.

"Hide me, Janet," he cried again, and so she flung her cloak about him and huddled there in the freezing wind.

All about them the Faery voices stormed at them out of the dark, while the icy wind tore at their bodies, so that they came near to death from cold and fear. Once again the eldritch voice screamed:

"If what I know this night, Tam Lin, I had known yestere'en
I'd have taken out thy heart of flesh and put in a heart of stone!"

And all this time, never a blade of grass moved, and never a leaf stirred in the wood.

The eastern hills grew red, and the voice came again:

"Adieu, Tam Lin! Had I known that a Lady had stolen thee
I'd have taken out thy two green eyes and put in two of treen!"

The first ray of Hallows-Day sun touched the rosebush above their heads, and the voice came in a last fading cry:

"Had I known but yesternight that which I know this day
I'd have paid my tithe seven times to Hell, ere you had
been won away!"

The first rays of the sun touched the well-stones and then their faces, and the voice and the wind were stilled.

Then Tam Lin stood on the hills of Carterhaugh in that long-ago dawn when the world was new, with Janet held to his breast.

"I will be your true love, Janet," says he, "forever and for a day." And he kissed her once for love, and once for joy, and once for always. Then he turned her to face her father's hall. But this time his hand stayed in hers,

for she held him fast,
to be her heart's desire.


*K. Reed Needles*

*This is the perfect tale for Hallowe'en. There is an old ballad called Tam Lin from which I have taken verses. Rosemary Sutcliff's version of the legend is written in The Armourer's House, and since that is the one I heard read to me often as a boy, it probably has the most influence on my version. Sutcliff, however, does not mention the illegitimate child, nor the attempt to destroy it, where the ballad does.*


ക


# The Story of Rose Latulippe


*Cric, crac, les enfants!*
*Parli, parlo, parlons!*

*Sac-à-tabi, sac-à-tabac,*
*A la porte, les ceusses qui ne m'écoutent pas!*

*Il y a bien longtemps* – a long time ago, in the little village of St Joachim, near Montreal, there lived *une jeune fille qui s'appellait Rose Latulippe. Elle était jolie* – so pretty! *Ravissante!* But unfortunately *elle était vaniteuse.* You know what that means? She was vain. *Elle aimait beaucoup regarder dans le miroir.* And that wasn't all. *Elle était coquette.* She liked to flirt with boys. Now, it wasn't that she was boy-crazy. *Ah, non!* She just liked boys to pay attention to her. Because when *les garçons*, when they paid attention, then *les autres filles, elles étaient jalouses*, they paid attention, and then *tout le monde faisait attention à Rose. Elle aimait ça!*

Now, Rose was engaged to be married. *Son fiancé, il s'appellait Gabriel Lafontaine.* And they were to be married *au printemps* – in springtime. But our story begins *en hiver*, before that, and on a very special evening for Rose and Gabriel and all the other citizens of St Joachim. *C'est le soir du Mardi gras.*

Mardi Gras, you know, *c'est une fête.* People still celebrate it. Parties, dancing, parades. In Rio de Janeiro, the Caribbean, New Orleans, and of course, Quebec. It's good for tourism; visitors spend a lot of money. But in the time of Rose and Gabriel, there was a different reason to celebrate. In St Joachim, people celebrated because the following day – *mercredi des Cendres*, Ash Wednesday – they wouldn't be able to celebrate anything! For that was the beginning of Lent, *le Carême*, forty days of penitence and sacrifice to prepare Christians for the holiest feast of the year – *le Pâques*, Easter. Nowadays, of course, for many Christians part of observing Lent means choosing something difficult to do. You might give up *frites* – french fries – for forty days. Or not watch your favourite TV program. Or not go to the movies. Or help with the dishes without being asked. Or not lose your temper when your little sister pesters you. Difficult things.

But for Rose and Gabriel, it was different. It was much stricter. Listen to what you *had* to give up for forty days long ago. *Pas de viande.* No meat for forty days. *Pas de beurre.* No butter. *Pas d'oeufs* – not a single egg. And here's the really hard one – *pas de sucreries.* That's right, *pas de bonbons, pas de tartes, pas de gâteaux. Quarante jours, c'est bien long!* And what's more, *pas de parties. Pas de musique, pas de danses, rien de rien!*

So you can imagine that on the evening before all that started, you'd have your last chance to eat all that rich food. And you'd serve it at a party with as much music and dancing stuffed in as possible. But there was only one thing; you know what time the party had to stop? Right, *minuit*, because after that it would be Lent.

Now, that year in St Joachim the Mardi Gras party was being held *chez Latulippe*. Monsieur Latulippe, *le papa de Rose*, he'd organized the evening; all the young people were coming, and of course *le violoneux*, the fiddler, Isidore Dubois. And before things got started, Monsieur Latulippe came over to Isidore, who was tuning his fiddle, and said, "*Isidore, n'oublie pas, ça se termine à minuit.*" And Isidore, he said, "*Ah, ne t'en fais pas!* I know very well we have to stop at midnight." And he took up *le violon* and *l'archet* – his bow, and began a reel.

*Et tout le monde dansait! Rose, elle dansait avec son fiancé, Gabriel. Elle aimait bien danser.* But after ten minutes of dancing with him, she tired of her partner and started to make eyes at Joe Charbonneau. So he came and danced with Rose, but after a while, she got bored and smiled over her partner's shoulder at Ovila Legaré, and he left his *petite amie* Catherine to dance with Rose. *Et Catherine, elle était jalouse,* and she told the other girls what Rose was doing, and now everyone was paying attention to Rose, *elle était bien contente, elle!*

And things continued in this fashion until about eleven o'clock, when there was a knock at the door. *Qui est-ce?* Everyone expected to come had arrived long ago. Ah, it was undoubtedly *le curé* – the priest, come to make a social call.

Monsieur Latulippe opened the door. *Mais, ce n'était pas le curé!* The man standing there was a tall, handsome stranger. *Le monsieur était très grand et très, très beau. Il était habillé de vêtements noirs: un grand chapeau noir, un costume noir, des gants et des bottes noirs. Il portait des moustaches noires aussi;* even his moustaches were black.

"*Que voulez-vous, monsieur?*" asked Monsieur Latulippe.

"Ah," said the stranger, "I was just passing through your village, and all at once I saw the lights and heard the music and I remembered, Mardi Gras! And since I'm a stranger here, I wonder if I might share the rest of the celebration with your guests!"

"*Mais bien sûr, monsieur,*" said Latulippe. "Nobody should be alone *le soir du Mardi gras! Entrez donc!*" So the stranger came in, and Monsieur Latulippe started introducing him to some of his guests, until he noticed that his visitor had not removed much of his outer clothing. "*Monsieur! Ne voulez-vous pas enlever votre chapeau? Vos gants?*"

"*Non, merci*," replied the stranger. "*Un rhume de cerveau* – I have a head cold, I'd prefer keeping my hat on. And as for my gloves, I'll leave them on too. *Une maladie de la peau*, a skin problem."

"*Comme vous voudrez, Monsieur*," said Latulippe. "But now, *je vous présente ma fille, Rose.*"

"*Ah, mademoiselle*," breathed the stranger. "*Je suis enchanté.*"

"*Enchantée, monsieur*," answered Rose. Ah *le monsieur était si beau, et si bien vêtu! Et il parlait si bien, si doucement!*

"*Mademoiselle Rose*," says the stranger, "*voudriez-vous m'accorder l'honneur de danser avec moi?*"

"*Danser avec vous … ah, monsieur, je serais ravie!* I'd be delighted," said Rose. Just think! He had asked no other girl to dance but her. She gave him her arm, and he led her to the centre of the room as Isidore, *le violoneux*, started another reel. And they began to dance.

*Mais quel beau danseur, ce monsieur!* Could he ever dance! *La gigue, le reel, le casse-reel, le cotillon, le tout!* He knew them all, and he never missed a step! And Rose, *elle aimait bien danser*, she followed him perfectly, and she knew that everyone in the room was watching them as they danced. But after a while, she forgot about everyone else, because of the way *le monsieur* was smiling down at her with his dark eyes. And as they danced, he drew her closer and closer to him, so he could whisper in her ear without anyone else hearing. And this is what he was saying: "*Ah, ma belle Rose, tu es la plus jolie.* You're the most beautiful woman in this room tonight. Won't you come away with me, now? Won't you be mine forever?"

"*Mais, monsieur*," said Rose, "*je suis déjà fiancée – à Gabriel Lafontaine!*"

"*Ah, oui, je l'ai rencontré, Gabriel*, I've met him. A nice enough lad, but – do you really want to marry him, and be stuck in this village for the rest of your life, where no one appreciates your charm, your beauty? *Ah, ma belle Rose!* If you were my wife, it would be so different! *J'ai une grande maison dans une belle ville.*

We would have parties all the time; all my friends – rich, influential people – would come to meet you. And I'd buy you everything – *le tout! Des robes, des bijoux, des fourrures!* Won't you be mine?"

"Ah, *monsieur*," said Rose. Nobody had ever spoken to her in that way, had ever made such promises! "I don't know what to say!"

"Don't say anything, *ne dis rien, ma belle*. Just dance with me," he replied. And Rose danced, and danced. She never once thought of changing partners or of flirting with another. So engrossed was she in her handsome stranger that she noticed nothing going on around her. That was a shame, because some rather unusual things were starting to happen at that party.

For one thing, there were a couple of little children there still awake and watching the dancers with their *maman*. They were really little, you know, *trois ans, quatre ans*. And the first time that Rose and the stranger danced really close to them, *ces petits*, they just pulled at their mother's skirts and said, "*Regarde, maman, le monsieur qui dance avec Rose Latulippe, il brûle. Pourquoi brûle-t-il?* Why is that man burning?" And their mother, she looked, but she couldn't see anything wrong, and she said "*Il ne brûle pas, vous êtes fous tous les deux, taisez-vous, taisez-vous!*" Of course, like all the adults in the room, she had lost her innocence long ago, and she couldn't see what her children could see so well. And another thing – *la tante de Rose*, Rose's old aunt. She lived with the family, and she was getting tired and wanted to get to bed. So she made her *bonsoirs* to everyone and went to her bedroom. It was right next to the room where everyone was dancing, but that didn't bother *la tante, elle était un peu sourde*; she was hard of hearing. As a matter of fact, when she knelt down to say her prayers, she had her bedroom door partly open. Now she liked to pray in a loud voice, and she prayed to a lot of people up in heaven. Anybody passing the door could hear her. "*Sainte Catherine, priez pour nous! Saint Joseph, priez pour nous! Saint Jean de Baptiste, priez pour nous!*" *Alors*, the stranger came dancing past with Rose in his arms, and he heard the holy words; all at once he turned his face away from Rose and looked through the bedroom door at Rose's aunt. And what a look, *quel regard!* It chilled her blood. But he danced away, and trembling, she continued her prayers, finishing with the Lord's Prayer, *le Notre Père* … "*Notre Père, qui êtes aux cieux, que votre nom soit sanctifié, que*

*votre règne vienne*" ... And the stranger came by her door once
more, and once again, *quel regard* ... almost *démoniaque, quoi!*

But the person at the party who was most upset was none of
these! It was Gabriel; you remember, *le fiancé de Rose?* He hadn't
had a dance with her since about seven o'clock, but it wasn't
that which bothered him. What really bothered him was that it
was now nearly midnight, and she had been dancing for about
an hour with the same partner, *le bel étranger*, paying attention
to none but him. Gabriel, *il était bien jaloux*. He couldn't stand
it. He wanted to go up to the pair of them and say, "*Écoutez,
monsieur, Rose Latulippe est ma fiancée et vous n'avez pas le droit
de danser si longtemps avec elle*," but he couldn't do it; the stranger
intimidated him and he didn't know why. Gabriel decided to
leave the party early. He stomped across the room, pulled open
the front door and walked out, slamming the door behind him.
There! He'd done it. He'd left his coat inside, but he was so
angry that his anger kept him warm.

And then, standing there in the snow, Gabriel noticed something. You know what it was? *Le cheval du monsieur*. Well, that
horse tied up at the post by Latulippe's door, it had to be the
stranger's horse. Gabriel had never seen it before. Besides, nobody
in St Joachim could afford a horse like that. It was a thoroughbred:
coal-black, *tout noir*, and beautiful – but there was something
wrong with it.

All at once Gabriel realized what it was. *C'était l'hiver*, it was
winter, *il y avait beaucoup de neige partout*, banks of snow everywhere, but – *sous les pattes du cheval* – under the horse's feet –
*plus de neige!* It was all melted, *toute fondue!*

"How could that be?" thought Gabriel. "*Comment se fait-il que
...*" and his gaze travelled up the horse's legs, up its body, to its
head. And Gabriel found himself looking *dans les yeux du cheval*,
right into the horse's eyes.

Oh, dear! There, where the eyes should have been, *deux charbons
ardents*, two burning coals, glowed at Gabriel. And Gabriel was
cold, colder than he'd ever been in his life. *Mais ce n'était pas
l'hiver*, it wasn't the winter that made him cold now, *c'était la
peur*. It was fear.

And Gabriel broke into a run. He ran down the road as fast
as he could, towards the house of the priest, *le presbytère*. He
banged on the door. "*Monsieur le curé, monsieur le curé, venez*

vite! *Reveillez-vous, reveillez-vous! Il y a quelque chose qui ne marche pas chez Latulippe!*"

But the priest wasn't asleep. *Ah, non!* He was wide awake and praying that none of his parishioners would dance after midnight, when Lent began. So he ran to the door. "*Gabriel, qu'est-ce qu'il y a?*"

"*Ah, mon père, mon père!*" Gabriel told the whole story, and when the priest heard the description of *le monsieur* who would remove neither his hat nor his gloves, he knew he had a business call to make! Quickly he draped his stole about his neck, took his crucifix from the wall, and rushed out the door towards Latulippe's house, *aussi vite que possible*, with Gabriel following right behind.

Meanwhile, *chez Latulippe*, the Mardi Gras party was still going full swing. *Isidore, le violoneux, il jouait encore, tout le monde dansait, Rose dansait encore dans les bras du beau monsieur.* And the stranger was whispering, "*Rose, ma belle Rose! Donne-moi ta promesse. Dis-moi que tu seras à moi pour toujours!*"

Well, Rose by then could hardly resist. But at that moment Isidore Dubois looked at the clock. *L'horloge manquait deux minutes à minuit.* Two minutes to midnight, two minutes before the beginning of Lent, when all the dancing must stop. So Isidore finished up the tune he was playing and put down his fiddle. But immediately *le monsieur*, he came over holding Rose by the hand.

"*Ah, monsieur le violoneux, une danse de plus!* Just one more dance, please!"

"*Mais non, je ne peux pas!* I can't – it's forbidden – *défendu* – during Lent!"

"But we still have two minutes left before Lent begins," urged the stranger. "And you haven't yet played the last dance. You know, the one in honour of our host, Monsieur Latulippe."

Isidore, he'd never heard of such a thing. He just stared. "You don't do that here?" continued the stranger. "Ah, but of course, I forgot this is the country. *Dans la ville*, in the city, where I live, our fiddler always dedicates the last dance to the host. A mark of respect, *un peu de politesse*. But I can't expect country people to have the same manners as city dwellers, forgive me."

Well, Isidore wouldn't stand for that! He was going to show this *citadin* that country people were just as polite as he. So he tapped on the bridge of his fiddle. "*Messieurs, mesdames, attention! Une danse de plus, à l'honneur de Monsieur Latulippe!*"

*Isidore, il jouait, tout le monde dansait, et le monsieur, il avait la*

*belle Rose dans ses bras.* "Rose," said he, "this is our last chance
to be together. *Je t'en prie, donne-moi ta promesse!* Won't you
come with me and be mine forever?"

And Rose, thinking of all his promises, all his flattery, wanting
to dance for the rest of her life with this wonderful stranger,
gazed up into his eyes. She didn't notice – the other dancers
didn't notice – even Isidore, proving what a well-mannered fiddler
he was, didn't notice that the minute hand of the clock had
twice crossed the twelve. It was after midnight! But Rose, unmind-
ful, clung to her partner and sighed, "*Ah oui, chéri, je te donne
ma promesse. Je serai à toi pour toujours – aïe!*" She shrieked in
pain. Something sharp had stabbed her right palm. She withdrew
her hand from her partner's and noticed her flesh was torn. Blood
was trickling from the wound. "*Mais, regarde!*" said she. "*Je me
suis coupée la main!* How could I have cut my hand? I wasn't
doing anything but dancing with you – ah!" She saw his black-
gloved hand, the hand that she had been holding. Oh, the glove
was still there, but from the tip of the middle finger, something
had cut through the black leather, something long, white, curved
to a sharp point, with blood on the tip. *Une griffe* – a claw!

She looked at him in horror. And do you know, *le monsieur,
il souriait encore.* Yes, he was still smiling. But it was no longer
*un sourire d'affection, de tendresse.* It was a smile of triumph.

"Aha, Rose Latulippe!" said he. "*Je t'ai fait danser après minuit.*
I got you to dance after midnight. And you will be mine forever,
as you promised!" And when he began to laugh, Rose finally
realized who her partner was. She screamed again and fell uncon-
scious at his feet. Isidore stopped playing. Everyone stopped dancing. And they all recognized their visitor. But not one of them
could come to Rose's aid. Everyone had celebrated after midnight,
during Lent. And the stranger knew his power. He bent down,
picked up Rose's limp body, and began to carry her to the door.
*Et il l'aurait emportée pour toujours,* he would have carried her
away forever; they never would have seen her again!

But at that moment the door opened and in came *le curé,*
brandishing his crucifix. He walked right over to the stranger and
said, "*Monsieur, je sais très bien qui vous êtes. Sortez de là!* I know
who you are, get out!"

The stranger took one step back. Then he said, "*Oui, je sors.
Mais pas tout seul.* I'm not going alone. *Rose Latulippe, elle*

*m'accompagne*. She's coming too; she's given me her promise and the contract has been sealed – in blood!"

"*Un contrat?*" echoed the priest. "You think you have a contract with her? *Vous avez tort, monsieur!* Your contract is invalid!"

"*Pas valable! Qu'est-ce que vous dites?*" roared the stranger.

"I'm saying," continued *le curé*, "that Rose was not free to make a contract with you because she made another one last week, to the Lord. Rose came to see me privately and said, 'Mon *père*, I think I have a religious vocation. I would like to leave the world and enter a convent of holy nuns, to pass the rest of my life in prayer and meditation.' And she made a solemn vow to do just that. So anything she said to you doesn't count!"

Everyone was stupefied. Was this possible – Rose Latulippe, *la vaniteuse, la coquette*, was to become a nun? *Mais non, impossible!* Rose was the last girl in the world to take the veil. Everyone knew there were no mirrors in the convent – or partners to dance with. Or boys to flirt with. The priest must have made a mistake!

But of course there was no mistake. The priest knew exactly what he was doing. *Il disait un petit mensonge.* He didn't like telling lies usually, but under the circumstances …

And, do you know, the stranger believed the priest. "*Une religieuse? Rose Latulippe? Ah, non! Quel gaspillage de temps!*" And he stamped his foot and – BOOM – *il y avait une explosion!* He disappeared from sight. Black smoke filled the room, and there was the odour of sulphur. It's the smell of *le malin* – the Evil One, you know. Rose fell from his arms, to be caught just in time by Gabriel. And there, in Latulippe's outer wall, was a hole just the size and shape of a man, through which the stranger had obviously made his exit. Rose came back to consciousness to learn that she had barely escaped the clutches of – *vous savez qui*.

Now, there are all sorts of endings to this story. Some say that Rose was so terrified by her experience that she gave up men completely and remained *vieille fille*. Others say that she did enter a convent, either through fear or penitence, and that she died there a few years later during an influenza epidemic. Still others will tell you that Rose finally married Gabriel, *comme prévu*, right on schedule, and having learned her lesson, became a model wife, *ni vaniteuse, ni coquette*. There are even those storytellers who say that the priest did not come in time and that Rose was taken away by the handsome visitor, never to return.

*Alors, les filles,* you can take the ending you choose. But if you're at a dance, and you're tapped on the shoulder by a good-looking man all dressed in black, with gloves to match, and if he wants you to dance with him, *que faites-vous?* All right, if you really want to dance with him, ask him to take off his gloves first, and get a good look at the length of his nails before you go any further. Even these days, one can't be too careful ...

    *Sac-à-tabac, sac-à-tabi,*
    *Le conte est fini!*

*Marylyn Peringer*

*This tale is reputedly of Norman or Breton origin. It has many variants among francophones and anglophones in North America. My version is based on bits and pieces from several sources, as well as my own imagination, which, I trust, has kept faith with the spirit of the traditional form of the story. The heroine was first christened Rose Latulippe by Philippe Aubert de Gaspé fils in his book Le Chercheur de Trésors (1837), the very first novel from Quebec. I always tell this story bilingually to keep the flavour of its French origin.*

છ

# The Magic Cat

This is one of a set of stories, of which there are a great many in China, about just and righteous officials who, by their courage and ingenuity and their caring for the welfare of the people, bring about an amelioration or a resolution of a situation that has been brought into existence by some arbitrary action by persons in power. Sometimes the latter are dishonest, and sometimes, as in this case, they're simply mistaken. Judge Bao is a figure who occurs in many of these stories, a well-loved figure. We call him

Judge Bao because he first made his mark as prefect of one county in China. The prefect is the person who's responsible for all aspects of the law. He's judge, administrator, lawmaker, all rolled into one. So we still call him Bao Gong, Judge Bao. Although by the time of this story, he's actually prime minister.

It was the time of the great Song Dynasty, and the Emperor Renzong was on the throne. Renzong was not a bad emperor, but sometimes he could do foolish things. At one point in his reign he decided that there were too many old people in China. So he issued a decree that all of the old people over a certain age were to be killed. Well, there was great grief and lamentation all over the country. But the Emperor's decree was absolute and must be obeyed. Who would dare to disobey it?

And so, with much grief, the decree was carried out. In every case but one. And who was that one? It was the prime minister of China, Bao Gong, Judge Bao. He could not bear to be parted from his old father, even though his father was over the age to which the Emperor's decree applied. So Judge Bao hid his father away in an inner secret place in his own mansions, and every day he would get up before dawn to attend court with all the other officials to the Emperor, and deal with the business of the nation. When he returned he would go to his father's chambers and ask after his health, as a filial son should.

One day, when Judge Bao was returning from court and coming in to speak with his father, his father looked at him and said, "You seem worried." "Well, I am," said Judge Bao. "We have a most peculiar situation in court, and no one can do anything about it. We have been visited by a plague of five incredible rats. They are running all over the court, eating up the grain in the imperial granary, going hither and yon in the kitchens. They've even gotten into the imperial concubines' quarters. And they're scaring the women, who are afraid that they might be going up their skirts. One has even had the temerity to run across the imperial throne. Nothing we have done can avail against them, and no one has been able to make a helpful suggestion."

"Well," said his father, "but that is very simple. What you must do is borrow the Jade Emperor's cat." "But the Jade Emperor is up in heaven!" said Judge Bao. "How am I going to get his cat?"

"Simple," said his father. "What you must do tonight is dream that you have gone up to heaven, and in your dream, speak to the Jade Emperor and persuade him of the seriousness of the situation. Then, if he gives you the cat, you can bring it back down, and tomorrow morning, take it into court."

So that evening Judge Bao did just that. He went up in his dream, and spoke most eloquently to the Jade Emperor about the tribulations and difficulties that the court was facing. Although the Jade Emperor was extremely reluctant, Judge Bao finally made a solemn promise that the cat would be returned as soon as the five rats had been dealt with. Then he was given the cat, returned to his mansion with it, and the next morning, took it into court.

Well, the minute that he came into the court and set loose that cat it set to work. One, two, three, four of those rats were dispatched on the spot. But the fifth rat was quicker than the others, and it ducked behind a broom. When the cat went to the left, the rat went to the right. And when the cat went to the right, the rat went to the left, until at one moment when the cat's attention was just slightly distracted, the rat turned and darted through a hole in the wall, and found safety, looking out with his nose still quivering.

Well, the cat planted himself instantly in front of the hole. That rat was not going to be able to get out. Judge Bao looked about and saw that the situation had been dealt with, if not completely resolved. So he went and reported to the Emperor. "Four rats have been killed, and the fifth rat is now imprisoned in a hole in the wall, with the cat guarding that hole."

"Ah," said the Emperor, greatly pleased. "You are my true and loyal official, Judge Bao. When no one else could think of a method to save the situation – this chaos that was created in our court – you were able to." "Well," Judge Bao thought to himself, "if I don't speak now there will never be another opportunity." So he fell to his knees and kowtowed before the Emperor, and said, "Your servant should die a thousand deaths. Ten thousand deaths! But that plan was not of my making."

"It was not?" said the Emperor. "Then whose was it?"

"It was the plan," said Judge Bao, "of my father."

"Your father?" said the Emperor, who of course was well aware of the age of Judge Bao's father. "Yes," said Judge Bao. "I could not bear to be parted from him, and even now he is concealed in an inner room in my mansions." Well, the Emperor thought long and hard, and he was silent for a while. Then he said, "I see. Those five rats were a plague that was sent down by the Jade Emperor to awaken me to the error of my ways. Our old people are the repositories of wisdom. From now on we should cherish and honour them."

He revoked his decree, and all over the country there was rejoicing. And that cat? Well, Judge Bao had promised to return the cat when all five rats were disposed of. But he needed the cat to guard that hole and keep the fifth rat from coming out. Finally he decided that he would have to break his word, and not return the cat. The cat stayed there all its life, guarding that hole and keeping the rat inside, and keeping order for the court. From that cat are descended all the cats in China.

And so sometimes when you see a cat nowadays chasing a broom, you know that it's remembering its ancestor, and how its ancestor was fooled by that fifth rat who got away by hiding behind a broom and then slipping quickly into the hole. And sometimes you'll hear a cat purring. Now we in the West think that when a cat purrs it's happy. But the Chinese know better. That cat is grumbling to itself. Not quite daring to speak aloud, but remembering the fate of its ancestor, it's saying, "*Xu song, bu song, Bao Gong, za zhong!* Promised return, not sent back. Judge Bao is a bastard rat."

## Kate Stevens

*I got into Chinese storytelling through a series of accidents; it all began with Ezra Pound. Pound was a marvellous poet in his own right, one who became excited by Chinese poetry. He turned some of China's poems into highly evocative English poetry that made me want to read the originals for myself. By the time I discovered that Pound's translations, wonderful though they were, had little to do with the original – in short, that I'd been diddled – I was already hooked. So I kept on going anyway.*

*A few years later, as a graduate student in Taiwan, I wandered into a teahouse, only to be captivated by the barely comprehended performance of a Beijing Drumsinger. When I raved about the soaring melodies and evocative acting to my landlady, Mrs Yeh replied, "Why don't you learn how to sing it?" After a brief struggle, the ham in me overcame the book-bound student; the singer became my teacher.*

*Thus began an exploration of Chinese narrative performing arts that has continued to the present day. Thirty-odd years later, I continue to be fascinated by the great treasure house of Chinese tales, sung or spoken, and by the skill of their tellers.*

*Most of my own stories come direct from China, be it from performers or from books. How often do you find a Chinese story in your kitchen? That is where a friend of mine, Wu Hua, told me "The Magic Cat." All because I had said, as we watched the antics of my own cat, "What a pity China doesn't have cat stories." The tale had been told her by her father, Wu Xiaoling, now in his early seventies, still resident in Beijing. He had heard it from his grandmother, so the story has at least a hundred-year history in the Wu family.*

*Searching the literature later, I've found other versions of this story; the core theme of how we treat our old people is widely known not only in China, but in India and Japan as well. But to me this version is special not only for the unique twists it gives the tale, but because it was found by my own cat in my own kitchen.*

☙

# A Miracle on Friday

How a hot potato pudding ever acquired supernatural powers is a problem best left to more subtle minds than ours. Learned scholars – natural scientists, theologians, medievalists – claim to have uncovered traces of a now lost continent said to have been ruled by a large rational potato, the sole surviving memory of which is enshrined in the phrase, "the Might has a thousand eyes." But of the supra-rational tuber, we have no evidence but this:

On a Friday afternoon in the winter of 1897, Mrs Yoshke Furmanovsky, a stout *hausfrau* of the Moldovanke, opened her oven door and plunged her fork into the kugel baking within, to see it if was ready. Her husband looked forward to nothing so much as his Friday night kugel – indeed, it was one of the great sorrows of Mrs Furmanovsky's life that he looked forward to the

kugel with somewhat more enthusiasm than to certain other Friday
night activities. He would rush home from *shul*, gobble down the
whole kugel, along with some chicken and fish, and then fall
straight to sleep, in despite of rabbinic injunctions concerning
private duties.

Mrs Furmanovsky, *nebekh*, tried everything. She put in fewer
potatoes, hoping to make the meal lighter, but her Sabbath frock
was fancy enough without a kugel tiara. She purchased herbs
guaranteed to wake the dead; her husband, *nebekh*, spent the
night in the outhouse. She made the tea extra strong, the soup
extra weak, the chicken extra lean, but by the time the weekly
glimmer stole into Mrs Furmanovsky's eye, old Yoshke – *nebekh*
– would be stretched out on the bed, as level and as useful as
a bench in the ritual bath.

So Mrs Furmanovsky decided to avenge herself on the whole
cursed race of kugelen in the only way she knew how: whenever
she went to test one, she would thrust her fork murderously into
the kugel's tender, yielding flesh, twisting it so hard that she
could almost hear the hapless concoction screaming for mercy.
*"Zoln ale kugelen geyn tsu di ale shvartse-yorn,"* she would mutter.
"Let every kugel go to hell. They've ruined my life ... I sweat,
I toil, I break my back like a slave in Egypt six days a week,
and *shabbes*, instead of a little *nakhes*, a little pleasure like everybody else, what do I get? A kugel bowl to be washed out with
my tears. They say that on *shabbes* you're supposed to get a
*neshome yeseire*, an extra soul. Nu, how can I get when my extra
lies there as useful, as useful, *vi bankes a toytn*, as cups on a
corpse? A plague on every kugel, and may the Lord deliver us
from them speedily and in our day, amen."

She was otherwise a very nice woman.

And her husband? A purblind tailor with the mind of a goose.
Honk, peck, eat; honk, peck, eat; pull a needle through a hole;
honk, peck, eat. Shortly after their marriage, Mrs Furmanovsky
began to suspect him of infidelity, so weak and inconsequential
was his desire. But when could he have had the time? He spent
all day in the shop, which was the front room of their meagre
apartment, and he spent all night chomping and shnorkhing. She
began to think that perhaps he was punishing her; perhaps she
had sinned against him in some way – she had no experience
in being a wife – and he was taking his revenge by denying her.

She bought potions and philtres, perfumes, negligees like the Russian women wore – all they produced was snores. Where some men had such strong evil inclinations as to be veritable mad dogs for the bed regardless of the time of the month, Yoshke Furmanovsky wasn't even inclined.

She sought reasons, excuses. A whole week he works from dawn to dusk, shut up in an airless and stifling room – OK, he's too tired. But Friday, Friday when he stops work at two o'clock, goes to the ritual bath, has a little time to relax and a day of relaxation to look forward to – Friday night stuck in her craw. Many women shared her problems during the week, but Friday night? Why else had God invented it? And Yoshke, after she had finally found the courage to ask him, on their eighth anniversary, Yoshke merely answered that he ate so well that he could think of nothing but sleep. And that kugel – so heavy and hearty, it warmed him so, that the vapours shot straight up to his brain, telling it to close his eyes so that Yoshke might savour the taste and aroma – undistracted.

"A-nu," said Mrs Furmanovsky, "from now on, no more potato kugel. It's coming between us. I have my rights as a wife."

"Wife," replied Yoshke, "if you should fail even one Friday night to fix me my favourite potato kugel, you will lose all your cherished rights. Oys wife! I will divorce you forthwith, and then we'll see about your wifely rights."

So Mrs Furmanovsky, who, when all was said and done, did love her husband, began to hate his kugel. Every Friday afternoon was a war between her, the potatoes, and the spices, with Mrs Furmanovsky always the loser. Loudly she lamented the fate which had kept her from being born in Ireland.

On the Friday afternoon in question, in the winter of 1897, Mrs Furmanovsky stuck her fork into the kugel with her usual vigour, gave it a twist and gleefully removed it, studying the tines for traces of kugel blood. Disappointed as always, she was about to shut the oven door, when the kugel, with an alacrity shocking in an inanimate object, leapt from the oven straight to the floor, and sank its teeth into Mrs Furmanovsky's ankle.

Mrs Furmanovsky was more shocked than pained; the kugel is known for its blunt, yielding teeth, and she had no trouble shaking it loose. Bits of kugel clung to her ankle, but no tooth marks were to be seen. Hungry for vengeance, she kicked at the errant pudding, only to see it leap cackling onto the table, where it sat smugly, humming "The British Grenadiers."

A woman of valour, this Mrs Furmanovsky. She grabbed her broom and set after the kugel like a hound to the fox. She cursed, she shrieked, the sound of the broom slapping the floor re-echoed through the kitchen, but the giggling kugel was always one step ahead, baiting her, egging her on in a *heimishen, geshmakenem* Yiddish, a down-home, *tasty* Yiddish: *"Me ret fun Aleksandr, un oykh fun Herkules,"* until Mrs. Furmanovsky, no Hercules, threw down her broom and sank to the floor in despair.

Casting her eyes heavenward, "Why me?" she cried. "What did I ever do to deserve this? The rest of the world lives in peace and quiet, while I, Khayke Furmanovsky, am condemned to do battle with a dancing kugel. If potatoes can sing, it's the end of the world. The messiah must be on his way. Soon all calves will have two heads and a stillborn child will assume the throne. Men will walk on their hands, horses become rabbis, and I … I will be murdered to death in my own kitchen by a kugel from hell."

"And this is how you say thank you?" asked the kugel angrily. It was reclining peacefully in one of the chairs, and fixed Mrs Furmanovsky in its gaze. "I come here to help you, and this is the thanks I get? Poked like a pig, chased like a thief, and cursed like a Cossack. I've got a good mind to get up and go right now, except that once I'm finished here maybe I can get out of this kugel and go back to the Garden of Eden where I belong. Kugel from hell! A *shvarts-yor af dir*, lady, I'll give you a kugel from hell!"

Mrs Furmanovsky's eyelids grazed the ceiling. "Oh my God, it's possessed yet."

"Possessed, shmossessed. If you'd shut up and listen for a minute, you'd understand the whole thing." And the kugel began its story. "When I was still on earth, I was a famous man. The rebbe of Dlugaszow, perhaps you've heard of me?"

The rebbe of Dlugaszow? Who hadn't heard of the holy rebbe of Dlugaszow? A saint, a wonderworker. He made the dumb to speak, the lame to walk, the barren to give birth. It was said that merely touching his walking stick or the hem of his garment was sufficient to ensure a man's prosperity all the days of his life. A dwarf who looked upon the rebbe's face one Yom Kippur night awoke the next morning a giant.

The rebbe of Dlugaszow. Sweet-tempered, kindly, and modest. He was never known to have lost his temper or to have uttered an angry word. And what people didn't know didn't hurt them. Once, shortly after his marriage, the future rebbe made the mistake of attempting to explicate certain rather complicated kabbalistic ideas to his wife. She was a simple, pious girl who wanted only to serve her husband, and she rapidly became lost in the chain of emanations he was describing. The young scholar looked at her bewildered countenance and spat in contempt. "The brains of a kugel, that's what you've got." Her tears so affected him that he vowed never again to insult or speak ill of any living creature.

This vow was never broken. But after a hundred and twenty years, when the rebbe came before the heavenly court, the *kategor*, the accusing angel, held this one incident up before the Judge as proof that the rebbe was not worthy of paradise. What would scarcely have been noticed on any other record was the sole blemish on this one, and as such, deserved to be treated with appropriate severity.

The Judge disagreed. True enough, the rebbe's sin *had* been a grievous one; true enough, his wife was left with a nervous tic for the rest of her life as a result of his outburst; still, he did not merit Gehenna. Rather, the rebbe's soul was to be returned to earth in the very form with which he had insulted his wife, *id est*, a kugel, and was there to wander about until such time as the rebbe, in the form of a kugel, was able – kugel-wise – to repair a breach of domestic harmony and thus counterbalance his own sin on the scales of justice.

"And so," continued the kugel, *"ot bin ikh.* Here I am, lady. Your cries have reached the ear of heaven, and it has been decided that the nature of your problem makes your household particularly well suited to my mission."

"Some kind of help you'll be," said Mrs Furmanovsky. "My husband will come in, take one look at you and gobble you up before you can say Rabbi Eliezer ben Horkanos, and I'll be back where I started from. Do me a favour and go somewhere else. Go to St Petersburg and poison the Tsar for all I care, just leave me in peace."

"Lady, I didn't ask to come here, so let's try to make the best of it. If I mess up here – straight to hell. And remember, lady,

I was a rebbe; I don't *know* anybody in hell." The kugel wept so piteously that Mrs Furmanovsky finally gave in. What did she have to lose?

The kugel paced the room for an hour or so, racking its brains to come up with a solution. Paced and racked and racked and paced until, "Hey Mrs! I got it! We'll scare your husband out of ever wanting kugel again for the rest of his life. We'll make him so scared of kugel that the merest mention of the word will set him to trembling and begging for mercy. And I know just how to do it ..."

Yoshke Furmanovsky found everything in order when he returned from the synagogue that night. The soup was on the table, and just as he was lifting the last mouthful to his lips, his wife brought in the kugel. Yoshke gazed at it affectionately, saliva dripping onto his beard as he prepared to consign it to his belly. He reached over, pulled the bowl towards him, and almost dropped dead of a heart attack when it told him to keep his hands to himself. Yoshke may have been a big *makher* at home, but everywhere else he was as timid as a rabbit. He would return from his occasional trips to the market with virtually every item offered him – no matter how much it cost, or how little he needed it – simply because he was afraid to say "no." Their tiny closet was stuffed with samovar-taps, flywheels, pot-lids. So when the kugel spoke, Yoshke cowered in his seat, awaiting further orders.

"I've had just about enough of you and your gluttony," barked the kugel. "Every Friday the same story. Wolf down the kugel so you can avoid your duty to your wife. Well, we kugelen are sick and tired of being made an occasion for sin by the likes of you, and we've decided to take matters into our own hands, so to speak. From this day forth, if you so much as try to swallow even a single morsel of any kugel whatsoever, that same morsel will tear your throat into a thousand pieces and scatter them to the four winds. Furthermore, if word should ever reach us that you have been ... remiss ... in your duties as a husband, a group of picked kugelen will see to it that you are deprived of your manhood. And remember, Yoshke, there are some things that grow, but don't grow back."

With that, the kugel leapt up, smacked him in the face, and strode over to the window. It sprouted wings and flew off, never to be seen again.

When Mrs Furmanovsky came in with the chicken, she found her husband pale and trembling. So sickly was he feeling, he averred, that he had lost all his appetite for food. And for food alone. He led Mrs F. out of the kitchen, and they lived normally ever after.

Nu. How the rebbe's soul came to lodge in a kugel, which is not, after all, an animate, organic unity, is a mystery that will never be solved. But that it did, and that in so doing saved the married life of Mr and Mrs Furmanovsky, this cannot be questioned. I have the story straight from Mrs Furmanovsky herself, and can see no reason to doubt it. For Mrs Furmanovsky, the sainted Mrs Furmanovsky, the Mrs Furmanovsky who realized her destiny as woman through the agency of a bunch of crushed potatoes to which the proper heat was at long, long last applied – Mrs Furmanovsky was my mother.

## Michael Wex

*This was composed in a fit of pique after a dispute with another storyteller, who did not consider some of my other work sufficiently "folktalish." "He wants folktales," I said to myself, "he'll get f'ing folktales." The idea of a talking kugel came to me from heaven.*

### Glossary

| | |
|---|---|
| *makher* | big *makher* – a big shot |
| *Moldovanke* | the old Jewish district of Odessa |
| *nebekh* | an exclamation of pity (cf. *nebbish*, a person about whom one says *nebekh*) |
| *shnorkhing* | snoring |
| *shul* | a synagogue |

⌘

# The Shivering Tree

Nanabush was walking; he'd been walking a long time. He'd been walking a long time and he was feeling very tired and thirsty.

"My, my, my," Nanabush says to himself, "I been walking a long time and boy oh boy am I tired and thirsty. It's a good thing I'm such a smart fellow and decided to follow this river. This way, if I get lost, I'll still know where I am even though I won't."

And he liked what he said to himself.

"Goodness me but I'm a bright fellow," Nanabush said to himself. And he had to stop in his tracks and smile and just shake his head, he was just so proud of himself for what he'd just said just before telling himself how bright he was.

"Well, Nanabush, you bright fellow, let's go down to the river and have a drink and rest our old bones for a year or two … heh, heh," Nanabush said to himself. And he agreed.

Feeling very proud of himself, Nanabush strutted down to the river. It wasn't far at all and when he got there Nanabush took a good long drink, threw some water in his face, and lay back on the sandy bank.

"It certainly is a big world," he thought. "Somewhere to the west of here are the Tall Mountains that mark the approach of the Home of the West Wind. Someday I'll go there, for I've a score to settle with that Old Fellow."

That's when his quick ears caught another sound above the voice of the river. It was another voice, a man's voice.

Nanabush sat up, fast.

"A man?" Nanabush thought. "That just can't be. No human being has come this far."

But it was a man. At least it looked like one. But that meant nothing back in those times; after all, Nanabush looked like a man – most of the time. But Nanabush was far from being human. But just who or what was this fellow anyway?

Like I said, the stranger looked human at least. He was tall and thin, clad in buckskins with long fringe that fluttered and shivered in the breeze. He wore warm leggings and moccasins as it was autumn and the weather getting colder.

The stranger was juggling something. Now that was interesting.

He was juggling with his eyes closed. And that was mighty interesting.

Nanabush stood up, slowly, never taking his eyes off the juggling stranger.

"Hello, Nanabush," The Juggler said, still juggling, his eyes still shut firmly. "It is Nanabush, isn't it?"

Nanabush felt insulted.

"Of course I'm Nanabush," Nanabush said. "Who else could I be?"

The Juggler, eyes still firmly shut, still juggling what now appeared to be a pair of small crystals, just smiled.

"Well, let me see now," The Juggler said, still juggling, his eyes still shut firmly. "You could be Me, seeing as I'm the only person in these parts, but as you are you and not me and I'm here to see it, I guess I'm me and you're you and you must be Nanabush, because I've heard you've been spotted in these parts and I'm the only person here who would have heard about you besides you."

Nanabush glared at The Juggler.

"It's a fortunate thing for you that I'm such a clever fellow," Nanabush said, "because if I wasn't I might've been confused by what you just said and I'd've become very angry."

The Juggler just kept on juggling, eyes closed and all.

Nanabush felt himself getting impatient.

"Well?" Nanabush said. "Are you going to tell me who you are?"

With a big, wide grin, The Juggler stopped what he was doing, opened his eyes and turned to Nanabush.

"Very well," The Juggler said, "I'm a juggler and conjuror and I am known as Restless As The Wind; but most people just call me The Juggler."

"I have never heard of you," Nanabush said. He didn't like this fellow at all. No sir, Nanabush didn't like him at all.

"I was just playing around with a couple of pieces of crystal," The Juggler said. "That was nothing at all. That was just ordinary juggling that a child can do, eyes closed or not. Just watch. I'll show you some real conjuring ... Look, Nanabush, look."

Quick as lightning, The Juggler plucked out his own eyes and started to juggle them, rapidly from hand to hand. He started to dance, leaping into the air, all the while juggling his eyes hand to hand, back and forth, back and forth, hand to hand.

Nanabush was stunned, couldn't move.

Now that in itself was something. It takes a great deal to shake up someone like Nanabush, and everyone knows that there just isn't anyone to compare with The Great Nanabush.

The Juggler kept it up. Juggling, hand to hand, back and forth, back and forth, hand to hand, dancing, leaping, juggling. Juggling his eyes.

"Stop," Nanabush said, shouting. "Stop, you're making me dizzy ... *stop it.*"

And, just as quickly as he had started, The Juggler stopped, came to a halt just like that, arms out wide, head back, just in time for his eyes to fall right straight into their sockets.

Nanabush's own eyes almost fell out, he stared so hard.

The Juggler grinned: boy, did he grin.

Nanabush still couldn't stop staring.

I don't blame The Great Nanabush one bit, my friends. A sight like that would be enough to jar anyone's preserves.

"Now that is most certainly conjuring at its best," Nanabush said, "and you may take that as the word of the very one who invented conjuring."

The Juggler grinned.

"Well, Great Nanabush, Father of Conjuring. Perhaps I can show my gratitude, indeed the gratitude of all of us Conjurors," The Juggler said, smiling. "Allow me to show you how it's done. Allow me to show you how to juggle one's own eyes in one's own hands."

Now that got to Nanabush. For great and powerful as he can be, Nanabush can make the odd blunder now and then, and when he does, it's usually a bad one. This was going to be one of the worst.

"I'm flattered," Nanabush said, smiling like a proud father. "And I'm never too old to learn."

How true that was. Nanabush was about to learn a lesson that he and we are never going to forget.

"Will you allow me, then, to show you how it is done?" The Juggler said, smiling.

"The honour will be mine," Nanabush said, stepping forward. "Show me how it's done, Nephew."

"Removing the eyes is the really dangerous part," The Juggler said. "You have to apply some pressure just below each eye, like this."

The Juggler demonstrated how it was supposed to be done. Using his thumbs, he applied some pressure underneath his eye-sockets and ... POP ... out came the eyes. Very quickly, but carefully, he caught the eyes and, quickly and just as carefully, placed them back in his sockets.

"Did you see that?" The Juggler said. "Now, very carefully, 'cause it's just the first time, try it yourself and on yourself. Not too fast. This is only the First Lesson."

Nanabush placed his thumbs under his eye-sockets, carefully applied some pressure.

"Good, good ... that's good," The Juggler said, directing and urging Nanabush. "Careful now ... be very careful."

Then ... POP ... out came Nanabush's eyes ... Then ... WHOOSH out shot The Juggler's right hand and grabbed Nanabush's eyes in mid-air.

"I've got them ... HA HA. I've got them," The Juggler cried, leaping into the air and spinning like a top. "I've got the most powerful charms of any conjuror in The North. I have the very eyes of Nanabush ... HA HA I have them."

Then, as quick as lightning, The Juggler turned and ran, ran faster than he'd ever run in his life, for Nanabush is still Nanabush, blind or not.

But Nanabush was blind. Even before The Juggler turned and ran, Nanabush had made a lunge forward, instinctively knowing that something had gone wrong.

As The Juggler ran off, laughing and whooping, Nanabush landed, face down in the river. Almost immediately, he was on his feet. Almost immediately he was the real Nanabush. He stood still, turned his fear into caution.

"I've been a fool, a vain, yes ... even a blind fool. With both my eyes in my head, I was blind," he said to himself. He stood still, silent. He listened. He began to take his bearings.

The river was in front of him. He turned his back to it.

"Until I regain my sight ... and I will regain my sight, I must feel my way about. I also need a weapon which I can use easily and quickly should one of my old enemies come upon me," Nanabush said to himself. "A staff, that's it. A big heavy staff, sharpened at one end; it'll act as a cane and a weapon. I must find my way to the bush."

So, stumbling over bits of driftwood and rocks, falling painfully but always getting right back up on his feet, Nanabush made his way towards the bush, feeling his way with his hands, carefully keeping his ears open for every sound.

"If a friend finds me, may he truly be a friend," Nanabush said. "If an enemy should come upon me, may he act with honour. If my enemy should save me, I will gladly be in his debt. If my enemy finds me and chooses to kill me, then fine, I will still owe him something, if only a good fight."

All around him was darkness. But he knew that to be a false darkness. The birds still sang and the warmth of the sun made itself felt on his body and he knew it to be daylight and he knew himself to be in full view of friend, foe, and stranger alike. But he stumbled on, into the bush. He knew he was in the bush, for he smelt pine needles and the odour of fallen leaves. He bent over and felt a pine cone beneath his hand.

"I must find a stout pole to carve into a pointed staff," he said, feeling about, moving more cautiously than before.

The forest was thick, for he continually bumped into trees and stumps.

"Trees, stumps, but no limbs of any good size," he thought. "At least one old enemy of mine has been at work here, Old Man Beaver and his clan."

Then his left hand touched on something, a young fallen tree, This was it. He ran his hands up and down the narrow trunk. This was exactly what he wanted. He pulled out his knife after using his great strength to break off an appropriate length of trunk. Carefully, he sat down and carefully, very carefully, he began to carve.

A staff alone won't be enough. Nanabush knew that. He'd have to find help from someone who knew the country, someone he could trust, someone who could be trusted as a guide.

But Nanabush had to concentrate on his carving. He had to be really, really careful or, in his blindness, he might cut a finger or two off.

So far, he hadn't given a thought to The Juggler.

He kept on carving, clumsily but carefully.

Then, suddenly, he stopped. Stopped everything. He had a

strong feeling that he was being watched. He tightened his grip on the knife.

Though he had no eyes with which to see, he still instinctively moved his head back and forth as if scanning the area around him. He was certain that he was being watched. The feeling was even stronger.

Then he heard the voice, a deep clear voice, from somewhere above him.

"Well?" The Voice said, "Why have you stopped? You were doing well."

Knife in hand, Nanabush leaped to his feet.

"Who is there?" he snapped. "If you're an enemy, come out and fight."

"Fight?" The Voice said. "I thought you were busy working with that piece of wood."

Nanabush recognized the voice. It was indeed the voice of an enemy; a very old enemy, too.

"Owl, so it's you," Nanabush said, more on his guard than ever. "Well. What are you waiting for? Come and fight."

"I'm an old warrior, not an old fool," Owl said. "There's a thousand eyes in these woods. If I fought you and if I slew you in the condition which you are in the whole of Creation would hear of it. You'd be honoured. I'd be disgraced.

"No, Nanabush. I'm no coward. I may be your enemy, but I would like to think that I'm a worthy enemy.

"Lower your weapon. There is no danger from me, you have my word as a Warrior and as the head of my clan."

Nanabush, on hearing this solemn oath, placed his knife back into its sheath.

"I know that you're blind," said the Owl. "So will others and soon, Nanabush. Others who may not be so generous. Something must be done to restore your vision to you."

"I'll find a way myself," said Nanabush. "I'm already far too much in debt to you, Owl."

"Not if we decide to be friends," Owl said. "I am willing, for I wish there to be peace for my children. If you agree, then it's done."

"Then it's done," Nanabush said.

Their friendship sealed, the two began to talk of Nanabush's trouble.

"There is a way to restore your vision," Owl said. "I will give you a pair of eyes. I will give you my eyes."

"But Owl, my friend. That will leave you with no eyes. You will be as blind as I now am," Nanabush said.

The Owl shook his head. If he could have smiled, he would have.

"Oh no, not me," Owl said, "You see, Nanabush, I have two sets of eyes. One set for daytime and another set for night. As most of my enemies are daylight hunters like the hawk, I'll do my hunting at night from now on. During the day, I'll rest and stay safely with my family. I'll need only one set of eyes then. The other set I give to you."

Owl told Nanabush to hold out his hands. Nanabush did so, and a pair of eyes dropped into Nanabush's hands. Then ... POP ... Nanabush dropped the eyes into his own sockets.

"They are perfect, Owl," Nanabush said, joyously but seriously, as befits a Warrior.

"From this day, Owl, the night is yours," Nanabush declared. "From this day and for all time, you will be the Bird of The Night. You will be my eyes at night. At night your vision will be sure and your flight safe and clear. You will be to night as the Eagle and the Falcon are to the daylight. You'll rule the night skies. And out of respect for the great favour you have done for me, all who hear you call at night shall show their respect. They must not mimic your call if they hear you; that is to say, they will not answer your call. For them to do so would be to mock you. Your call will be my message in the night that I, Nanabush, never sleep but with my ears open, that even at night I watch those whom I protect and that I keep a watch out for those who would do harm to The Creation. So call out at night, Owl, my friend and my Emissary."

Their friendship sealed for all time, Owl and Nanabush bade each other good hunting and a long life. And so they parted, Owl with his new honours, Nanabush with his new eyes.

Springtime.

Springtime, and Nanabush was home. New eyes and everything. "The World is very beautiful this day," Nanabush said to himself as he walked along. "All is green and fragrant with new life and the birds are back. Yes, this is truly a beautiful day."

"Can't wait till the butterflies come out," Nanabush said. "My, but it's a wonderful day. Good thing that I have my eyes to see it all."

Then came that little voice that is sometimes to be heard in the back of Nanabush's mind. "Ah, Nanabush, but they weren't always your eyes, were they?" Nanabush remembered, of course. He remembered where his new eyes had come from and he remembered also what had happened to his old eyes. For the first time in months he thought of The Juggler. That ruined his day.

"The Juggler," Nanabush thought. "If I ever again meet up with that thieving rascal, he will regret the day his parents met. He will need more than an extra pair of eyes when I get through with him."

His day was ruined, he sat down and sulked. He couldn't help but think of The Juggler, couldn't think of anything else.

In the days which followed, Nanabush was obsessed with his strange enemy. He talked of little else. He began to worry his friends and his family.

His Grandmother advised him to stop thinking about The Juggler.

"You still have a great deal of work to do in this world," Grandmother said. "You've much to do. You are the teacher, the helper of all living things. Go about your work, Grandson. Don't seek out enemies. They will find you soon enough if they are not cowards."

So Nanabush carried on as always. Sometimes sure of himself, sometimes blundering, but always leaving his mark somewhere, somehow, on the world around him, making it more and more like the world we know today.

Then, one afternoon in late summer, he felt in need of a drink of water. He was deep in the woods at this time, but he knew where there was a clear, cold pool of water not far from where he stood. Picking up his kit, he made his way through the bush. He'd just about reached the pool when he saw, through the bushes around him, that another was at the pool.

A man.

A tall, thin man.

A tall thin man who was juggling a pair of crystals hand to hand, back and forth, hand to hand, back and forth.

Nanabush's eyes narrowed; he clenched his teeth.

"I must think this out," Nanabush said to himself. "I must think quickly, though. I may not get another chance at this rascal; besides, in addition to being my enemy, he's a Sorcerer and a dangerous one. Who is to tell how much damage he has done to others besides me? This fellow is very dangerous and I must do something about him."

Quickly and quietly, as only he can do it, Nanabush changed his appearance. He took on the appearance of an old man. Then he stepped out into the open.

The Juggler gave him a quick glance but kept right on juggling.

"Good day, Old One," The Juggler said. "I'd wish you long life but it seems a good number already have done so."

"So they have, Nephew," Nanabush said. "And they did so out of respect."

"Forgive me if I sound disrespectful," The Juggler said, continuing to juggle, "but I'm a very happy fellow these days and I sometimes don't give thought to what I'm saying. It could be that you've heard of me. I'm The Juggler. My name is Restless As The Wind.

"So," Nanabush said. "You are the fellow Nanabush is looking for, the one who stole Nanabush's eyes."

"That's me all right, Old One," The Juggler said. "Tell Nanabush if you like to. Maybe I'll take his ears this time."

"He'll find you without my telling him," Nanabush said, trying to hold back a smile. "He is no longer blind, by the way. A friend gave him a new pair of eyes."

The Juggler stopped his juggling.

Nanabush, still looking like an Old Man, stepped over to the pool and took a drink of water.

"So, he's got new eyes, has he?" The Juggler said, trying not to sound as scared as he was beginning to feel. "Well, good for him. If he comes to me, I just might take his new eyes, too. I did it before and I can do it again."

Nanabush stood up.

"So you're a mighty, powerful fellow?" Nanabush said. "You think that you can beat Nanabush?"

"I am a Great Sorcerer," The Juggler said. "I can defeat anything or anyone."

"Can you beat me?" Nanabush said.

"Anyone or anything," The Juggler said, trying very hard to sound brave.

"I've heard that you can juggle with your eyes out of your head. That you don't need eyes to see," Nanabush said.

The Juggler grinned, popped out his own eyes and juggled them, hand to hand, back and forth, hand to hand, back and forth. Then he stopped, threw his head back. Then he tossed his eyes into the air. Up went his eyes, down they came and ... plunk ... landed safely in their sockets.

"Is that good enough for you, Old One?" The Juggler said, grinning at Nanabush.

But it wasn't Nanabush as an old man standing there. It was Nanabush as The Juggler remembered him.

"Well. If it isn't The Great Nanabush himself," The Juggler said, grinning and trying to sound (and feel) braver than he really was.

"I've already seen that trick," Nanabush said. And he was grinning too.

"So, Nanabush, are you tired of your new pair of eyes already?" The Juggler said. "If you want to save us both some time and work, you can just hand your eyes over to me right now."

"If you really want my eyes, you're going to have to work for them, Nephew," Nanabush said.

"Fine by me. Just tell me how," The Juggler said.

"Very good, Nephew. Nothing fancy – I'll toss my eyes to you and you catch them," Nanabush said. "If you catch them, you get to keep them. If you miss you won't owe me a thing. All or nothing. Fair enough."

"Too easy," The Juggler said. "No real challenge. Tell you what, Nanabush. I'll seal my eyes shut. How does that sound?"

"Fine by me, Nephew," Nanabush said. "But I warn you. I'm going to be throwing from quite a distance, from the very rim of the world itself."

"Ha. Go to the rim of the world. Even that wouldn't be far enough. I'd know when it's coming. I'll just stand here and wait. You're the one who'll have all the work to do. If you want to walk all the way to the edge of Creation just to toss a couple of eyes, that's fine by me, I'll catch them. I never miss," The Juggler said proudly.

With a shrug of his shoulders, The Juggler obtained some sap from a nearby tree. This sap he used to seal his eyes shut. Then he stood calmly and with very great confidence.

"Well, Nanabush. I'm ready if you are. Be on your way. It's a long walk, but I'll wait. When victory is a sure thing, I can wait," The Juggler said. Then he folded his arms in front of his chest and said no more.

Nanabush walked away.

Nanabush walked away, but not to the rim of the world. He just plain walked away and didn't look back.

Nanabush went about his work of making the world what it was meant to be. He never gave The Juggler another thought. Why?

Because Nanabush knew that The Juggler, like all Sorcerers, was a vain fellow more than eager to show off his power no matter how long it took. The Juggler said he'd wait and so he did.

He's still waiting. And he will wait for all time, until The End of Time. Oh, it's not at all difficult to find him. He's very well known. He's easily recognizable.

His name, you recall, is Restless As The Wind. It's a very descriptive name. He's still to be seen standing, day in, day out, standing, rooted to the spot, his fringes and hair swaying and shivering constantly in the wind, at the slightest breeze or draught. Even when the air is perfectly still.

To pass the long hours away, you see, The Juggler, Restless As The Wind, has taken the form of a tree. A tree that never rests, whose leaves and branches still shake and shiver even when the air is still and quiet.

He's become the Shivering Tree.

The Poplar Tree.

And that's the way it is to this good day.


## John McLeod

*None of the stories about the Great Nanabush takes place in this part of the province. The Old People brought all the Nanabush stories with 'em from our old home at Bowating (Sault Ste Marie) and I guess they never really got around to making up any new ones. Oh, the stories change a little, that's bound to happen, someone adds something to a story to make it funnier or more exciting, or someone leaves something out that he doesn't like or maybe it doesn't suit the reason for his telling the story.*

*This one starts off a long way from here, oh, way off over in*

*Manitoba, and way back before the first groups of our people set foot in that part of the world. I've added certain details and whole episodes, but I am, after all, a storyteller, not an archivist.*

ᘡ

# Such a Land Does Not Exist

There was a woman once who had a son. And as the boy grew up he noticed that everyone around him, except himself, had a father. But this didn't bother him; this didn't bother him until one day when he went to the market and overheard a boy say, "Look, there's Ivan who doesn't know who his father is or if he has one at all."

When Ivan heard this, he made up his mind that he would not rest until he knew who his father was. So he went back home and told his mother what he heard and asked her what she knew.

"Your father is dead," she said.

And she told Ivan all about his father and the kind of man he was and how he died.

"But will he never come back?" asked Ivan.

"No, my son, your father will never come back. But one day we will go to him. Death comes to us all and takes us back to where we began."

"But if God has given someone life," said Ivan, "why does he give it away to Death?" And without waiting for an answer he said, "Mother, I will go. I will search the ends of the world, of the universe if necessary, to find a place where God does not give life away to Death."

When Ivan told her what he had in mind to do, she tried to tell him it was no use, that there was nothing for it but to make do. But when she saw that he was resolute, she filled a basket with food for him and gave him her blessing.

"Whether you should go east or west, or north or south; over the mountains or across the Steppes, I don't know. But you will never see your father again, and you will want to come back home in the end."

And with that, Ivan started out, and straight from the door of his mother's house he went. He had been going from the quick of daylight to the fall of dark, and everywhere he went he asked the same question: "Is this a land where God does not give life away to Death?" And the answer he received was always the same: "No, when man, woman, or child leaves this world, it is Death who takes them away."

And seven years passed and Ivan had not found a land where the life that God gives is everlasting.

Then one day while Ivan was walking across a field he came upon an old man with a white beard down to his chest, and beside him a red stag. The deer's antlers spread far into the sky, disappearing in the clouds.

Ivan called to the old man, "Is this a land where Death does not take the life that God has given?"

The old man shook his head. "Such a land does not exist," he said. "But God has sent this deer to earth so that the heavens may rest upon its antlers. This deer will live for some years to come. And I will feed this deer until its great horns reach the heavens. Stay with me and you will live until the heavens are supported."

"You mean that I will live only as long as the deer lives," said Ivan.

"Yes," said the old man. "But if you stay with me you will live a long time, longer than you would expect to live were you not here."

"And how long will that be?" asked Ivan.

"About one hundred years."

"No," said Ivan. "I will not let Death take my life."

And Ivan turned away from the old man and the stag and set off again, travelling over mountains, and through steppes, marshes, and woods.

And then one day, while walking through a rocky and desolate mountain region, Ivan met an old man with a white beard down to his middle. The old man was standing beside a hole in the earth that spread so deep and wide that Ivan thought it must end in the land of the dead. Above the bottomless pit rose a great rocky mound that reached up into the sky, and on the summit sat an enormous black bird.

Ivan called out to the old man, "Is this a land where Death does not take the life that God has given?"

The old man ran his gnarled fingers through his beard. "Here Death enters the world too," said the old man. "But if it is a long life you want, you have come to the right place. God has sent the black bird to fill this hole with the soil and stones from these mountains. The bird and I will live until that is done. Stay here and you too will live until the pit is full."

Ivan looked at the black bird and then back to the old man. "How long will it take the bird to fill the hole?"

"About two hundred years," said the old man, "and what man would want to live longer than that?"

"Two hundred years is not long enough," said Ivan. "I want only a land where Death never comes." And with that, Ivan turned his back on the old man and the bird and set off again.

Whether it was a long road or a short road he travelled I can't tell you, but one day he came to a barren land cut through by a great river. On the banks of the river there stood an old man with a white beard down to his knees.

And Ivan said to him, "For years I have been searching for a land where life never ends. Have I found it?"

"No," said the old man, "as far as I know there is no such land. But stay here with me and you will live longer than any man could hope for."

The old man pointed to a small duck floating in the grey-green water. "God has sent this duck to drink up the water which has long poisoned the land. It will take the duck another three hundred years to drink up the water of this river. Only then will the duck and I die. If you stay with us you too will live until the river is dry, and what man would want more time than that?"

"I do," said Ivan. "I will live forever or not at all."

And off he went again looking for a land of everlasting life.

Ivan made his way over a vast mountain range and came at last to the sea. The shore was smooth and carpeted with white sand. Upon the sand stood a magnificent glass house. Ivan walked about the house, trying to get a glimpse of what was inside. But it was as if water had condensed upon glass walls, and he could not see in. He put his hands upon the glass to get a closer look, and to his wonder a panel of glass lifted at his touch.

Ivan stepped across the threshold. As he walked about, his skin drew taut and his mouth went dry. Never before had he seen such a house. Then he saw her, lying on a bed of glass, a young woman as beautiful as the sun rising over the sea. She sat up in her bed as he approached. And Ivan asked her the same question he had asked the old men.

"Why do you want to find such a land?" she asked. "Life does not last forever. What you seek is nowhere to be found. But why not stay with me here?"

"I didn't travel about the world to find you," said Ivan, "but a place where Death never touches."

"You will not find such a place," said the young woman.

A smile spread across her face. "Tell me, if you can, how old do you think I am?"

Ivan looked at the young woman. He gazed and gazed at her gleaming skin and at her hair that grew both dark and fair. And he suddenly forgot about his search. In an instant, the thought of death dimmed and vanished.

"You can't be more than eighteen years old," he said.

"Ah, you are wrong," she said, "you are wrong. I came into the world on the first day of creation, when God separated light from dark. I am Beauty. And I will always look as you see me now."

Beauty paused and stroked her hair. "Stay with me, will you?" she said at last. "Stay with me."

Ivan stayed with Beauty. And she was happy to have him for she was no longer alone. And the years passed, but for Ivan there was no time and he knew nothing of change.

Then one day, early in the morning, Ivan woke with a start. He had been dreaming of his home, of his mother and of the people he knew. He woke with a longing to see them that did not pass even when he saw the face of Beauty.

"I miss my mother and my friends," said Ivan. "I must see them again."

"You can't," said Beauty shaking her head. "You have chosen to stay here. And so much time has passed since you arrived, so much has changed. What you'd find is not what you left."

"But I must try to see them, whatever you say, if only for a visit," said Ivan.

Beauty sighed. "I should never have asked you to stay with me. I knew you would want to return. Very well then, do as you wish," she said, "but listen carefully to what I say."

She reached into a basket and from it removed three apples.

"Take these three apples and keep them with you. Neither eat the apples nor linger in any one place on your way home. When you reach your mother's village and have seen what you must see, make your way back here to the sea. Then you must eat the apples."

Ivan threw his arms about Beauty, placed the apples in his bag, and set off on his journey home. After some time he came to a long, narrow valley, green with grasses and cut here and there with crumbling pillars of rock. Walking along the edge of the valley he came upon two piles of bones. One was larger than the other. The place reminded him of the old man and the duck he had seen on his way to the sea. Ivan felt a knot in his chest, and he understood then what Beauty had meant about time. The duck and the old man were long dead and the land was now filled with life. The world had indeed changed, time had moved beyond any number of years he could have imagined. Yet he felt compelled to go on.

He travelled slowly and one day he came to a great rocky desert where there stood, apart from anything else, a mound no taller than himself. At the top were the bones of a bird, still standing. Tears came to his eyes as he realized that he had reached what had once been the bottomless pit. The black bird had filled it and died. And he knew that he would find nothing that he recognized when he returned home. Still he did not want to turn back.

In time Ivan came to a field where the now dead stag stood, the heavens supported by its antlers. Ivan was not surprised to see the dead stag. He walked on without stopping.

At last he came to what he knew in his heart to be the village where he had grown up. Everything was different. He recognized no one. The houses were made of concrete rather than stone. He walked about searching for a trace of what was once his home. And everyone he met he would ask about his mother, but everyone said they knew nothing of her.

After a long search, during which Ivan felt his life run out of him, he came to a patch of land overrun by nettles. A few stones, round and covered with moss, lay in a pile. Perhaps, thought Ivan, this had once been the wall of his house.

There was nothing for him here, so Ivan left the village and started on his long journey to the sea. And on the way he passed the ancient stag whose antlers supported the heavens, and the black bird that had filled the hole in the earth, and the duck that had long ago consumed the poisonous river. Then one day, just before dawn, Ivan reached the sea.

As soon as he stood upon the sand, Ivan took the apples from his sack and began to eat the first one. Immediately a beard dropped from his chin to his feet. His legs felt weak. In the distance he saw the glass house. Ivan ate the second apple. His knees buckled and he fell to the sand.

Beauty left her house of glass then, and walked over to Ivan. She placed him in her lap as if he were a baby, and fed him the third apple. In an instant, Ivan turned to dust. Death had come at last to take the life that God had given Ivan, the life that Death had been so long denied.

Beauty gathered the dust in her hands and carried it to the edge of the sea. There she stopped, as the sun cut through the night sky in glorious pinks and spread its light richly upon the sea and land. A new day; the rhythm of life and death continued; and Beauty cast the dust into the sea.

And if you had been there and had looked into the face of Beauty, you would not have known whether it was with a smile or a frown that she cast the dust into the sea.

### Ray Gordezky

*I first came across a Russian version of this story in* Caucasian Folk Tales *by Adolf Dirr (translated into English by Lucy Menzies). That was many years ago, and I paid little attention to it at the time. Italo Calvino's telling of an Italian version in* Italian Folktales *brought me back to the story. I have taken something from each version to make my own.*

# The Sphinx and the Way to Thebes

He didn't know anything about the city, but one day the Wanderer set out for Thebes.

There was only one way to Thebes and he knew that the Sphinx lay along this road. And he knew also that those who came through the desert to go to Thebes were given a riddle by the Sphinx and that anyone who couldn't answer it had to die.

Anyway, he crossed the desert. Do you want to go to Thebes? asked the Sphinx.

I want to go to Thebes.

You know that you won't see the gates of the city if you can't solve my riddle?

Yes, I know, but I want to go to Thebes.

You know that there's still time to turn back?

Yes, I know that.

All right, then, listen. What is it: in the morning it goes on four legs, at noon on two, and in the evening on three. What is it?

The Wanderer thought for just a moment. Then he smiled and said softly: I could give you the answer, but I don't want to.

Why don't you want to give me the answer, if you know it, especially if you want to go to Thebes?

I could give you the answer, but your riddle doesn't please me.

Why doesn't it please you? It's hard, and many people have died because of it.

Your riddle doesn't please me because the answer is better than the question. So I won't cheapen the answer by giving it to you.

Then you must die. My eyes will kill you like lightning.

Your eyes won't kill me, Sphinx, because I know the answer you want to hear. But you don't deserve to hear that answer.

How can you prove that you know it?

I'll prove it by giving you a riddle. Listen, Sphinx, what is it: it's made of dust and breath. In the morning it searches for everything, at noon it searches for something also made of dust and breath, in the evening it searches for itself. Then it returns to dust and breath again. What is it?

I don't want to answer your riddle, Wanderer. Because it isn't a true riddle. I think you'll have to die.

Why do you say it isn't a true riddle? It's better than yours.

It doesn't have the form of a true riddle. There are no numbers in it.

All right, then, I'll give it to you again, this time with numbers. It'll be a little more confusing this way, though. Listen. What is it: in the morning it is the smallest of three riddles, at noon it is one of two, in the evening it is left alone. Yet it was alone the whole day. What is it?

There's no answer to that riddle, Wanderer.

Oh yes, there's an answer, but you don't know it.

Well, Wanderer, I can see that you've tried. You can go even though you've evaded my question. You've amused me with your sayings and so I'll let you go to Thebes.

I wasn't trying to amuse you, Sphinx. You aren't being consistent if you let me go to Thebes. Because if you can't answer my riddle, and it was only one that I gave you, then you don't know if I can answer yours. You betray your weakness right there, Sphinx.

Go quickly, Wanderer, or my eyes will kill you.

Your eyes can't touch me, Sphinx. You heard the words but missed their meaning. You have no answer, though you always ask a question.

Wanderer, you don't realize that you're pushing your luck when you speak in riddles. As I listened to you in silence, I was patient, not weak. I understand my riddle, and I know the answer to it.

You think you know, but you're wrong. Now I'll give you one last riddle, in the form that pleases me the most. Only then will I go to Thebes. Sphinx, what is it: it has two eyes, but it pits them against nature. It has a mouth that can only promise. It has no heart, yet it wants to live. And it's like this in the morning, at noon, and in the evening. It has a riddle, which it uses to kill, but the riddle will live when it itself is dead. What is it?

The face of the Sphinx remained unfathomable, and it appeared for a moment as if it were growing accustomed to that condition. And so it froze. A line ran across its forehead like a snake. A part of its nose slowly fell away, and the Wanderer saw that a change had taken place and that the Sphinx was now completely made of stone. And then he knew that he had killed it.

The Wanderer leaned against the rocks, and there was no room between him and the rocks. He didn't want to go to Thebes any more. It isn't good to know so much of riddles, he thought, and: it isn't good to have no heart in the evening.

The Wanderer sat leaning on the Sphinx, as on a mountain, for a night, a day, through a cycle of the moon. He woke and he slept but took no nourishment – and so he died.

Wanderers on the way to Thebes find him there, partially covered by sand. They go on – no riddle stops them.

And since that time, many, oh so many wanderers have come to Thebes.


## Gary Hophan

*While at university I came upon this story by Wieland Schmied, fell in love with it, and translated it. Twenty years later it was the first story I told to an audience of storytelling listeners.*

*I am publishing this translation with the kind permission of Wieland Schmied.*

∽

# Epilogue: The Listener's Tale

Dunyazad, kid sister, your part in the story is so easily and often forgotten. There you were, sitting by the royal bed the night Shahrazad must wed that mad King Shahriyar. He was the gender-cidal monarch who sought revenge on all womankind by taking a virgin bride each night and chopping off her head each morning. And why? Because he was afraid that she would betray him as his first wife had done (quite spectacularly, with a big slave named Mass'ood, naked by the open-air fountain, with girl-slaves and boy-slaves joining in the festivities). This reign of horror lasted until the very night your sister was to be his bride.

And there you were, beside that dreadful bed, waiting while the King and Queen did as men and women do; and then, in the stillness following, you asked Shahrazad the question you asked her every night, the question you must ask this one more time: "Sister, would you tell me a bedtime story?"

And she: "Do you agree, O King?"

And he, suffering from habitual sleeplessness, agreeing.

And Shahrazad speaking the words she always spoke, the words you'd heard so many times before:

> "Come, little sister, come near
> Leave behind all of your fear
> Darkness comes and night is near
> But dawn shall find you sleeping here."

And so the storytelling began. There were tales of wonder to make the hours of night pass pleasantly; stories of the great ones and the lowly ones of this earth; ancient histories; modern spoofs; and tales of that other great insomniac, the Caliph Harun al-Rashid, who wandered his city of Baghdad at night in disguise, listening by the windows of bedchambers, by the gates of gardens, seeking the secret tales of his own city.

The King listened as your sister told each tale only halfway through, and so strong was his desire to hear the story's end he kept postponing your sister's death. It seems we humans long to know what happens next – as in the story of the Jalandhar garbagemen:

Dateline: New Delhi, 1988. The garbagemen of Jalandhar have gone on strike in this city in Punjab to protest the cancellation of a popular television series. The series is based on the Hindu epic the *Ramayana* and is the most popular show on Indian television. Its 78-week run is scheduled to end this month, but the Jalandhar garbagemen demand an extension to show *what happened to Lord Rama's two sons*. Municipal officials fear the workers' refusal to collect garbage could spread disease.

Shahriyar listened to Shahrazad's stories. He heard how Harun al-Rashid wandered the streets of Baghdad, eavesdropping by palaces and wretched hovels; and how the truth he found spoke in many accents but rarely the one he expected to hear; and how the truth appeared in half-light, moonlight, firelight, tender and violent, resigned or passionate, but never predictable; and how to hear the stories of his own city the great Caliph must needs leave the gates of his palace and risk finding truths he cannot control but only accept.

On the one thousand and first night you, Dunyazad, brought in the three children your sister had borne.

And she: "Spare my life for the sake of our children, husband of mine. My stories are ended."

And he: "Your tales, O Queen, beloved wife, have healed my madness. You have shown me that women are wise and tender, chaste and eloquent. My grief and rage are ended, for I see now that the two things men cannot control are destiny and a woman's soul. May all your ancestors be blessed and may your descendants find favour with Allah; for me, this one thousand and first night is more radiant than the day itself ..." (and so on in like manner, for Shahriyar had become a storyteller himself by now).

So the storyteller was spared. And what a party there was to celebrate the joy of King Shahriyar and his storytelling Queen!

And who should you meet there, and love, and wed, but the King's younger brother Shahzaman; and so find yourself in your own marriage bed and no longer beside your sister's.

You lived, the four of you, happily for a very long time – until, as they say, you too were visited by the Destroyer, the one who cuts down mighty kings and humble folk too, the one who waits for us all at the end of our journey.

Dunyazad, kid sister, greatest listener of them all, you give all storytellers the courage to begin.